JESUS
A New Vision

Spirit, Culture, and the Life of Discipleship

Marcus J. Borg

HarperSanFrancisco

A Division of HarperCollins*Publishers*

ALSO BY MARCUS J. BORG

Conflict, Holiness and Politics in the Teachings of Jesus

For Esther and Marianne,
two women who have graced my life

FIRST HARPERCOLLINS PAPERCOVER EDITION PUBLISHED IN 1991.

Library of Congress Cataloging-in-Publication Data

Borg, Marcus J.
   Jesus, a new vision : spirit, culture, and the life of
discipleship / Marcus J. Borg — 1st Harpercollins papercover ed.
      p.   cm.
   Reprint. Originally published: San Francisco : Harper & Row,
©1987.
   Includes bibliographical references and indexes.
   ISBN 0–06–060814–5 (alk. paper)
   1. Jesus Christ—Person and offices.   2. Jesus Christ—
Significance.   I. Title.
[BT202.B644   1991]
232—dc20   91–55090
                                                                 CIP

98   RRD(H) 15 14

Contents

Preface

This book attempts in a scholarly and nondogmatic way to say, "This is what the historical Jesus was like, this is what he taught, and this is what his mission was about." It seeks, in short, to sketch a portrait of what Jesus was like as a figure of history before his death.

My purpose is twofold. First, I want to present a synthesis of modern Jesus scholarship that is accessible to the general reader, whether Christian or among the interested inquirers. At the same time, I wish to make a serious scholarly case for a particular image of the historical Jesus that is considerably at variance with the dominant scholarly image. This twofold purpose accounts for the book's character. On the one hand, I presuppose no familiarity with the academic discipline of New Testament studies or with theological language. On the other hand, I seek to provide enough support for the positions taken so that they can be considered seriously by other scholars.

I have a third purpose as well. The two focal points of the book, Spirit and culture, enable us to see some of Jesus' significance for our time. For us, whether in the church or not, his life is a vivid testimony to the reality of Spirit, a reality affirmed and known in virtually every society prior to the modern period. But this reality is poorly understood and often discounted in the modern world, not only in the academy but even in much of the church.

For the church and Christians in particular, among whom I number myself, knowledge of what the historical Jesus was like can be a potent source of renewal. Not only is he a witness to the reality of Spirit as an element of *experience*, but his passionate involvement in the culture of his own time—his "social world"—connects two realities which Christians have frequently separated. Throughout the centuries as well as in our own time, Christians have tended to view culture as having little or no religious significance, or as largely negative in its significance. But it was not so for Jesus. He sought the transformation of his social world.

The Jesus who emerges in these pages is thus deeply spiritual and deeply political. He is spiritual in that his relationship to the Spirit of God was the central reality in his life, the source of all that he was; we cannot glimpse the historical Jesus unless we take with utmost seriousness his relationship to the world of Spirit. He is political in the same sense that the mainstream of his tradition was political: concerned about creating a community within history whose corporate life reflected faithfulness to God. What happens in history matters to the God of Jesus and his tradition.

This book is simultaneously polemical and apologetic. It is polemical in that it is critical of much that is central to modern culture; and apologetic in that it seeks to show how the gospel portraits of Jesus, historically seen, *make sense*. From his life and teaching flow a convincing and persuasive understanding of reality. The challenge which the historical Jesus presents is not the sacrifice of the intellect, but the sacrifice of something much deeper within us. Christianity has very little to do with believing forty-nine impossible things before breakfast—as the late Bishop John Robinson puckishly described the impression that people commonly have of what it means to be a Christian; but it has everything to do with taking seriously what Jesus took seriously.

My study of the historical Jesus began over two decades ago in graduate school and has continued through fifteen years of teaching in both university and church settings. The present book builds on that study and interchange and is indebted to many people, some of whom I know only through books, others more personally. In particular, it builds on my book *Conflict, Holiness and Politics in the Teaching of Jesus*. Directed primarily to other scholars, it emphasized Jesus' relationship to his social world, especially as renewal movement founder and prophet. The present volume broadens the focus of that book, even as it seeks to be accessible to a broader readership.

The reader needs no particular faith orientation to understand this book. I generally avoid language which depends on the Christian belief system for its meaning; when I do use the language of "insiders," I explain what it means in terms not drawn from the Christian language and belief system.

Thus it addresses both the interested inquirer who may well be outside of the church, even as it also addresses the Christian who wants to reflect about what it means to follow Jesus. For the first reader, the book sketches a credible picture of the historical Jesus; for the second reader, it also sketches a picture of the life of discipleship.

I began my scholarly study of Jesus (and theology) as an "unbelieving son of the church." Raised within the church, convinced that Christianity was exceedingly important, committed to studying and teaching it—even preaching it, respecting and loving it—I did not yet understand (and therefore did not believe) its central claims. The study has continued through the glimmering of understanding and the birth of belief, still embryonic but growing. To some extent, the book reflects this journey. I have dared to presume that some of the difficulties I encountered have also been issues for my readers. The book incorporates both parts of my journey. What is stated in it makes sense to me both in the context of my unbelieving past and in the context of my believing present.

Finally, I wish to express my appreciation to the Stewart Foundation at Oregon State University for providing me with release time in which to write. I also wish to thank a number of individuals at Oregon State: Mrs. Pat Rogerson, secretary of Religious Studies, who helped to create that most valuable of commodities, time; Professor Nicholas Yonker, my chairman, who supported me in many ways; and Hans Michael Vermeersch, my student assistant. Students in courses at both Oregon State University and Carleton College helped shape the material. A visiting professorship at the University of Puget Sound unexpectedly provided some extra time for writing. Finally, I am grateful to my editor, Roy M. Carlisle of Harper & Row San Francisco, who saw potential in a preliminary outline; and to my wife, Marianne Wells Borg. In addition to being my best conversational partner about the ideas in this book, she provided me with constant encouragement and nourishment.

NOTES

1. Marcus Borg, *Conflict, Holiness and Politics in the Teaching of Jesus* (New York and Toronto: Edwin Mellen Press, 1984).

1. Introduction
Clearing the Ground:
Two Images of Jesus

The historical Jesus is of interest for many reasons. Not least of these is his towering cultural significance in the nearly two thousand years since his death. No other figure in the history of the West has ever been accorded such extraordinary status. Within a few decades of his death, stories were told about his miraculous birth. By the end of the first century, he was extolled with the most exalted titles known within the religious tradition out of which he came: Son of God, one with the Father, the Word become flesh, the bread of life, the light of the world, the one who would come again as cosmic judge and Lord. Within a few centuries he had become Lord of the empire which had crucified him.

For over a thousand years thereafter, he dominated the culture of the West: its religion and devotion, its art, music, and architecture, its intellectual thought and ethical norms, even its politics. Our calendar affirms his life as a dividing point in world history. On historical grounds alone, with no convictions of faith shaping the verdict, Jesus is the most important figure in Western (and perhaps human) history.[1] Thus, simply as a matter of intellectual or historical curiosity, it is interesting to ask, "What was this towering cultural figure like as a historical person *before* his death?"

For Christians, the question is significant for an additional reason. Jesus is not simply a historical person, but the founder and central figure of their religion. Millions of Christians confess him each Sunday to be both Lord and Christ. Moreover, within the church, Christians talk about "following Jesus," about "the life of discipleship" (which means to follow after Jesus), and about "imitating Christ," as the apostle Paul and other Christian saints put it. Thus what Jesus was like as a historical figure would seem to be not only interesting but important, for what he was like provides the content of what following him means. Though Jesus is ultimately more than a model for the life of discipleship in the Christian tradition, he is not less. As we shall see, what he was like is a potent challenge and invitation to both our culture and the church.

Yet, despite the fact that "Jesus" is a household word, and despite his importance for the Christian life, what he was like as a historical figure before his death is not widely known, either in our culture or within the church itself. Instead, what he was like is seriously obscured by two dominant images of Jesus: the first dominates the popular imagination within both the church and culture, the second has dominated much of New Testament scholarship in this century. Each of these images provides its answers to the three central questions about the historical Jesus: his *identity* (who was he?), his *message* (what was central to his proclamation or teaching?), and his *mission* (what was his purpose, what did he himself hope to accomplish?). But the answers provided by the popular and dominant scholarly images hide rather than reveal what Jesus was like. In order to be able to see Jesus afresh, we need to become aware of the images that obscure our vision.

THE POPULAR IMAGE OF JESUS

The popular image is most familiar to Christian and non-Christian alike: the image of Jesus as a divine or semidivine figure, whose purpose was to die for the sins of the world, and whose life and death open up the possibility of eternal life. Its answers to the three questions of identity, purpose, and message are clear. As the divinely begotten Son of God, he was sent into the world for the purpose of dying on the cross as a means of reconciliation between God and humankind, and his message consisted primarily of inviting his hearers to believe that what he said about himself and his role in salvation was true.

The image is widespread, with degrees of sophistication and

elaboration. Billboards and evangelists proclaim, "Jesus died for your sins," suggesting that this was his purpose in a nutshell. Much of Christian preaching takes the popular image for granted. The celebration of the major Christian festivals in our culture reinforces the image. Christmas, with wise men and shepherds and angels, a manger and a star and a virgin, tells the story of his wondrous birth and thus calls attention to his divine identity; Easter focuses on his triumph over death.

The popular image has its roots deep in the past, indeed in the language of the New Testament itself. Among the gospels, its primary source is John, probably the most loved and familiar gospel. There Jesus speaks of his identity in the most exalted terms known in his culture, especially in the magnificent series of "I am" statements: "I am the light of the world," "I am the bread of life," "I am the resurrection and the life," "I am the way, the truth, and the life," "Before Abraham was, I am."[2]* The self-proclamation of his own identity in the "I am" statements is buttressed by other passages in John: "The Father is in me and I am in the Father," "He who has seen me has seen the Father," "I and the Father are one."[3] In a single verse, the fourth gospel sums up Jesus' identity, purpose, message, and the proper response to him: "For God so loved the world that he gave his only Son, that whoever believes in him should not perish but have everlasting life."[4]

The roots of the popular image also lie in the development of Christian theological thought and piety in the centuries following the composition of the New Testament. The creeds of the church express that development. The Apostles' Creed proclaims that Jesus was "God's only son our Lord, who was conceived by the Holy Ghost, born of the Virgin Mary, suffered under Pontius Pilate, was crucified, dead and buried; on the third day he rose again from the dead; he ascended into heaven from which he shall come to judge the living and the dead." In the Nicene Creed, Jesus is spoken of as "the only begotten Son of God, begotten of his

---

* All biblical references are from the Revised Standard Version. See notes at the end of each chapter for citations.

Father before all worlds, God of God, Light of Light, very God of very God, begotten, not made [that is, not *created*], being of one substance with the Father." There, his purpose is described very simply, "Who for us men and *for our salvation* came down from heaven . . . and was crucified for us under Pontius Pilate."

Throughout the Middle Ages and into the modern period, this image of Jesus as divine savior and Lord dominated Western worship, thought, art, and devotion. Centuries of Christians have taken it for granted that this image depicts what he was like as a historical figure. No wonder this image is so deeply rooted in the Christian imagination, as well as in our culture generally. Christian and non-Christian alike share it; what separates them is not the image, but whether or not they believe the image to be true.

THE COLLAPSE OF THE POPULAR IMAGE IN BIBLICAL SCHOLARSHIP

The popular image, certainly, is widely accepted. Yet as an image of the historical Jesus—of what Jesus was like as a figure of history before his death—the popular image is not accurate. Indeed, it is seriously misleading. This statement, surprising though it is to many people (including many within the church), is a bedrock conclusion of mainstream New Testament scholarship.[5]*

The conclusion flows out of the meticulous study of the New Testament documents over the past two centuries, most of it done by Christian scholars. Of primary importance for the collapse of the popular image in scholarly circles is the sharp contrast between the portraits of Jesus in John's gospel and the other three gospels (Matthew, Mark, and Luke), collectively known as the *synoptic* gospels (from the Greek root "seen together") because of their many similarities. John differs sufficiently that his gospel must be seen separately.

---

* Editor's note: Notes indicated by a number in boldface type (e.g.[**12**]) contain further discussion; Those notes set in regular roman type (e.g.[12]) are bibliographic citations.

According to John, as already noted, Jesus spoke often and openly about his exalted identity and purpose. However, the synoptics contain a very different picture. According to Mark, still judged to the earliest gospel by most scholars, Jesus never proclaimed his exalted identity; it did not constitute part of his public teaching or preaching. The silence of Jesus about his own identity is matched by a corresponding silence on the part of the other human actors in Mark's narrative. Indeed, on only two occasions was there an exchange between Jesus and those he encountered regarding who he was. Both occasions were private, not public, and both were near the end of the ministry.[6] Throughout, Mark's gospel is dominated by "the Messianic secret"; though Mark clearly believed that Jesus was the Messiah, his messiahship was a secret during the ministry. In short, in Mark the proclamation of Jesus' own identity and of the saving purpose of his death was not the message of Jesus. He did not proclaim himself.

When once this fundamental contrast between John and Mark was seen, a great historical "either/or" presented itself to scholars. Either the historical Jesus openly proclaimed his divine identity and saving purpose (John), or he did not (Mark). To put the issue most directly, Jesus could not *consistently* proclaim his identity and at the same time *not* do so. Thus the question became, "Which image of Jesus is more likely to be like the historical Jesus, John's or Mark's?" The nearly universal answer given by scholars was "Mark."[7] With that answer, the popular image's basis *as a historical image* disappeared. The image of Jesus as one who taught that he was the Son of God who was to die for the sins of the world is not historically true.

The historical preference for Mark, with the implication that John is not very historical, is disturbing to some Christians. Indeed, it was to me when I first encountered it. John's gospel and the image of Jesus which derives from it seemed to be the core of what I as a Christian was supposed to believe. The first Bible verse I learned was the famous John 3:16: "For God so loved the world that he gave his only begotten Son . . . ." The notion that Jesus did not say that, and that he did not proclaim himself as a divine figure, was unsettling. Moreover, it seemed to invalidate John's gospel, implying that John was a "false" account of the ministry of Jesus.

In one sense, that is true; for the most part, John cannot be used as a source of information about the historical Jesus. But rather than invalidating John's gospel, that realization enables us to see more clearly what John's gospel is. Instead of it being a picture of the historical Jesus, it is about the risen living Christ of Christian experience. John's gospel comes out of the experience of the Christian community in the decades after Easter. In it, the historical traditions about Jesus are thoroughly transformed by the early Christians' ongoing experience of the risen Christ. John's gospel is the church's memory transfigured.

In their own experience, these Christians knew the living Christ as the light of the world who brought them out of darkness, as the bread of life who nourished them with spiritual food, as the vine whose life coursed through them, and as the way and the truth which brought them to new life. And thus John portrayed Jesus as all of these: as light, bread, vine, the way and the truth, God's "Word" become flesh. The remarkable affirmations about Jesus in John's gospel are a powerful testimony to the reality and character of the living Christ. Rather than being the self-proclamation of Jesus, they flow out of the post-Easter experience of the early church, and their truthfulness is testified to by the experience of Christians ever since. John's gospel is "the spiritual gospel," as was recognized already by the Christian writer Clement of Alexandria near the end of the second century; it speaks of the significance of Christ in the spiritual life of Christians.[8]

What is true of John's gospel is true of the popular image in general. Both are the product of projecting later Christian convictions, grounded in the experience of Christ through the centuries as a living divine reality, back into the period of the ministry itself. The risen living Christ does possess the qualities of divinity; he is "very God of very God," one with the Father, and therefore everywhere-present, all-powerful, and all-knowing. But though these statements are true about the risen Christ, they are not true about the historical Jesus. Clearly, Jesus as a figure of history was not "omnipresent," but was always in some particular place—in Nazareth, on the road, in Jerusalem, or elsewhere. Similarly, even though remarkable powers flowed through him, as we shall see later, he was not "omnipotent," as even the gospels recognize.[9] Neither should we suppose that he was "omniscient." As a first-century Jew who learned what he knew in the context of his own culture and experience, presumably he shared many of the beliefs of his contemporaries, including beliefs about the world which we now think of as erroneous. The risen Christ, "seated at the right hand of God," does share all of the qualities of God. But the historical Jesus did not.

The projection of divine qualities back onto Jesus is very ancient. Not only can we see this to some extent in the New Testament itself, but it became especially prominent in what are known as the "apocryphal" gospels.[10] There Jesus *as an infant* is already portrayed as having superhuman knowledge and power. From his crib, he points at the animals and makes them talk; on his journey into Egypt as a baby, he saves his parents from a dragon by killing it; as a five year old, he makes clay birds and then turns them into real birds. Clearly, what is happening here is that the experiential knowledge that the risen Christ is divine is unreflectively projected back onto the human Jesus.

The tendency continues in the modern world. Some years back, a well-known evangelist suggested that Jesus would have been the world's greatest athlete, and speculated about how quickly he could have run the mile. Behind this somewhat strange suggestion is the notion that Jesus was a divine being with superhuman powers. But the portrait of Jesus as a divine "superhero" has nothing to do with historical reality. Indeed, to the extent that the popular image sees Jesus as a divine being who merely seemed to be human, the popular image is not only nonhistorical but also was declared to be heretical by the early church.[11]

In short, the image of the historical Jesus as a divine or semi-divine being, who saw himself as the divine savior whose purpose was to die for the sins of the world, and whose message consisted of proclaiming that, is simply not historically true. Rather, it is the product of a blend produced by the early church—a blending of the church's memory of Jesus with the church's beliefs about the risen Christ. The former was seen through the window provided by the latter. They remembered Jesus with the "eye of faith," that is, in the light of Easter and afterward.

The blend was both natural and legitimate. It is what happens when a religious community looks back on its founder in light of their ongoing experience of him; and it is legitimate in that it speaks of what Christ is in the Christian life. Moreover, the image has nurtured the lives of millions of Christians over the centuries. However, if what is wanted is a reasonably clear image of the historical Jesus, then one must use a historical method which seeks to separate out the church's later beliefs from the traditions about Jesus found in early Christian documents. If one wants historical answers to the questions of Jesus' identity, mission, and message, one must first set aside the answers given by the popular image.

All of this is old news to anybody who has attended seminary or divinity school in the mainstream churches. It is also familiar to most people who have taken a religion course in a nonsectarian college. Yet it is still news to many (and perhaps most) people in our culture and in the church. In part, this is simply because of the endurance which popular images possess. But it is also because mainstream biblical scholarship has not generated a persuasive alternative image of the historical Jesus. Instead, the image which has dominated New Testament scholarship throughout much of this century has made Jesus seem both strange and irrelevant.

THE DOMINANT SCHOLARLY IMAGE OF JESUS

The realization that the popular image is not historical led to the "quest for the historical Jesus" in biblical scholarship.[12] If the historical Jesus did not proclaim himself as the Messiah and the Son of God, the divine savior who was to die for the sins of the world—if that was not his purpose and the content of his preaching—what then was he like, and what was his mission and message? Though the quest in the twentieth century produced a wide diversity of answers to these questions, two traits emerged as dominant emphases in mainstream scholarship.

INCREASING HISTORICAL SKEPTICISM

First, there was an increasing historical skepticism about whether we can know the answers to these questions with any degree of probability. To some extent, this skepticism flowed out of the increasingly meticulous study of the origins of the gospels, especially form criticism and redaction criticism.

This century's scholarship has made it clear that not only John but also the synoptic gospels reflect the experience and beliefs of the early church. *Form criticism*, emerging after World War I, studied the way the traditions about Jesus were shaped during the three or more decades that they circulated in oral form before being written down. *Redaction criticism*, developing largely after World War II, analyzed Matthew, Mark, and Luke as individual documents, as well as carefully comparing how each handled individual texts. Correctly treating the gospels as the products of particular authors writing for particular communities, redaction criticism focused attention upon the meaning intended by the *gospel writers themselves*, and not upon the history behind the gospel.

Together with form criticism, redaction criticism has made it even more clear that every story and word of Jesus has been shaped by the eyes and hands of the early church. By making us more aware of the ways the gospel writers and the early Christians before them during the oral period shaped their material in accord with their own needs and purposes, form and redaction critics have also made us more aware of the difficulties involved in using gospel texts as sources of information about the historical Jesus.

The historical skepticism ignited by the careful study of the texts has been fueled by the multiplicity of diverse portraits of Jesus constructed by scholars, ranging from a fairly traditional understanding of Jesus as the servant and Son of God to Jesus as a political revolutionary, or as one who expected the immediate end of the world, or as the center of a mushroom cult.[13] These widely divergent portraits, all claiming to be based on the use of an objective historical method, have reinforced the notion that we really cannot know much about Jesus at all, and the corollary notion that it is possible to construct almost any portrait of Jesus one wishes. Prudent scholars thus tended to avoid the quest for the historical Jesus; indeed, the middle portion of this century is commonly described in the history of scholarship as the period of "no quest."[14] All that we can know directly, it was affirmed, is the Christ proclaimed in the preaching (or *kerygma*)[15] of the early church. All attempts to go behind the *kerygma* involve one in highly subjective speculation. Obtaining knowledge of the historical Jesus thus was seen as both exceedingly difficult and theologically irrelevant.

THE IMAGE ITSELF: JESUS AS ESCHATOLOGICAL PROPHET

This strong mood of historical skepticism was accompanied (somewhat inconsistently) by a near consensus concerning what little can (and cannot) be known about Jesus. Despite the diversity of portraits, there was considerable unanimity within the scholarly mainstream. Its answers to the three questions of Jesus' identity, message, and mission together comprise an image of Jesus which became almost taken for granted in much of scholarship over the past sixty years.

Regarding Jesus' own sense of identity, the growing historical skepticism produced a consensus. Whether Jesus thought of himself as having any special exalted identity—as "Messiah" or "the Son of God"—we cannot know because of the very nature of the documents. When we do find such statements in the gospels (and they are few in our earliest sources), the careful historian (even if he or she is also a Christian) must suspect them as the post-Easter perspective of Jesus' followers projected back into the ministry. They may well be *theologically* true—that is, statements which appropriately describe what Jesus had become in the life of the post-Easter church—but they may not be taken as historically accurate statements of what was said during the ministry itself. So also with the statements (again, relatively few in our earliest sources) speaking of "dying for the sins of the world" as Jesus' purpose or intention. Thus the image of the historical Jesus as the divine savior who knew himself to be such, and whose mission was to complete that purpose, disappears. How Jesus thought of himself and his purpose must be inferred from his message, not from statements which speak directly of who he was.

According to the consensus, from such an examination of Jesus' message and mission we may surmise that he was an "eschatological prophet" or perhaps even "*the* eschatological prophet." The phrase needs some unpacking. *Eschatology* is that branch of theology which concerns the "end time"—the end of the world, last judgment, and the dawning of the everlasting kingdom. An eschatological prophet is one who announces the end. There is some evidence that some in the Jewish tradition near the time of Jesus anticipated such a prophet, "one like unto Moses" or perhaps even greater than Moses, who would appear immediately before the end of time. To say that Jesus was the eschatological prophet is to say that he saw himself as the prophet of the end who proclaimed the end of the world *in his own time* and the urgency of repentance before it was too late. That was the core of his message and mission.

The consensus image of Jesus as eschatological prophet was grounded in the claim that the "Kingdom of God" was at the center of Jesus' own message. So Mark describes Jesus' mission in his advance summary at the beginning of his gospel: "The Kingdom of God is at hand, therefore repent!"[16] However, the consensus image also depends upon a *particular interpretation* of the phrase "Kingdom of God," namely that "Kingdom of God" is to be understood eschatologically as referring to the "final" Kingdom which would bring an end to earthly history as we know it, the "end of the world."

This eschatological understanding of Jesus and of the Kingdom of God had its origin primarily in the work of Albert Schweitzer (1875–1965) at the beginning of this century.[17] He is most familiar to us as a world-famed medical missionary, Nobel prize recipient, and a modern "saint." But as a young man Schweitzer, prior to going to Africa, wrote two brilliant books that decisively shaped

Jesus studies for the rest of the century.[18] Calling attention to the element of crisis running throughout the gospels and the statements about the coming of the "Kingdom of God" and "the Son of man" who would bring all earthly history to a close, Schweitzer argued that Jesus expected these events in the immediate future and saw his death as playing a decisive role in bringing about the end. Jesus was mistaken; the end did not come, and he died perhaps realizing his mistake.[19]

Though Schweitzer's work initially created a sensation and still strikes many as outlandish when they first hear of it, his basic image of Jesus as eschatological prophet gradually became the consensus understanding among scholars. Stripped of some of its details, it became the dominant image in German New Testament scholarship and, through the influential role played by German scholarship, in much of North American scholarship.[20] To be sure, scholars also recognized that Jesus spoke of the Kingdom as present and not only future, but the future imminent Kingdom continued to be emphasized. The image of Jesus as one who proclaimed the end of the world and the urgency of repentance remained.

Especially indicative of the consensus is the treatment of Jesus by the Roman Catholic theologian Hans Küng. At the heart of his best-selling book *On Being a Christian* is a very lengthy section on the historical Jesus—about half of the book's six hundred pages.[21] Illustrative of the consensus precisely because he is not a New Testament scholar but a systematic theologian, Küng's treatment is based upon his perception of the consensus of New Testament scholarship.[22] Running throughout his account, thick with incisive insights and powerful phrases which catch some of the passion of the gospels themselves, is the picture of Jesus as one who expected the end of the world in his generation.

Though the scholarly image of Jesus as eschatological prophet is known only in relatively narrow circles, it has had its effect upon the life of the church, primarily through the education provided to clergy. In addition to learning that the popular image is not historical, students in the seminaries of mainstream churches over the past several decades have basically learned two things about Jesus: one, we cannot know much about him; and two, what we can know is a bit shocking and largely irrelevant to the life of the church. The image of Jesus as mistakenly expecting the end of the world in his own time and calling people to repent because the end was near does not lend itself well to Christian preaching and teaching. Never have I heard a preacher say in a sermon, "The text tells us that Jesus expected the end of the world in his time; he was wrong, but let's see what we can make of the text anyway."

As a consequence, among mainstream clergy there is often a strange silence about what Jesus was like as a historical figure. Christian preaching about Jesus is left to those who still think of the popular image as historical and who can therefore proclaim that image with confidence. When mainstream clergy do preach about Jesus, understandably they tend to emphasize the *kerygma*, the message of the early church about Jesus, and not Jesus himself. No wonder the popular image has remained so dominant, for Christians are typically not exposed to a persuasive and compelling alternative image.[23] What is known is an unhistorical image, believed by some, disbelieved by others.

Thus the two dominant currents of twentieth-century scholarship on Jesus—historical skepticism and eschatological emphasis—have made the historical Jesus seem irrelevant. There is a widespread impression that what the historical Jesus was like is not only difficult to know but also of no theological consequence—that is, of no significance for us today, whether we are in the church or outside it. Schweitzer said so explicitly, and much of subsequent New Testament scholarship has essentially agreed: the historical Jesus is irrelevant.[24]

There is some truth to this position. Knowledge of the historical Jesus is not *essential*. Being a Christian does not require having accurate historical information. Generations of Christians, taking the gospel portraits at "face value" as historical accounts, have had incorrect historical beliefs about Jesus without harm to their faith or piety. Christianity does not consist primarily of having correct beliefs about the historical Jesus, but consists of having a relationship with the living Christ.

Yet what the historical Jesus was like is not irrelevant to the Christian faith, even if historical knowledge about him is not essential, a *sine qua non*. There is a long tradition in the church that the lives of the saints are edifying, that is, instructive and informative for the Christian life. At the very least, the historical Jesus should be significant for this reason. Surely what he was like as a historical figure is as interesting as the lives of St. Francis, or Gandhi, or Dietrich Bonhoeffer. In what ways Jesus is relevant is to a large extent the purpose of the rest of this book and the alternative image of Jesus which it describes.

TOWARD A THIRD IMAGE

Several developments in New Testament studies in recent years pave the way for a new historical image of Jesus. First, there are signs of major cracks in the scholarly image of Jesus as eschatological prophet. Significantly, the consensus regarding Jesus' expectation of the end of the world has disappeared. The majority of scholars no longer thinks that Jesus expected the end of the world in his generation.[25]

The erosion of the consensus has been due to several factors, including especially an emerging conviction that the "coming Son of man" sayings (which are the central foundation stones for saying that Jesus expected the imminent end of the world) are not authentic, that is, that they do not go back to Jesus but are the product of the early church.[26] Moreover, if Jesus did not expect the imminent end of the world, then it follows that "Kingdom of God" must be given a meaning other than its eschatological one. The collapse of the consensus makes it possible to ask, "If Jesus was not an eschatological prophet whose mission and message were to proclaim the nearness of the end and issue the call to repentance, what then was he like and what was his purpose and proclamation?"

Second, there has been a renaissance of historical Jesus scholarship in the past decade. The period of "no quest" which dominated the middle portion of this century has given way to a new interest.[27] Fueled in part by a fresh emphasis on incorporating insights and models from the study of social and religious behavior provided by many disciplines (especially the social sciences, anthropology, and history of religions), the present quest seeks to broaden the somewhat narrow focus on literary and historical method that has marked traditional scholarship. As one scholar put it, "The interdisciplinary quest for the historical Jesus has just begun."[28]

Third and finally, there are signs that the extreme historical skepticism that has marked most Jesus study in this century is abating. Though it is true that the gospels are not straightforward historical documents, and though it is true that every saying and story of Jesus has been shaped by the early church, we can in fact know as much about Jesus as we can about any figure in the ancient world.[29] Though we cannot ever be certain that we have direct and exact quotation from Jesus, we can be relatively sure of the *kinds* of things he said, and of the main themes and thrust of his teaching. We can also be relatively sure of the kinds of things he did: healings, association with outcasts, the deliberate calling of twelve disciples, a mission directed to Israel, a final purposeful journey to Jerusalem.

Moreover, as we shall see, we can be relatively certain of the kind of person he was: a charismatic who was a healer, sage, prophet, and revitalization movement founder. By incorporating all of this, and not preoccupying ourselves with the question of whether Jesus said *exactly* the particular words attributed to him, we can sketch a fairly full and historically defensible portrait of Jesus.[30]

The portrait sketched in this book is organized around two primary categories: Part One treats Jesus' relationship to Spirit; Part Two treats his relationship to culture. The choice of Spirit and culture as the two organizing principles is not arbitrary, for they were the two central realities in the life of Jesus. He had an intensely vivid relationship to the world of Spirit, to that "other reality" sometimes spoken of as the sacred, or the holy, or the other world, or simply as God. That relationship was the source of his power and teaching, his freedom, courage, and compassion, and of his urgent mission to the culture of his day. For Jesus, culture was basically the historical life of his own people, the "social world" of first-century Palestine. With that social world he was deeply involved, not only living in it and to some extent shaped by it, but also intensely concerned with its shape and direction. He radically criticized it, warned it of the historical consequences of its present path, and sought its transformation in accord with an alternative vision. A person of Spirit, he sought the transformation of his own social world.

In addition to Spirit and culture, there are four other organizing categories. These four are what might be called "religious personality types," and are known cross-culturally as well as within the history of Israel. Though the terminology varies from culture to culture, they are the charismatic healer, sage, prophet, and renewal or revitalization movement founder. The term *charismatic* has a diversity of meanings, some of which can be misleading. Most basically, it means a person who is in touch with the power of the Spirit and who becomes a channel for the power of the Spirit to enter the world of ordinary experience.[31] *Sages*, known in all traditional cultures, are teachers; they are "the wise" who teach a way of life. *Prophets* know the "mind" or "will" of the other world and announce that to their people. Finally, a *revitalization movement founder* stands within a tradition and either calls it to return to some earlier form or to a radicalized form. Jesus, we shall see, was all of these.

By looking at the traditions about Jesus in the illumination provided by these categories, we will not only be able to see him with considerable clarity as a historical figure, but we will also be able to see his extraordinary relevance for both contemporary culture and the church. He provides us with a way of seeing reality that is very different from and yet more comprehensive than the modern vision, and a model of being human at sharp variance from the modern model.

Thus Jesus has an intellectual as well as spiritual relevance. Indeed, he challenges much of what we take for granted. For Christians who seek to mold their lives of discipleship around what it means to follow Jesus, what Jesus was like should be of more than passing interest. To follow Jesus means in some sense to be "like him," to take seriously what he took seriously. Though this is primarily a historical study, it is done with the recognition that the figure of Jesus has been significant to generations of Christians, and with the conviction that he is of continuing and indeed crucial importance to the life of both church and culture. With this conviction in mind, this book seeks to recover the vision of Jesus, a vision which can provide us with an alternative vision of life.

NOTES

1. For a masterful survey of Jesus' role in culture, see Jaroslav Pelikan, *Jesus Through the Centuries* (New Haven: Yale University Press, 1985; paperback edition published by Harper & Row, 1987).
2. John 9:5, 6:35, 11:25, 14:6, 8:58.
3. John 10:38, 14:9, 10:30.
4. John 3:16.
5. Mainstream biblical scholarship is the approach to Scripture taught in the seminaries of the mainstream churches. It is the product of using a historical method on the books of the New Testament, treating them as human documents rather than as divine documents guaranteed to be infallible by God. Beginning in the seventeenth century and accelerating through the nineteenth and twentieth centuries, it is now the approach to Scripture taught in the theological schools of the majority of Christian churches (including, for example, Roman Catholics, Presbyterians, Methodists, United Church of Christ, Disciples of Christ, Episcopalians, the majority of Lutherans, and some Baptists).
6. The two occasions are reported in Mark 8:27–30 and 14:53–65. In the first instance, shortly before Jesus and his disciples began the final journey to Jerusalem, and in a setting where his disciples were alone with him, Peter said, "Thou art the Christ" (Mark 8:29; "Christ" is the Greek word for the Hebrew "Messiah," which means roughly "the anointed one of God"). This, the first time that any follower of Jesus in Mark called him by an exalted title, contrasts sharply with John 1:29–51, where already in John's opening chapter both John the Baptist and several of Jesus' disciples applied the grandest titles to Jesus: Lamb of God, Son of God, Messiah (Christ), King of Israel. Strikingly, Jesus responded to Peter's affirmation by ordering the disciples to say nothing about it to anyone (8:30), a restriction that was to last until after Easter (see Mark 9:9). Thus in Mark, neither Jesus nor his disciples proclaimed Jesus' identity during the ministry.

  The second occasion in Mark was at the secret hearing before the high priest the night before Jesus was executed; in response to the high priest's question, "Are you the Christ, the Son of the blessed?", Jesus said, "I am" (Mark 14:61–62). Noteworthy is the fact that the high priest virtually had to "drag" the statement out of Jesus, plus the fact that the Greek and Aramaic phrase behind "I am" can be translated either "I am" or "Am I?" It is interesting that both Matthew and Luke interpret Jesus' response as ambiguous (see Matthew 26:64 and Luke 22:67–68).

Regardless of how one interprets Jesus' response, the fact remains that Mark nowhere portrays Jesus proclaiming his identity *as part of Jesus' own message.* (It should be noted that the *spirit world* knows who Jesus was, even during the ministry; the voice "from heaven" at his baptism and transfiguration speaks of him as God's "beloved Son," and evil spirits recognize him as "Son of God" and "holy one of God." But it remains true there is no human proclamation of Jesus' identity in Mark's gospel, either by Jesus or others.)

7. The contrast was first developed by Johann Gottfried Herder in 1797. Through the influence of David Friedrich Strauss's two-volume *Life of Jesus* (1835) it became one of the foundational conclusions of Jesus scholarship. The reason for preferring Mark to John as more *historical* is quite simple. It is easier to account for a theological development from a Jesus who did not explicitly proclaim himself (Mark) to a portrait in which his identity is explicitly proclaimed (John) that it is to account for the reverse process. If Jesus did consistently proclaim his identity, as John reports, what motive could an early Christian author such as Mark have had for saying that Jesus did not preach about who he was?

8. The literature on John's gospel is voluminous. For an excellent introduction, see Robert Kysar, *John: The Maverick Gospel* (Atlanta: John Knox, 1976).

9. See, for example, Mark 6:5.

10. The "apocryphal" gospels were gospels written by early Christians in the first few centuries of the church which did not make it into the New Testament. See E. Hennecke and W. Schneemelcher, *New Testament Apocrypha*, two volumes (Philadelphia: Westminster, 1963, 1965).

11. The heresy is known as "docetism," from the Greek word *dokeo*, which means "to appear" or "seem." Docetism is the notion that though Jesus *appeared* to be human, he was really God. Ironically, one of the earliest heresies is still thought by many people, Christians and non-Christians alike, to be the orthodox Christian position.

12. The beginning of the theological and historical movement known as the "quest for the historical Jesus" is typically dated in 1778 with the anonymous and posthumous publication of an essay by Hermann Samuel Reimarus (1694–1768), available as "Concerning the Intention of Jesus and His Disciples" in H. S. Reimarus, *Fragments*, edited by C. H. Talbert and translated by R. S. Fraser (Philadelphia: Fortress, 1970), 59–269. For a history of the quest up to 1900, see above all Albert Schweitzer, *The Quest of the Historical Jesus* (New York: Macmillan, 1968; first published in German in 1906, and in English in 1910). For a treatment which includes the present century, see John Hayes, *From Son of God to Superstar* (Nashville: Abingdon, 1976).

13. For surveys of the diverse portraits, see especially Hayes, *From Son of God to Superstar*, and John Bowman, *Which Jesus?* (Philadelphia: Westminster, 1970).

14. See, for example, the history of Jesus research as sketched by W. Barnes Tatum, *In Quest of Jesus* (Atlanta: John Knox, 1982), 63–97.

15. *Kerygma* is a Greek word which means "preaching" and has become a technical term referring to the early church's post-Easter message about Jesus. It is often emphasized that the purpose of the gospels is essentially kerygmatic and not

historical, and whatever history they may contain has been thoroughly overlaid by the *kerygma* of the church. Scholars during the "no quest" period affirmed both the near impossibility as well as the theological unnecessity of trying to go behind the *kerygma*.

16. Mark 1:15. These are the first words attributed to Jesus in Mark, his "inaugural address," and presumably Mark intends them as a shorthand summary of Jesus' message and mission. It is Mark's answer to the question, "What was the *core* of Jesus' proclamation?"

17. Often cited as Schweitzer's most influential predecessor is Johannes Weiss, *Jesus' Proclamation of the Kingdom of God*, edited and translated by R. H. Hiers and D. L. Holland (Philadelphia: Fortress Press, 1971; first edition published in German in 1892, second edition in 1900).

18. See his *The Mystery of the Kingdom of God* (New York: Schocken Books, 1964, originally published in German in 1901); and *The Quest of the Historical Jesus*.

19. For Schweitzer, however, the story of Jesus did not end there. Instead, Schweitzer spoke movingly of the spiritual Christ who still speaks to us, concluding his treatment of Jesus with what have been called the most famous words of twentieth-century theology:

He comes to us as One unknown, without a name, as of old, by the lake-side, He came to those men who knew Him not. He speaks to us the same word: "Follow thou me" and sets us to the tasks which He has to fulfil for our time. He commands. And to those who obey Him, whether they be wise or simple, He will reveal Himself in the toils, the conflicts, the sufferings which they shall pass through in His fellowship, and, as an ineffable mystery, they shall learn in their own experience Who He is. (*Quest*, 403)

The words have even been set to music by Jane Marshall as "He Comes to Us," an anthem for use in Christian worship.

For Schweitzer, the living Christ called him to Africa, even though Schweitzer's understanding of the historical Jesus as one who was profoundly misled by the eschatological beliefs of his day left Jesus firmly anchored in his own time. No wonder Schweitzer wrote that Jesus is "a stranger to our time" (*Quest*, 401). For Schweitzer, the historical Jesus thus became theologically irrelevant; only the Christ who still speaks to us is relevant for theology.

20. It is found in the work of Rudolf Bultmann (1884–1976), arguably the most influential New Testament scholar throughout much of this century; in Günther Bornkamm's *Jesus of Nazareth* (New York: Harper, 1960; originally published in German in 1956), probably the most widely read scholarly book about Jesus written in the last thirty years; and, in various forms, in the work of such influential scholars as Joachim Jeremias, Werner Kümmel, Hans Conzelmann, R. H. Fuller, and the early works of Norman Perrin. British scholarship, represented especially by C. H. Dodd, has resisted the consensus.

21. Hans Küng, *On Being a Christian* (Garden City, New York: Doubleday, 1984), originally published in German in 1974.

22. For Küng, as his sources indicate, that consensus is based almost exclusively on German scholarship; as already noted, German scholarship (at least until very recently) has been the dominant voice in biblical scholarship in this century. See also Bruce Chilton in his recent treatment of "Kingdom of God" research, *The*

Kingdom of God in the Teaching of Jesus (Philadelphia: Fortress, 1984), who speaks of a consensus reached by midcentury that the Kingdom was to be understood eschatologically.

23. See my essay, "The Historical Jesus and Christian Preaching" in *The Christian Century* (August 28–September 4, 1985): 764–767.

24. See the well-known epigram created by Rudolf Bultmann: only the *das* ("thatness") of Jesus matters, not the *was* ("whatness"); that is, all that matters theologically is *that* Jesus was, not *what* Jesus was. The "facts" of his life are theologically irrelevant. Bultmann's position is not universally held, but it is typical and influential.

25. In the spring of 1986, I conducted a mail poll of seventy-two active Jesus scholars, members of the Jesus Seminar inaugurated by Robert Funk and members of the Historical Jesus Section of the Society of Biblical Literature. The two samples thus fairly represent contemporary mainstream scholarship. Combining the two groups, 59 percent of those responding think that Jesus did *not* expect the end of the world in his generation. It should be noted that all of the scholars were in North America; a poll of German scholars would, I suspect, show that the consensus still exists in Germany. For the poll itself and detailed results, see my "A Temperate Case for a Non-Eschatological Jesus," published in *Society of Biblical Literature: 1986 Seminar Papers* (Atlanta: Scholars Press, 1986), 521–535, and in the journal of the Jesus Seminar, *Foundations and Facets Forum*, volume 2, number 3 (September 1986): 81–102, especially 98–100. The same poll was taken at the October 1986 national meeting of the Jesus Seminar at Notre Dame, with even more decisive results. Of the thirty-nine scholars voting, nine said they thought Jesus did expect the end of the world in his own time, thirty said they did not.

26. In addition to the essay referred to in the previous note, see also my "An Orthodoxy Reconsidered: The 'End-of-the-World Jesus,'" in *The Glory of Christ in the New Testament* (Oxford: Oxford University Press, 1987), 207–217, and my *Conflict, Holiness and Politics in the Teaching of Jesus* (New York and Toronto: Edwin Mellen Press, 1984), 221–227.

27. In addition to the large number of books published in recent years on the historical Jesus and related subjects (for example, the social setting of first-century Palestine), the "renaissance" is pointed to by two organizational developments. In the Society of Biblical Literature, the major professional organization for mainstream biblical scholars, a new "consultation" was formed in 1981 and became an official "section" in 1983, devoted to the study of the historical Jesus. In 1985, Professor Robert Funk founded "The Jesus Seminar," now constituted by over one hundred "Fellows" committed to investigating the traditions about Jesus. The Jesus Seminar has already attracted considerable national attention, not only in scholarly circles but in the public media. See its journal, *Foundations and Facets Forum*, which began publication in 1985.

28. A remark made by Bernard Brandon Scott at the annual meeting of the Historical Jesus Section of the Society of Biblical Literature in Chicago in December 1984. For bibliographical essays about this rapidly growing development in New Testament studies, see Paul Hollenbach, "Recent Historical Jesus Studies and the Social Sciences," *Society of Biblical Literature 1983 Seminar Papers* (Chico, CA: Scholars Press, 1983), 61–78; Bruce Malina, "The Social Sciences and Biblical Interpretation," *Interpretation* 36 (1982), 229–242; Philip Richter,

"Recent Sociological Approaches to the Study of the New Testament," *Religion* 14 (1984), 77–90; Robin Scroggs, "The Sociological Interpretation of the New Testament," *New Testament Studies* 26 (1980), 164–179. See also the volume in the *Semeia* series devoted to this topic: John H. Elliott, ed., *Semeia 35: Social Scientific Criticism of the New Testament and Its Social World* (Decatur, GA: Scholars Press, 1986).

29. In some respects, the quest for the historical Jesus as a historical enterprise is no different from the quest for the historical Caesar or the quest for the historical Buddha. Though we know of these figures only in traditions preserved by their respective communities, we do not therefore conclude that we can know nothing about them. Our sources for the historical Jesus are at least as good. To be sure, there is more of a "theological overlay" in the sources about Jesus because of the early church's convictions regarding his ultimate stature, but this does not render historical knowledge impossible.

30. To a large extent, the methodological skepticism of this century has flowed from beginning with the *sayings* of Jesus, especially those with a christological significance (that is, those which directly or indirectly make a statement about Jesus' ultimate status). But to make the historical difficulties involved in assessing these sayings *paradigmatic* for all historical knowledge of Jesus goes beyond sound historical judgment. See the astute methodological remarks of E. P. Sanders, *Jesus and Judaism* (Philadelphia: Fortress, 1985), 3–13, and A. E. Harvey, *Jesus and the Constraints of History* (Philadelphia: Westminster, 1982), 5–10.

31. This meaning of the term must be distinguished from two other common meanings. In popular usage within the church today, it has become virtually synonymous with having the gift of tongues. That usage is too narrow; the term properly denotes a Spirit-filled person who may or may not speak in tongues. It is also to be distinguished from a second use, widespread in secular culture: to refer to a person (often in the political or entertainment world) who has unusually captivating or magnetic appeal.

I. JESUS AND THE SPIRIT

2. The Context: The Spirit-filled Heart of Judaism

When I was a young teacher in my mid-twenties, an older colleague delighted in characterizing modern theology as "flat-tire" theology —"All of the *pneuma* has gone out of it." The irony of his comment depended on the double meaning of *pneuma*, a Greek word meaning both air and spirit.[1] I understood his point, but I wasn't sure I agreed with it. For me, modern theology was a joy: insightful, challenging, liberating.

Though I still see modern theology as a treasure of great value for both church and culture, I also see that my colleague's statement was (and is) largely correct, not only about theology in general but also about biblical scholarship and historical Jesus studies in particular.[2] Within scholarly circles, Jesus' relationship to the world of Spirit is seldom taken seriously.[3] Attention is directed to what he *said*, and sometimes even to what he *did*, but seldom is attention paid to what he *was*.

What Jesus was, historically speaking, was a Spirit-filled person in the charismatic stream of Judaism. This is the key to understanding what he was like as a historical figure. In an important sense, all that he was, taught, and did flowed out of his own intimate experience of the "world of Spirit."

THE "WORLD OF SPIRIT"

The notion of a "world of Spirit" is a vague and difficult notion in the contemporary world. By it I mean another dimension or layer or level of reality in addition to the visible world of our ordinary experience. This notion of "another world," understood as *actual* even though nonmaterial, is quite alien to the modern way of thinking. The modern worldview or "picture of reality" sees reality as having essentially one dimension, the visible and material realm.[4] Deeply ingrained in all of us who have grown up in modern Western culture, this worldview makes us skeptical about another reality. For most contemporary people, believing in another reality requires "faith," understood as affirming that which on other grounds is doubtful.[5] The "world of Spirit" is not part of our taken-for-granted understanding of reality, not part of our worldview.

But the notion of another reality, a world of Spirit, was the common property of virtually every culture before ours, constituting what has been called the "primordial tradition."[6] Appearing in a multiplicity of cultural forms, indeed in virtually as many forms as there are cultures, it was almost a "cultural universal," the "human unanimity" prior to the modern period. Essential to it are two claims.

First, in addition to the visible material world disclosed to us by ordinary sense perception (and modern science), there is another level of reality, a second world of nonmaterial reality, charged with energy and power. This basic division of reality into two levels can be spoken of in many ways—as the sacred and the profane, the holy (or "numinous") and the mundane, God and "this world," and so forth.[7] What is most important is the notion of another level or levels of reality rather than any particular set of terms. Moreover, the "other world"—the world of Spirit—is seen as "more" real than "this world." Indeed, the "other reality" is the source or ground of "this world."

Second, and very importantly, the "other world" is not simply an article of belief, but an element of experience. That is, the notion of another reality does not have its origin in prescientific speculation about the origin of things, or in primal anxiety about death or the need for protection, but is grounded in the religious experience of humankind.[8] It is not merely believed in, but *known*.

To put this second claim somewhat differently, the world of

Spirit and the world of ordinary experience are seen as not completely separate, but as *intersecting* at a number of points.[9] Many cultures speak of a particular place as the "navel of the earth," the umbilical cord connecting the two worlds.[10] Some cultures speak of the two worlds intersecting in particular historical events. But it is especially in the experience of individuals that the "other world" is known. In every culture known to us, there are men and women who experience union or communion with the world of Spirit, either "entering" it or experiencing it coming upon them. Those who experience it frequently and vividly often become mediators between the two worlds in a variety of cultural forms: as healers, prophets, law-givers, shamans, mystics. Such men and women are charismatics in the proper sense of the word: people who know the world of Spirit firsthand.

THE PRIMORDIAL TRADITION IN THE BIBLICAL TRADITION

The cultural tradition in which Jesus lived took for granted the central claims of the primordial tradition: there are minimally two worlds, and the other world can be known. At the heart of the Jewish tradition, indeed constituting it, was Israel's story of the intersection between the world of Spirit and the world of ordinary experience. For that is what Israel's scriptures were. The Hebrew Bible is Israel's story of events which were seen as disclosures of Spirit, of people who were experienced as mediators of Spirit, of laws and prophetic utterances which were believed to have been given by the Spirit.

This multilayered picture of reality runs throughout the Bible. The opening verse of Genesis portrays the visible world as having its origin in Spirit, in God: "In the beginning God created the heavens and the earth." Importantly, Spirit is not seen as abstract and remote, as a hypothetical first cause.[11] Rather, the world of Spirit is seen as alive and "personal," populated by a variety of beings: angels, archangels, cherubim, seraphim. At its center (or height or depth) is God, often spoken of as personal: as father, mother, king, shepherd, lover. Nonanthropomorphic terms can also be used: fire, light, Spirit.

It is difficult to know how literally we should take this language. Language about "the other world" is necessarily metaphorical and analogical, simply because we must use language drawn from the visible world to try to speak of another world constituted by very different realities and energies. If anything is to be communicated at all, it must be by analogy to what we know in the ordinary world, or in images drawn from the ordinary world. Thus God is *like* a father or mother, *like* a king, *like* a shepherd, *like* fire; but God is not *literally* any of these things. Yet, though the language is metaphorical, the realities are not.

Moreover, this other world is not *literally* somewhere else. It is not the localized heaven of the popular imagination. Though God can be spoken of as a being "up in heaven," the tradition makes it clear that God and the world of Spirit are not literally elsewhere. Rather, according to the tradition, God is everywhere present. To use somewhat technical but useful theological language, for the biblical tradition God is *immanent* (everywhere present, omnipresent), even as God is also *transcendent* (not to be identified with any particular thing, not even with the sum total of things). As omnipresent and immanent, God and the world of Spirit are all around us, including within us. Rather than God being somewhere else, we (and everything that is) are in God.[12] We live in Spirit, even though we are typically unaware of this reality.[13]

BIBLICAL MEDIATORS BETWEEN THE TWO WORLDS

Israel affirmed that the world of Spirit was *known*. It intersected with "this world" at many points: historically, especially in the exodus and the return from exile, though also in other central events of her history; cultically, in the temple of Jerusalem, which was seen as the navel of the earth connecting this world to the other world which was its source; and personally, in the devotional and spiritual experiences of ordinary people and especially in Spirit-filled mediators such as Moses and the prophets. It is this tradition of Spirit-filled mediators that is most significant for understanding the historical Jesus.

From start to end, the Bible is dominated by such figures, beginning with the Genesis stories of the patriarchs, the "fathers" of Israel. Abraham saw visions and entertained heavenly visitors. Jacob had a vision of a fiery ladder connecting the two worlds, with angels ascending and descending on it. Afterwards he exclaimed, "This is the gate of heaven" — that is, the doorway into the other world.[14] In the last book of the Bible, the vision of John begins with a similar image: "I looked and lo, in heaven, an open door."[15] What is true of the beginning and end of the Bible is also true of its great figures throughout the tradition.

The first five books of the Bible (the Pentateuch) center on Moses, the central human figure of Israel's history, indeed her "founder." According to the brief obituary at the end of Deuteronomy, he "knew God face to face." According to Exodus, he repeatedly ascended the mountain of God (symbolizing the connection between the two worlds?) and there was given the words which he imparted to his followers as "divine law." On one occasion after coming down from the mountain, we are told, his face actually glowed with the radiance of the holy which he had encountered.[16] Throughout the Pentateuch, Moses functions as a mediator between the two worlds: as divine law-giver, as channel of power from the world of Spirit, and as intercessor on behalf of his people.[17]

The experience of the other world and the role of mediation are also central to the prophets, including Elijah as well as the classical prophets. Though a much more shadowy figure than Moses, Elijah was one of the central heroes of the Jewish tradition. Like Moses, he was frequently in the wilderness and sojourned to the sacred mountain, where he also experienced a theophany (an experience of God or "the holy"). Even as the stories about him emphasize the issues of social justice and loyalty to God which characterize the later prophets, he is also clearly portrayed as a "man of Spirit": he traveled "in the Spirit" and was a channel for the power of Spirit as both a healer and rainmaker. At the end of his life he was carried into the other world by "chariots of fire."[18]

One hundred years later, in the eighth century B.C., the mission of the prophet Isaiah began with an overwhelming experience of the other world:

In the year that King Uzziah died I saw the Lord sitting upon a throne, high and lifted up; and his train filled the Temple. Above him stood the seraphim; each had six wings: with two he covered his face, and with two he covered his feet, and with two he flew. And one called to another and said: "Holy, holy, holy is the Lord of hosts; the whole earth is full of his glory." And the foundations of the thresholds shook at the voice of him who called, and the house was filled with smoke.[19]

In the temple, the sacred place connecting the earth to the other realm, Isaiah momentarily "saw" into the other world: a vision of God upon the divine throne, surrounded by strange, unearthly six-winged creatures. But he did not simply "see" into the other world; he was, in a sense, *in it*, for he became a participant in the scene: "Then flew one of the six-winged creatures to me, having in his hand a burning coal which he had taken with tongs from the altar. And he touched my mouth and said, 'Behold, this has touched your lips.'"[20]

The image of seeing into another world is also used to describe the origin of Ezekiel's mission as a prophet some 150 years later: "In the thirtieth year, in the fourth month, on the fifth day of the month, as I was among the exiles by the river Chebar, *the heavens were opened and I saw visions of God.*"[21] Alternatively, prophets spoke of the Spirit descending upon them: "The Spirit of the Lord *fell upon me*," or "The Spirit of the Lord God is *upon me.*"[22] The direct encounters with the world of Spirit reported by Isaiah and Ezekiel generally characterized the prophets. They spoke of knowing and being known by God, of seeing visions, of being present in the "heavenly council."[23]

In Jesus' day, the stream was not frozen in the past, but continued to flow. In the century before and after Jesus, the charismatic phenomenon continued in a number of Jewish "holy men" active primarily in Galilee.[24] Known for the directness of their relationship to God and the length and effectiveness of their prayer, they were delegates of their people to the other world, mediating the power of the Spirit especially as healers and rainmakers. The two most famous, Honi the Circle-Drawer and Hanina ben Dosa, were both compared to that earlier person of the Spirit, Elijah.

They had power over demons, who recognized and feared them. Among the healings credited to Hanina, active around the middle of the first century A.D., one involved a cure from a distance. He healed the son of Rabbi Gamaliel who was mortally ill with a fever, despite the fact that Hanina was in Galilee and Gamaliel's son was in Jerusalem, some one hundred miles away.

These charismatics were known for their intimacy with God. Some were even heralded as "son of God" by a "heavenly voice": "The whole universe is sustained on account of *my son* Hanina."[25] The role of intercession characteristic of the Spirit-filled tradition appears in a saying attributed to Honi (first century B.C.) which also uses the language of sonship: "Lord of the universe, thy sons have turned to me because I am as a *son of the house* before thee."[26] As "son of the house," he was sought by the other "sons" as an intercessor with the world of Spirit.[27]

The most famous follower of Jesus in the generation after his death was also a Spirit-filled mediator. Near the middle of the first century the apostle Paul wrote about his own journey into the world of Spirit:

I know a man in Christ [Paul is referring to himself] who fourteen years ago was caught up to the third heaven—whether in the body or out of the body I do not know, God knows. And I know that this man was caught up into Paradise—whether in the body or out of the body I do not know, God knows—and he heard things that cannot be told, which man may not utter.[28]

Notable is the picture of reality as having several layers, the image of entering it, the uncertainty whether the experience was "in the body" or out of it, the notion of Paradise as a realm that can be entered in the present, and the ineffability of the other world, which is filled with realities that cannot be adequately described in language drawn from this world. Paul's conversion is also best understood as a charismatic experience,[29] and he was, according to Acts, a healer, a channel for power from the world of Spirit.

Thus the stream in which Jesus stood, going back through the prophets to the founder and fathers of Israel, as well as the stream which issued forth from him, centered on Spirit-filled mediators who bridged the two worlds. The stream was the source of the tradition; its literature, both the Hebrew Bible and the New Testament, clusters around them. Indeed, in the specific sense of the term used here, the heart of the biblical tradition is "charismatic," its origin lying in the experience of Spirit-endowed people who became radically open to the other world and whose gifts were extraordinary.

THE COLLISION WITH OUR WAY OF SEEING

Even people familiar with the Bible are often unaware how much the experience of the other world pervades it. Because the notion of another realm or dimension of reality, and of people who can be mediators between the two worlds, is alien to our way of seeing, we need to return to this theme as we draw this chapter to a close.

Those of us socialized in the modern world have grown up in a culture with a largely secularized and one-dimensional understanding of reality. Though remnants of a religious worldview remain, the dominant worldview in the modern period flows from the scientific and technological revolution of the last few centuries. For us, perceiving reality within the framework of this worldview, what is real is essentially the material, the visible world of time and space. What is real is ultimately made up of tiny bits and pieces of "stuff," all operating in accord with laws of cause and effect which can be known. Reality is constituted by matter and energy interacting to form the visible world. In short, there is but one world.

As we grew up, the process of learning this worldview was largely unconscious. We were not directly instructed in the subject of "worldview," but it was the presupposition for all subjects. Moreover, we are not normally conscious of its presence or function within our minds. As a fundamental picture of reality, the modern worldview is like a map laid over reality, conditioning both our experience and understanding. We pay attention to what it says is real. The depth of this worldview in us, the taken-for-granted way in which it affects our understanding, is remarkable, even in people with a religious upbringing.[30]

This nonreligious one-dimensional understanding of reality makes the other world and the notion of mediation between the two worlds unreal to us. Though we may grant that unusual healings do occur, we are inclined to think that some psychosomatic explanation is possible. Though we grant that exceptional people may indeed enter a trancelike state and experience a journey into another world, we are inclined to view their experience of nonordinary reality as purely subjective, as an encounter with merely mental realities within the psyche, or as hallucinations. To put it mildly, the "other world" is no longer taken for granted as an objectively real "other reality." Indeed, within the modern framework, frequent and vivid experiences of another reality mark a person as clinically psychotic.

Even biblical scholarship in the modern period has generally not known what to do with the category of "Spirit." Most biblical scholars work within the modern academy, whose canons of respectability include a methodology that assumes the truthfulness of the modern worldview. Typically spending eight or more years in college and graduate school and often remaining as teachers, we often measure our time in the academy in decades rather than years. Texts that report "paranormal" happenings, whether they be visions of another realm or miracles, are either largely ignored or else interpreted in such a way that they do not violate our sense of what is possible or real.[31] Thus, because we do not know what to do with the world of Spirit, we tend not to give it a central place in our historical study of the biblical tradition.

But the reality of the other world deserves to be taken seriously. Intellectually and experientially, there is much to commend it. The primary intellectual objection to it flows from a rigid application of the modern worldview's definition of reality. Yet the modern view is but one of a large number of humanly constructed maps of reality. It is historically the most recent and impressive because of the degree of control it has given us; but it is no more an absolute map of reality than any of the previous maps. All are relative, products of particular histories and cultures; and the modern one, like its predecessors, will be superceded.

Already there are signs of its eclipse. Within the theoretical sciences, the modern worldview in its popular form has been abandoned.[32] At macro and micro levels, reality behaves in strange ways that stretch the popular worldview beyond its limits. The "old map" is being left behind. Of course, this does not prove the truth of the religious worldview, but it does undermine the central reason for rejecting it. The worldview that rejects or ignores the world of Spirit is not only relative, but is itself in the process of being rejected. The alternative to a one-dimensional understanding of reality can claim most of the history of human experience in its support. People throughout the centuries, in diverse cultures, regularly experienced another realm which seemed to them more real, powerful, and fundamental than the world of our ordinary experience. Not only is there no intellectual reason to suppose the second world to be unreal, but there is much experiential evidence to suggest its reality.[33]

In any case, quite apart from the question of ultimate truth, it is necessary to take seriously the reality of the world of Spirit if we wish to take the central figures of the Jewish tradition seriously. To try to understand the Jewish tradition and Jesus while simultaneously dismissing the notion of another world or immediately reducing it to a merely psychological realm is to fail to see the phenomena, to fail to take seriously what these charismatic mediators experienced and reported. For many of us, this will require a temporary suspension of our disbelief. As we shall see, Jesus' vivid experience of the reality of Spirit radically challenges our culture's way of seeing reality.

NOTES

1. I believe that he was quoting or paraphrasing Karl Barth, though I am not aware whether it is published somewhere in Barth's writings or whether it is anecdotal.

2. See the excellent statement by Stanley Hauerwas and William Willimon in "Embarrassed by God's Presence," *The Christian Century* (January 30, 1985): 98–100. They argue that both the modern church and modern theology are pervaded by the "practical atheism" of our time, that way of seeing and living which takes it for granted that there is no reality beyond the visible.

3. There are exceptions, to which I am indebted. Two studies from the last decade stand out: Geza Vermes, *Jesus the Jew* (New York: Macmillan, 1973), which treats the Jewish charismatic tradition contemporary with Jesus, and J. G. Dunn, *Jesus and the Spirit* (Philadelphia: Westminster, 1975), a scholarly study of texts and traditions relevant to Jesus' relationship to the Spirit.

4. Of the many books which treat the subject of the modern worldview (or *Weltanschauung*, a German term which often appears even in books written in English), I have found two to be especially useful: W. T. Stace, *Religion and the Modern Mind* (Philadelphia: Lippincott, 1952), and Huston Smith, *Forgotten Truth: The Primordial Tradition* (New York: Harper & Row, 1976).

5. Though this is not the place to develop the point at length, the term "faith" has thus undergone a subtle but decisive shift in meaning in the modern period. For many people, faith now means "believing in the existence of God." In earlier times, it didn't take "faith" to believe *that* God existed—almost everybody took that for granted. Rather, "faith" had to do with one's *relationship* to God— whether one *trusted* in God. The difference between faith as "belief in something that may or may not exist" and faith as "trusting in God" is enormous. The first is a "matter of the head," the second a "matter of the heart"; the first can leave one unchanged, the second intrinsically brings change.

6. The phrase comes from Huston Smith, *Forgotten Truth*; see also his *Beyond the Post-Modern Mind* (New York: Crossroad, 1982). Other scholars have developed the same basic understanding, but I find Smith's phrase "primordial tradition," as well as his exposition of the notion, to be especially illuminating and helpful.

7. See, for example, Mircea Eliade, *The Sacred and the Profane* (New York: Harcourt, Brace and World, 1959; originally published in French in 1956); and Rudolf Otto, *The Idea of the Holy* (New York: Oxford University Press, 1958; first published in German in 1917), who introduced the term "numinous" as a way of speaking of the "holy," understood *not* as a moral term meaning righteous or pure but as a designation for the overpowering mystery (the *mysterium tremendum*) that is experienced in extraordinary moments.

8. In addition to the works by Smith, Eliade, and Otto already referred to, see William James's classic study *The Varieties of Religious Experience* (New York: Macmillan, 1961; originally published in 1902). James finds the origin of belief in an "unseen" world in the experience of "religious geniuses" who experience *firsthand* the realities of which religion speaks, and carefully distinguishes this primal experience from what he calls "secondhand" religion, the beliefs that people acquire through tradition; see especially 24–25, though the distinction remains important throughout his book.

9. To use Eliade's terms for a moment, the two worlds intersect in "theophanies" (manifestations of God) and "hierophanies" (manifestations of the holy). Otto speaks of experiences of the *numinous* (that is, of the holy or *numen*, a Latin term for "God"), which underlies phenomena.

10. For example, the temple at Delphi in Greece was seen as the "navel of the earth," the *axis mundi* connecting the two worlds; for other examples, see Eliade, *Sacred and Profane*, 32–47.

11. This is what the notion of God as creator has become in much of the modern world. Beginning with the deists of the seventeenth century, the concept of God began to function primarily as an intellectual hypothesis to account for the origin of everything. In cultural retrospect, this development may be seen as part of the process whereby Western intellectual culture weaned itself (or "fell," depending upon one's point of view) from a religious worldview to a secular worldview.

12. Neither the Old or New Testament uses abstractions such as omnipresence or transcendence, but the notion is clearly present. Classic Old Testament texts which point to the omnipresence of God are Psalm 139:7–10, 1 Kings 8:27, Isaiah 6:3 ("the whole earth is full of his glory"). The notion of the immanent *Logos* at the beginning of John's gospel points in the same direction, as do the words attributed approvingly by Luke to Paul in Acts 17:28: "In God we live and move and have our being." God is not elsewhere"; we live in God.

13. See Smith, *Forgotten Truth*, 21: The "higher levels (of the primordial tradition) are not literally elsewhere; they are removed only in the sense of being inaccesible to ordinary consciousness." Or, to paraphrase William James in *The Varieties of Religious Experience*, we are separated from this other world only by the *filmiest screens of consciousness*; see especially 305, 331, 335, 401.

14. Genesis 28:17. For other experiences of the patriarchs involving contact with the other world, see, for example, Genesis 12:7–9, 15:1–17, 17:1–2, 18:1–33, 26:23–25, 32:22–31.

15. Revelation 4:1. The author of the book tells us that he received this vision while he was "in the Spirit" (1:10), presumably a state of nonordinary consciousness in which he momentarily "saw" into the other world. Revelation, part of the New Testament, is of course not in the *Hebrew* Bible, but it reflects the same worldview.

16. Exodus 34:29–35.

17. See especially Exodus 32:7–14 and Numbers 14:13–19.

18. Though most of the Pentateuch concerns Moses, only a few chapters in the books of Kings speak of this ninth-century prophet: 1 Kings 17–19, 21; 2 Kings 1–2.

19. Isaiah 6:1–4.

20. Isaiah 6:6–7.

21. Ezekiel 1:1.

22. Ezekiel 11:5, Isaiah 61:1

23. Almost all of the Spirit-filled mediators mentioned in the Hebrew Bible are men. No doubt this is because the religion of ancient Israel was dominated by men. "Official" religious positions such as priest, prophet, and sage were restricted to men and, so far as we know, all of the biblical authors were men. Given this, it is noteworthy that the tradition does mention two charismatic women by name: Deborah the judge and Hulda the prophet. So also in other

cultures dominated by patriarchy, though religious functionaries may have been male, the Spirit seems to show no gender preference.

24. For this whole section on Jewish "holy men" at the time of Jesus, see especially Vermes, *Jesus the Jew*, 65–78, 206–213. Also relevant are E. E. Urbach, *The Sages* (Jerusalem: Magnes, 1975), volume 1, 97–123; and, earlier, A. Büchler, *Types of Jewish Palestinian Piety* (New York: KTAV, 1968; first published in 1922), 87–107, 196–252.

25. From the Babylonian Talmud: B. Taan. 24b, B. Ber. 17b, B. Hul. 86a, all cited by Vermes, *Jesus the Jew*, 206. Vermes also notes that Rabbi Meir was called "Meir *my son.*"

26. From the Mishnah, M. Taan. 3.8, cited by Vermes, *Jesus the Jew*, 209.

27. Besides being known as people whose concentration in prayer was great and as mediators of divine power, they shared a number of other characteristics. Vermes notes that they were relatively detached from possessions, perhaps because the other world had a reality compared to which the preoccupations of this world seemed trivial. They were also suspected of being inadequately concerned about the laws of their tradition (like many before and since whose awareness of the other realm is direct and experiential). Finally, though not restricted to Galilee, they seem to have been largely a Galilean phenomenon. Hanina, for example, was from a town in Galilee about ten miles from Nazareth.

28. 2 Corinthians 12:2–4. See also 1 Corinthians 12–14, where Paul speaks about the "gifts of the Spirit," some of which clearly involve direct relationship to the world of Spirit.

29. It is described three times in the book of Acts: 9:1–8, 22:6–11, 26:12–18.

30. In a poll which I have taken in both university and church settings for about ten years, 90 percent of the participants regularly reply to stories of paranormal phenomena such as walking on burning coals in South Asia and Polynesia with, "It violates my sense of what is possible." Their sense of what is possible flows from the modern one-dimensional understanding of reality, in which everything must be explicable by chains of cause and effect within the material world, simply because that is the only world that we see as "real."

31. Rudolf Bultmann's proposal for "demythologizing" the New Testament is a case in point. Recognizing that the New Testament writers often use the language of a three-story universe (heaven as "up," hell as "down," earth in the "middle"), Bultmann rightly stresses that such language is not to be taken literally (heaven is not really "up," and so forth). When the early Christians spoke of Jesus ascending into heaven or descending into hell, they could not have been describing a literal up-and-down motion through space. But, as Bultmann continues, it becomes clear that demythologizing involves not only a deliteralizing of the three-story universe, but also a collapse of the world of Spirit itself. That, too, does not conform to the modern worldview. See especially his essay, "New Testament and Mythology," in H. W. Bartsch, *Kerygma and Myth* (New York: Harper & Row, 1961; originally published in German in 1941), 1–16.

32. For a useful summary, see Smith, *Forgotten Truth*, 96–117. See also Ian Barbour, *Issues in Science and Religion* (New York: Harper & Row, 1971), 273–316; and Fritjof Capra, *The Tao of Physics* (Berkeley: Shambhala, 1975).

33. The historical and anthropological evidence is very strong. Not only are there

frequent accounts of subjectively entering the other world, but paranormal happenings in this world are also reported. Paranormal healings are overwhelmingly attested in both the ancient and modern world. Clairvoyance is also quite well-authenticated, and even something as bizarre as levitation is reasonably well-grounded.

3. The Spirit-filled Experience of Jesus

Given the subsequent historical importance of Jesus, it is remarkable that his public activity was so brief. The synoptic gospels imply that his ministry lasted only a year, the gospel of John that it lasted three years, or a bit more. Which is correct, we can no longer know, but both agree that it was brief, extraordinarily so. The Buddha taught for forty-five years after his enlightenment, Muhammad for about twenty years. According to Jewish tradition, Moses led his people for forty years. But Jesus' ministry was brief, a light flashing momentarily but brilliantly like a meteor in the night sky. What was he like?

Jesus was born sometime during the waning years of Herod the Great, who died in 4 B.C. Nothing is known about his life prior to the beginning of his ministry as a mature adult, except by inference.[1] He grew up in Nazareth, a hill town in the northern province of Galilee, some twenty miles inland from the Mediterranean Sea, fifteen miles from the Sea of Galilee to the east, and roughly one hundred miles north of Jerusalem. Most of his neighbors would have been farmers who lived in the village and worked the fields nearby, or workers in the relatively small number of trades necessary to support agricultural life. He may or may not have been a carpenter; both "carpenter" and "carpenter's son" were used metaphorically within Judaism to mean "scholar" or "teacher."[2]

We may surmise that he experienced the socialization of a typical boy in that culture. Growing up in a Jewish home, most likely he attended school from roughly age six to at least twelve or thirteen, as a system of "elementary education" was widespread in Palestinian Judaism. His "primer" would have been the book of Leviticus. Whether he had formal training as a teacher of the Torah[3] beyond the schooling given to every boy, we do not know.

As a boy and young man, Jesus almost certainly attended the synagogue (a place of Scripture reading and prayer in local communities) every Sabbath, and perhaps on Mondays and Thursdays as well. As a faithful Jew, he would have recited the *Shema* upon rising and retiring each day, the heart of which affirmed: "Hear O Israel: The Lord our God is one Lord; and you shall love the Lord your God with all your heart, and with all your soul, and with all your might."[4] Presumably, he participated in the Jewish festivals and went on pilgrimages to Jerusalem. From the gospels, it is clear that he was very familiar with his Scriptures, the Hebrew Bible. He may have known it from memory, a feat not uncommon among the learned. The Psalms were probably his "prayer book."

That is about all we can know about Jesus prior to his emergence as a public figure, despite attempts to fill in the missing years in later apocryphal gospels and occasional scholarly speculations. Suggestions that Jesus lived among the Essenes,[5] or studied in Egypt, or traveled to India, or somehow came in contact with the teaching of the Buddha, are not only without historical foundation but also unnecessary. We need not go beyond the mainstream of the Jewish tradition to find a "home" for everything that is said about him.

THE SOURCE OF JESUS' MINISTRY: THE DESCENT OF THE SPIRIT

When Jesus does appear on the stage of history as an adult, the first episode reported about him places him directly in the charismatic stream of Judaism. His mission began with a vision from the other world and the descent of the Spirit upon him. At about the age of thirty, early in the governorship of Pontius Pilate,[6] something impelled Jesus to go to a wilderness preacher of repentance named John and known ever since as "John the Baptist." All of the gospels (as well as Acts) connect the beginning of Jesus' ministry to his baptism by John.

Known to us both from the New Testament and from the Jewish

historian Josephus,[7] John stood in the charismatic stream of Judaism. His style of dress emulated Elijah, and his contemporaries compared him to a prophet.[8] Renowned for his eloquent and passionate call for repentance, John proclaimed that it was not sufficient to be "children of Abraham," but called the Jewish people to a more intense relationship to God sealed by a ritual of initiation.[9] Crowds flocked to this charismatic, some to be baptized.

Jesus was among them. As he was being baptized by John, he had a vision.[10] It is very tersely described: "He saw *the heavens opened* and *the Spirit descending upon him like a dove.*"[11] The language recalls earlier experiences of the other world in the Jewish tradition. Like Ezekiel some six centuries before, Jesus saw "the heavens opened," momentarily seeing into the other world, as if through a door or "tear." Through this door he saw "the Spirit descending upon him," echoing the words of an earlier Spirit-filled one: "The Spirit of the Lord is upon me."[12]

The vision was accompanied by a "heavenly voice" which declared Jesus' identity to him: "Thou art my beloved Son; with thee I am well-pleased." About the historicity of the baptism and the vision itself, there is little reason for doubt. Unless we think that visions simply do not happen, there is no reason to deny this experience to Jesus. However, about the "heavenly voice" there is some historical uncertainty, simply because the words so perfectly express the post-Easter perception of Jesus' identity. As such, they must be historically suspect as the product of the followers of Jesus in the years after Easter.

Yet how we interpret the words affects the historical judgment. If "beloved Son" is taken to mean "unique" Son of God in the sense in which the church uses that term, then the phrase must be viewed as historically suspect. But if it is given the meaning which similar expressions have in stories of other Jewish charismatic holy men, then it is historically possible to imagine this as part of the experience of Jesus. For they too had experiences in which a "heavenly voice" declared them to be God's "son."[13] If read in this way, the words not only become historically credible but are a further link to charismatic Judaism.

Whatever the historical judgment concerning the "heavenly voice," the story of Jesus' vision places him in the Spirit-filled heart of Judaism. It reflects the multi-layered understanding of reality which was part of the belief system and actual experience of his predecessors in his own tradition. Indeed, standing as it does at the beginning of his ministry, the vision is reminiscent of the "call narratives" of the prophets. Like them, his ministry began with an intense experience of the Spirit of God.

THE COURSE OF JESUS' MINISTRY: A PERSON OF SPIRIT

Jesus' ministry not only began with an experience of the Spirit, but was dominated throughout by intercourse with the other world.

VISIONS

The vision of the descent of the Spirit was followed immediately by another visionary experience or sequence of experiences. According to both Mark and the tradition behind Matthew and Luke, the Spirit "drove" or "led" Jesus out into the wilderness. Mark's account is very brief: "And Jesus was in the wilderness forty days, tempted by Satan; and he was with the wild beasts; and the angels ministered to him."[14]

Matthew and Luke agree that he spent a forty-day solitude in the wilderness, where he was tested by the lord of the evil spirits and nourished by beneficent spirits. They add that Jesus fasted and had a series of three closely related visions.[15] In the first, Jesus was tempted by Satan to use his powers to change stones into bread. In the second and third, Jesus and Satan traveled together in the spirit world. The devil took Jesus to the highest point of the temple in Jerusalem, and then "took him up and showed him all the kingdoms of the world in a moment of time."[16] Throughout, Satan tempted Jesus to use his charismatic powers in self-serving ways and to give his allegiance to him in exchange for all the kingdoms of the world.

Both the setting and the content of the visions are noteworthy. Like Moses and Elijah and other Jewish holy men, Jesus journeyed into the wilderness, alone, beyond the domestication of reality provided by culture and human interchange. There, in a desolate desert area near the Dead Sea, he underwent a period of extended solitude and fasting, practices which produce changes in consciousness and perception, typical of what other traditions call a "vision quest." Indeed, the *sequence* of initiation into the world of Spirit (the baptism) followed by a testing or ordeal in the wilderness is strikingly similar to what is reported of charismatic figures cross-culturally.[17]

The synoptic gospels report one more visionary experience of Jesus. According to Luke, in the middle of the ministry, a group of Jesus' followers exclaimed: "Lord, even the demons are subject to us in your name!" Jesus responded, "I *saw* Satan fall like lightning from heaven."[18] The passage uses language typically used to introduce a vision ("*I saw,*"), though the passage could also be a metaphorical exclamation about the defeat of Satan.

We do not know if Jesus had other visions. The fact that none are reported may be without significance. Presumably, Jesus would not routinely report such, but would do so only if they served some purpose in his teaching.[19] The rest of the New Testament frequently reports visions, suggesting that the early church continued to experience reality in the same Spirit-filled way that Jesus did.[20]

PRAYER

Among the reasons that we in the modern world have difficulty giving credence to the reality of Spirit is the disappearance of the deeper forms of prayer from our experience. Most of us are aware primarily of a form of prayer in which God is addressed with words, whether out loud in the context of public prayer, or internally in private prayer. Such "verbal prayer" is typically relatively brief, ordinarily no longer than a few minutes, perhaps sometimes longer in private devotion.

But verbal prayer is only one form of prayer in the Jewish-Christian tradition. Indeed, it is only the first stage of prayer;

beyond it are deeper levels of prayer characterized by internal silence and lengthy periods of time. In this state, one enters into deeper levels of consciousness; ordinary consciousness is stilled, and one sits quietly in the presence of God. Typically called contemplation or meditation, its deepest levels are described as a communion or union with God.[21] One enters the realm of Spirit and experiences God.

For a variety of reasons, this form of prayer has become quite unfamiliar within the modern church. Though preserved in religious orders, by a few groups such as the Quakers, and by individuals scattered throughout Christian denominations, it has largely disappeared as part of the experience of most people in modern culture.

The tradition in which Jesus stood knew this mode of prayer. Moses and Elijah spent long periods of time in solitude and communion with God. Nearer the time of Jesus the Galilean holy men regularly spent an hour "stilling their minds" in order to direct their hearts toward heaven.[22] Meditation also is found in Jewish mysticism. Though most familiar to us from the medieval Kabbalah, Jewish mysticism stretches back to the *merkabah* ("throne") mysticism of Jesus' time and before.[23] For the *merkabah* mystics, contemplative prayer was the vehicle for ascending through the heavens to the ultimate vision of beholding the throne of God— that is, of experiencing the kingship of God.

The gospels portray Jesus as a man of prayer who practiced this form of prayer increasingly unknown in modern Western culture.[24] Like Moses and Elijah, he regularly withdrew into solitude for long hours of prayer: "In the morning, a great while before day, he rose and went out to a lonely place and there he prayed." Another time, "After he had taken leave of them, he went into the hills to pray."[25] Luke reports that Jesus on occasion prayed all night.[26] Such lengthy hours of prayer accompanied by solitude do not imply verbal prayer, but contemplation or meditation, the stilling of the mind and directing of the heart toward God reported of Hanina ben Dosa and others in the Jewish spiritual tradition. Jesus practiced one of the classic disciplines for becoming present to the world of Spirit.

The intimacy of Jesus' experience of Spirit is pointed to by one of the distinctive features of his prayer life: his use of the word *Abba* to address God.[27] An Aramaic word used by very young children to address their father, *Abba* is like the English "Papa." Within Judaism, it was common to refer to God with the more formal "Father," but rare to call God *Abba*. The most plausible explanation of Jesus' departure from conventional usage is the intensity of his spiritual experience, a supposition supported by the parallel within Judaism. Namely, *Abba* is used as a term for God in traditions reported about Jewish charismatics contemporary with Jesus.[28] Thus at the heart of Jesus' prayer life was the experience of communion with God.

"THE SPIRIT OF THE LORD IS UPON ME"

The image of Jesus as a Spirit-filled person in the charismatic stream of Judaism is perfectly crystalized in the words with which, according to Luke, Jesus began his public ministry:

The Spirit of the Lord is upon me, because he has anointed me to preach good news to the poor. He has sent me to proclaim release to the captives and recovering of sight to the blind, to set at liberty those who are oppressed, to proclaim the acceptable year of the Lord.

About these words, quoted from an earlier charismatic, Jesus said, "Today this scripture has been fulfilled in your hearing."[29] Though the passage as a whole is often attributed to Luke and not to Jesus himself,[30] the picture of Jesus as one "anointed by the Spirit" succinctly summarizes what we find in the gospels. From his baptism onward, through his ordeal in the wilderness, and continuing throughout his ministry, his life and mission were marked by an intense experiential relationship to the Spirit.

Thus far we have been speaking about Jesus' *internal* life: his prayer life, the visions he experienced, his sense of intimacy with God. We also see his connection to the world of Spirit in central dimensions of his public life: in the impression he made on others, his claims to authority, and in the style of his speech.

THE IMPRESSION JESUS MADE ON OTHERS

In his classic book about the experience of the holy or the *numinous*, Rudolf Otto describes the *numinous presence* that frequently is felt in charismatic figures by those around them. There is something uncanny about such figures which evokes awe and amazement and impresses people with the feeling of another world. There may be something authoritative about the way they speak, penetrating about the way they see, powerful about their presence.[31]

Such was true of Jesus. A verse in Mark vividly conveys the impression he made, the "cloud of the *numinous*" that was present around him: "And they were on the road, going up to Jerusalem, and Jesus was walking ahead of them; and they were amazed, and those who followed were filled with awe."[32]

As a teacher Jesus made a striking impression, very different from the official teachers: "They were astonished at his teaching, for he taught them as one who had *authority*, and not as the scribes."[33] Behind the Greek word for authority lies the rabbinic term for the power or might of God, the *Gevurah*: "He speaks from the mouth of the *Gevurah*,"[34] that is, from the mouth of power or Spirit.

Popular opinion associated him with earlier charismatic figures, with Elijah or the prophets or John the Baptist.[35] The aura of "otherness" around him may explain the reaction of his family on one occasion: "They went out to seize him, for they said, 'He is beside himself,' " that is, insane.[36] Even his opponents granted that there was a spiritual power at work in him, but interpreted it as coming from "Beelzebul, the prince of demons."[37]

Not surprisingly, he attracted crowds. "The whole city was gathered around the door," people "could not get near him because of the crowd," "a great crowd followed him and thronged about him."[38] Such language is only what we would expect in the early church's account of his ministry, but it also undoubtedly conveys the historical impression which he made. Jesus was widely known as a charismatic figure, and it was this reputation as a man of Spirit that drew the crowds which flocked around him.

JESUS' OWN SENSE OF AUTHORITY

Jesus himself was aware of this power or authority which others sensed in him. When some of the religious leaders in Jerusalem questioned him about his authority, Jesus responded with another question: "I will ask you a question; answer me, and I will tell you by what authority I do these things. Was the baptism of John from heaven or from men?"[39] Was the authority of John "from heaven," from the "other world," or from men? Though unexpressed, Jesus' own view is clear: implicitly he claimed the same authority as John, one grounded neither in institution nor tradition but in the Spirit.

Similarly, Jesus was aware of the power of the Spirit flowing through him. In the context of casting out a demon, he identified the power as the Spirit of God: "If it is by *the Spirit of God* that I cast out demons, then the Kingdom of God has come upon you."[40] On another occasion, after a woman had touched his garment in order to be healed, he perceived that *power* had gone out of him.[41]

The style of Jesus' teaching also shows an awareness of a *numinous* authority not derived from tradition. It is seen in his emphatic and unusual "I say unto you" statements, often prefaced in an unprecedented manner with "Amen" ("truly," "certainly"), a solemn formula which normally followed a statement.[42] Sometimes his emphatic "I say unto you" was incorporated into a contrast with the words of the tradition using the pattern, "You have heard that it was said . . . but I say to you."[43] Thus the language of Jesus indicates an awareness of a tradition-transcending authority, one from the mouth of the Spirit.

Moreover, he called disciples, an action which points to his sense of charismatic authority even as it also testifies to the deep impression he made on people. Though it was relatively common for a teacher within Judaism to have devoted students, the phenomenon of discipleship is different and uncommon, involving an uprooting and a following after. The stories of the call of the disciples describe with compact vividness the imperative of Jesus' call, the immediacy of their response, and the radical rupture from their previous lives:

And passing along by the Sea of Galilee, Jesus saw Simon and Andrew casting a net in the sea. And Jesus said to them, "Follow me." And immediately they left their nets and followed him. And going on a little farther, he saw James the son of Zebedee and John his brother, who were in their boat mending the nets. And immediately he called them; and they left their father Zebedee in the boat with the hired servants and followed him.[44]

Later, one of them exclaimed: "Lo, we have *left everything* and followed you."[45] The phenomenon of discipleship is located within the charismatic stream of Judaism, occurring in response to a charismatic leader.[46]

Given all of the above, it is not surprising that Jesus had a prophetic consciousness. Not only did some of his contemporaries put him in the prophetic tradition, but he also twice referred to himself as one, albeit somewhat indirectly. In his home town, he said, "A prophet is not without honor, except in his own country." Later, he said, "It cannot be that a prophet should perish away from Jerusalem."[47] Identifying himself with the prophets, Jesus saw himself in the tradition of those who *knew* God.[48]

THE TRANSFIGURATION

Some of his disciples reportedly experienced a strange episode which underlines the connection between Jesus and the world of Spirit. According to Mark, shortly before Jesus began his final journey to Jerusalem, the inner core of the disciples momentarily saw him transformed, his form and clothing suffused with light. Jesus "led them up a high mountain apart by themselves; and he was transfigured before them, and his garments became glistening, intensely white. And there appeared to them Elijah with Moses; and they were talking to Jesus."[49]

The details link Jesus to the world of the charismatics. Like Moses before him, he momentarily "glowed" with the radiance of the Spirit (stories of "glowing" holy men are also reported elsewhere). With him were seen Elijah and Moses, the two great charismatic figures of the Jewish tradition.[50] Of course, it is very difficult to know what to make of the story historically. Did the disciples actually have this experience, or is the whole narrative a symbolic statement of Jesus' identity? But even if the narrative is viewed as the creation of the church, it remains significant that the tradition associated Jesus with the two great men of Spirit of Israel's history.

JESUS' OWN SENSE OF IDENTITY

Jesus himself, his contemporaries, and the gospel writers all identified him with the charismatic stream of Judaism, as having a consciousness akin to the prophets. Did he also think of himself with the exalted titles with which the early church proclaimed him after Easter? Did he think of himself as the Messiah (Christ)? Or as "the Son of God"? As already noted, historical scholarship has tended to give a negative answer.[51] But, as with the "heavenly voice" at his baptism, the historical judgment hinges in part upon the sense in which these terms are understood.

If "Son of God" is used in the special Christian sense which emerges in the rest of the New Testament (by the time of Paul and John, preexistent with God from before creation; by the time of Matthew and Luke, conceived by the Spirit and born of a virgin), then almost certainly Jesus did not think of himself as *the* Son of God. But if "son of God" is given the meaning that it carried within Judaism at the time of Jesus, then it is possible he did. There, "son of God" was used in three different contexts to refer to three different entities, though with a common nuance of meaning. In the Hebrew Bible, it referred to Israel as a whole or to the king of Israel.[52] Contemporary with Jesus, the image of God as father and a particular person as God's son was used, as already noted, in stories about Jewish charismatic holy men. All three uses have one element in common. All designate a relationship of special intimacy with God—Israel as the chosen people, the king as the adopted son, the charismatic as one who knows and is known by God.

In this Jewish sense, Jesus may have thought of himself as "son of God." He clearly was aware of a relationship of special intimacy. His use of the term *Abba* has as its corollary the term "son." There are also a number of passages which may plausibly be attributed to him where he uses father-son imagery to speak at least indirectly of his relationship to God. Finally, the use of the image by other Jewish charismatics contemporary with him, with whom he shared much in common, provides a context in which the term is not only appropriate but virtually expected.

Moreover, there is a web of associations connecting this experiential awareness of intimacy with God with the term Messiah. "Messiah" (*Mashiah*) in the Jewish Scriptures means simply "anointed," that is, "smeared with oil." Such anointing was part of the coronation of the king of Israel, who thereby became God's "son." Jesus was aware of both "sonship" and being anointed by the Spirit, as we have seen. Thus the phrases "anointed by God," "son of God," and the term "Messiah" are all closely related.

We cannot know if Jesus made these associations himself; no saying which does this explicitly can be confidently attributed to him. Moreover, we may surmise that he did not spend a great deal of time thinking about who he was. Finally, of course, it does not matter whether he thought of himself as Messiah or Son of God, for whether or not he was does not depend on whether he thought so.[53] Yet our exploration of his life as a Spirit-filled person shows that the church's exalted designations of him were not an arbitrary imposition, but had roots in the historical experience of Jesus himself.

Jesus' intense relationship to the world of Spirit thus not only enables us to glimpse what he was like as a historical figure, but also enables us to understand the origin and appropriateness of the titles with which he was later proclaimed. Clearly, Easter played the major role in leading the followers of Jesus to describe him in the most glorious terms known in his culture. Yet the seeds of the church's proclamation lie in the experience of the historical Jesus, even if the full-grown plant needed the experience of Easter to allow it to burst forth.

The cumulative impression created by the synoptic gospels is very strong: Jesus stood in the charismatic tradition of Judaism which reached back to the beginnings of Israel. Matthew, Mark, and Luke all portray him as a Spirit-filled person through whom the power of Spirit flowed. His relationship to Spirit was both the source and energy of the mission which he undertook. According to these earliest portraits, Jesus was one who knew the other world, who stood in a long line of mediators stretching back to Elijah and Moses. Indeed, according to them, he was the climax of that history of mediation. Moreover, as we shall see, Jesus' relationship to the world of Spirit is also the key for understanding the central dimensions of his ministry: as healer, sage, revitalization movement founder, and prophet.

NOTES

1. Two of the gospels, Mark and John, say nothing at all about Jesus before the ministry, not even about his birth. Matthew and Luke do include accounts of his birth and early childhood, though in somewhat different form from each other (see Matthew 1–2 and Luke 1–2). Moreover, the accounts contain many symbolic elements (for the meaning of the word *symbolic*, see chapter 4, pages 59–60). Symbolic elements can be based on actual historical occurrence, but how much is historical we can no longer know. For a compact treatment of the birth stories, see W. Barnes Tatum, *In Quest of Jesus* (Atlanta: John Knox, 1982), 108–112; for a full treatment, see Raymond Brown's authoritative *The Birth of the Messiah* (Garden City, New York: Doubleday, 1977).

2. See Mark 6:3, Matthew 13:55, and Geza Vermes, *Jesus the Jew* (New York: Macmillan, 1973), 21–22.

3. *Torah* in Hebrew means "divine teaching or instruction" and is most commonly translated "law." It has a range of meanings, sometimes referring to the first five books of the Bible (or "Pentateuch"), as in the phrase, "the *law* and the prophets." It can also refer to the 613 specific written laws contained in the Pentateuch, or, more broadly, to those laws plus the "oral law" which expands the written laws. To be trained in the Torah refers both to being familiar with the content of the law as well as with the methods of interpretation and argumentation.

4. Deuteronomy 6:4–5; included in the recitation were Deuteronomy 6:4–9, 11:2–21, and Numbers 15:37–41.

5. The Essenes were a Jewish monastic group; see chapter 5, page 88.

6. According to Luke 3:23, he was "about thirty" when he began his ministry; according to John 8:57, Jesus was "not yet fifty." Though not being fifty is consistent with being about thirty, the former is an odd way of saying the latter. On other grounds, the younger age is to be preferred; the tradition that Jesus was born in the last years of Herod the Great (died in 4 B.C.) is reasonably strong. Thus, at the beginning of his ministry, Jesus was probably in his early to mid-thirties. Pilate was the Roman governor of Judea from A.D. 26 to 36; Jesus was probably crucified in A.D. 30, with his ministry beginning a year or a bit more before.

7. The writings of Josephus are one of our primary sources for first-century Jewish history. As a young man, Josephus was a Jewish general in the great war against Rome, which broke out in A.D. 66. Captured by the Romans in Galilee early in the war, he spent most of the rest of his life (perhaps another thirty-five years) in Rome, where he wrote his multivolumed *Jewish Antiquities* and *History of the Jewish War*, as well as two more minor works. Though Josephus refers to John the Baptist, he apparently does not refer to the ministry of Jesus; the only direct reference is in a passage which is believed to be a Christian addition. The standard translation of Josephus is now the Loeb Classical Library edition, nine volumes, translated by H. St. J. Thackeray, R. Marcus, and A. Wikgrin (Cambridge: Harvard University Press, 1958–1965).

8. According to Mark 1:6, John wore "camel hair" (presumably a camel skin) and a leather girdle; for a similar description of Elijah, see 2 Kings 1:8. For a "hairy coat" as the mark of a prophet, see Zechariah 13:4. For John as prophet, see Mark 11:32, Matthew 11:9 = Luke 7:26.

9. Mark 1:4–6, Matthew 3:7–10 = Luke 3:7–9. Ritual immersion in water (both in Judaism and other cultures) can have two different meanings. When repeated frequently (as it was among the Essenes), it has the meaning of a washing or purification. When it is a once-only ritual (as it apparently was for John) it may also be a purification, but its primary meaning is as an initiation ritual which symbolizes and confers a new identity. "Once-only" baptism was also known in Judaism; when a Gentile converted to Judaism, he or she was baptized (and if male, circumcised as well). But it is important to remember that John's baptism was intended for people who were already Jewish.

10. It is historically unlikely that John recognized Jesus at the time as an extraordinary or Messianic figure. According to Mark, Luke, and Q ("Q" is a designation used by scholars to refer to material found in very similar form in *both* Matthew and Luke, but not in Mark; "Q" is thus presumed to be an early collection of traditions about Jesus that predates both Matthew and Luke, and which may be earlier even than Mark), there is no such recognition. The common image in Christian circles of John as primarily a forerunner of Jesus who self-consciously knew himself to be such, and who recognized Jesus as "the coming one," is based on the gospels of John and Matthew. According to John 1, the Baptist proclaims Jesus as the Lamb of God, Son of God, even as one who preexisted him. But John's gospel cannot be taken historically, as already noted. Matthew 3:14 reports a snippet of conversation between Jesus and John; John says, "I need to be baptized by you, and do you come to me?" However, this (and Jesus' response) is almost certainly an insertion by Matthew into the story. Apart from these historically suspect references in John and Matthew, there is no reason to think that John believed Jesus to be "the coming one" at an early stage of the ministry. John's question from prison later in the ministry ("Are you he who is to come or shall we look for another?" Matthew 11:3 = Luke 7:19, and thus "Q" material), is therefore to be read as the dawning of curiosity or hope, not as the beginning of doubt.

11. Mark 1:10. According to Mark, the experience was private to Jesus. There is no indication that the crowd or John saw anything; and the "heavenly voice" in the next verse is addressed to Jesus alone ("*Thou* art . . ."). Matthew and Luke both change the text slightly, apparently making the experience of Jesus more public. According to Matthew, the voice declared Jesus' identity to the crowd (3:17);

according to Luke, the Spirit descended in "bodily form" (3:22). But Mark presents it as an internal experience of Jesus; it is not thereby less real.

12. See Ezekiel 1:1 and Isaiah 61:1. See also Isaiah 64:1 for the image of a "tear" or "rent" in the heavens: "O that thou wouldst *rend* the heavens and come down. . . ."

13. See chapter 2, page 31.

14. Mark 1:13.

15. Matthew 4:1–11 = Luke 4:1–13.

16. Luke 4:5 = Matthew 4:8. Such travel is found elsewhere in the Bible. Ezekiel, for example, reports, "The Spirit lifted me up between earth and heaven, and brought me in visions of God to Jerusalem" (Ezekiel 8:3; see 11:1–2). For Elijah's travels "in the Spirit," see 1 Kings 18:12; cf. 2 Kings 2:11–12, 16. In the New Testament, see Acts 8:39–40. J. R. Michaels, *Servant and Son* (Atlanta: John Knox, 1981), 50, comments, "Jesus' journeys to the Holy City and to the high mountain belong in the same category as the journeys of Ezekiel." The phenomenon is widely reported in traditional cultures. See, for example, John Neihardt, *Black Elk Speaks* (Lincoln: University of Nebraska Press, 1961), and the books of Carlos Castaneda; even if Don Juan is regarded as a fictional character, as some have argued, his portrait is based on solid anthropological research. Such journeyings probably involve what are sometimes called "out-of-body" experiences.

17. Stephen Larsen, *The Shaman's Doorway* (New York: Harper & Row, 1976), 61–66. See also a section entitled "The Road of Trials" in Joseph Campbell, *Hero with a Thousand Faces* (Cleveland: World, 1956), 97–109. On shamanism more generally, see Mircea Eliade, *Shamanism: Archaic Techniques of Ecstasy* (New York: Pantheon, 1964); and W. A. Lessa and E. Z. Vogt, *Reader in Comparative Religion: An Anthropological Approach*, third edition (New York: Harper & Row, 1972), 381–412.

18. Luke 10:17–18.

19. The vision at his baptism may well have been his "call story" (the Old Testament prophets apparently thought it important to tell such stories), and the temptation narrative seems to have a teaching function in addition to reporting an experience.

20. This occurs very frequently in the book of Acts, and the whole of the book of Revelation is presented as a series of visions.

21. The difference between communion with God and union with God is subtle and perhaps not important. Both are mystical states, and both are known in the Jewish-Christian tradition. In union with God, all sense of separateness (including the awareness of being a separate self) momentarily disappears and one experiences only God; in communion with God, a sense of relationship remains. Communion is typically associated with Western mysticism and union with Eastern mysticism, though the contrast is not as sharp as the typical association suggests. See Peter Berger, ed., *The Other Side of God* (Garden City, New York: Anchor, 1981). For the "polarity" within Judaism, see especially the essay by Michael Fishbane, "Israel and the Mothers," 28–47. For communion mysticism in the East, see the most popular form of Hinduism, *bhakti*.

22. Mishnah Ber. 5.1; see A. Büchler, *Types of Jewish Palestinian Piety* (New York: KTAV, 1968; first published in 1922), 106–107.

23. For a history of Jewish mysticism reaching back to the time of Jesus and earlier,

see especially the work of Gershom Scholem, *Major Trends in Jewish Mysticism* (New York: Schocken Books, 1946), and *Jewish Gnosticism, Merkabah Mysticism, and Talmudic Tradition*, 2d ed. (Hoboken: KTAV, 1965). A connection between apocalypticism and visions of or journeys into another world is increasingly affirmed in studies of Jewish apocalyptic. See, for example, John J. Collins, *The Apocalyptic Imagination* (New York: Crossroad, 1984), who speaks of two strands of tradition in Jewish apocalypses, one visionary and one involving otherworldly journeys.

24. For an excellent summary of Jesus and prayer, including bibliography, see Donald Goergen, *The Mission and Ministry of Jesus* (Wilmington: Michael Glazier, 1986), 129–145. Goergen's book arrived too late to be incorporated significantly into the present book, but I highly recommend it as one of the best recent works on the historical Jesus.

25. Mark 1:35, 6:46.

26. Luke 6:12. Luke emphasizes the role of prayer in Jesus' life more than the other evangelists; in addition to 6:12, see 3:21, 5:16, 9:18, 9:28–29, 11:1. However, the picture is not due simply to Lucan redaction, as is clear from the references to Jesus' prayer life in the other gospels.

27. See Mark 14:36. Though this is the only occurrence of the Aramaic *Abba* in the gospels (which were written in Greek), it may lie behind the unadorned "Father" in Luke's version of the Lord's Prayer (Luke 11:2). A consensus of scholarship affirms its authenticity. That it was also part of the prayer life of first-century Christians is indicated by the appearance of the word in Romans 8:15 and Galatians 4:6, remarkable in letters composed in Greek for Greek-speaking audiences. It is reasonable to assume that early Christian usage derived from Jesus' own practice. The classic study of *Abba* is J. Jeremias, *The Prayers of Jesus* (Naperville, IL: Allenson, 1967), though Jeremias overemphasizes its distinctiveness, arguing that it was *unique* to Jesus (an argument perhaps motivated by theological considerations).

28. See Vermes, *Jesus the Jew*, 210–213.

29. Luke 4:18–21, quoting Isaiah 61:1–2; see also Isaiah 58:6.

30. Even by quite conservative scholars, Luke 4:18–30 is commonly attributed to Luke and categorized as "inauthentic" (that is, not among the actual words of Jesus). To a large extent, this is because the placement of the sermon is so obviously the product of Luke's compositional work: these verses replace Mark's account of Jesus' "inaugural address" (Mark 1:15: "The Kingdom of God is at hand"). Moreover, the verses identify one of Luke's central themes: Luke stresses the presence of the Spirit in Jesus more than the other gospels. Thus it seems to be Luke's advance summary of who Jesus was and the thrust of his ministry. However, the possibility remains that Jesus did use these words with reference to himself at some other time in his ministry (perhaps even in the context of a synagogue reading—there is nothing improbable about the scene); though Luke is responsible for inserting the story at this point in the narrative, it is not necessarily created by Luke. Moreover, even if Luke did create the story, it aptly describes what we have seen to be true on other grounds. Whether Luke was reporting or creating tradition, he has seen well.

31. Rudolf Otto, *The Idea of the Holy* (New York: Oxford University Press, 1958; first published in German in 1917), especially 155–159. On 158, Otto writes, "The point is that the 'holy man' or the 'prophet' is from the outset, as

regards the experience of the circle of his devotees, something more than a 'mere man.' He is the being of wonder and mystery, who somehow or other is felt to belong to the higher order of things, to the side of the numen itself. It is not that he himself teaches that he is such, but that he is *experienced* as such" (italics added). See also Otto's *The Kingdom of God and the Son of Man*, translated by F. V. Filson and B. L. Woolf (Grand Rapids, ca. 1938), especially pages 162–169, 333–376.

32. Mark 10:32. As Otto puts it, in "these few masterly and pregnant words," Mark states "with supreme simplicity and force *the immediate impression of the numinous that issued from Jesus*." *The Idea of the Holy*, 158; italics added.

33. Mark 1:22.

34. On *Gevurah*, see E. E. Urbach, *The Sages* (Jerusalem: Magnes, 1975), 80–96; for his interpretation of this verse, see 85–86.

35. Mark 6:14–16, 8:28; Matt. 21:11; Luke 7:12.

36. Mark 3:21. The Greek text means literally, "He is out of himself," that is, ecstatic, a nonordinary state often characteristic of holy men, easily mistaken as dementia.

37. Mark 3:22–30, Matthew 12:24–32, Luke 11:14–23.

38. Quoted phrases are from Mark 1:33, 2:4, and 5:24; the motif runs throughout the gospels.

39. Mark 11:27–33. The narrative, in which Jesus puts his opponents in a dilemma, is also an excellent example of Jesus' skillful repartee in debate.

40. Matthew 12:28 = Luke 11:20. Matthew has "Spirit of God," Luke has "finger of God"; however, the two expressions are synonymous.

41. Mark 5:30.

42. On "Amen," see J. Jeremias, *New Testament Theology*. (New York: Scribner, 1971), 35–36. According to his tables, it appears thirteen times in Mark, nine times in Q sayings, nine times in Matthew only, and three times in Luke, as well as twenty-five times in John. Thus all strata of the gospel tradition attest to it.

43. See the six antithetical statements found in the Sermon on the Mount, Matthew 5:21–22, 27–28, 31–32, 33–34, 38–39, 43–44. Some scholars accept the antithetical formulation of only the first, second, and fourth as authentic (for example, Bultmann, *The History of the Synoptic Tradition* [New York: Harper & Row, 1963], 134–136). For a defense of the antithetical form as original to all six, see Jeremias, *New Testament Theology*, 251–253.

44. Mark 1:16–20; see also the call of Levi in Mark 2:13–14.

45. Mark 10:28.

46. See Martin Hengel, *The Charismatic Leader and His Followers* (New York: Crossroad, 1981; originally published in German in 1968). Hengel finds Matthew 8:21–22 especially illuminating, and notes that it echoes the call of Elisha by Elijah in 1 Kings 19:19–21.

47. Mark 6:4, Luke 13:33.

48. For a superb and passionate exposition of prophetic consciousness (including the prophet as one who knew God), see Abraham Heschel, *The Prophets* (New York: Harper & Row, 1962), especially volume 1.

49. Mark 9:2–4, Matthew 17:1–8, Luke 9:28–36. Matthew calls the experience a vision.

50. Moses and Elijah are significant *not* because they represent "the law and the

prophets," as is often stated in commentaries, for they were *not* symbolic of the law and prophets in the time of Jesus. Rather, they were the two great holy men of the Jewish Scriptures.

51. See chapter 1, pages 10–11.

52. Examples of it referring to Israel as a whole: Hosea 11:1, Exodus 4:22–23; referring to the king of Israel in particular: Psalm 2:7, 2 Samuel 7:14.

53. This is an important point. To use a very mundane example, George Washington is legitimately referred to as "the father of his country" even though he presumably did not think of himself in those terms. Similarly, from a Christian point of view, Jesus is legitimately spoken of as the Messiah, *even if* he did not think of himself as such.

4. The Power of the Spirit: The Mighty Deeds of Jesus

Perhaps no aspect of the gospel portrait of Jesus poses so many difficulties for the modern mind as the tradition that he was a "wonder-worker," a performer of "miracles." As a culture, we do not take it for granted that there are "miraculous powers" at work in the world, and we are suspicious of events that seem to require an explanation that transcends what we take to be the "natural" laws of cause and effect. Except in cases where a psychosomatic explanation seems possible, miracles violate the modern sense of what is possible.

Within the church itself there is uncertainty about the miraculous elements in the gospels. Christians in mainstream churches, those most open to the intellectual spirit and genuine achievements of the modern age, share in our culture's suspicion and tend to ignore the miracle stories of Jesus or else to interpret them in such a way that no violation of the modern understanding of what is possible occurs. More "conservative" and fundamentalist Christians tend to insist that the miracles *really* happened and suspect those who are uncertain about their historical actuality as not really believing in the power of God. Some even argue that the miracles "prove" that Jesus was divine, turning them into an element in a tight rational argument. For charismatic Christians, the emphasis is different. Rather than seeing the miracles as unique and thus as "proofs" of who Jesus was, they are convinced that the same "gifts of the Spirit" are still accessible and operative today. Understandably, they find no difficulty believing that such powers flowed through Jesus.

Modern biblical scholarship has developed its own characteristic approach.[1] Concerned with the meaning of the miracle stories as part of the *early church's story of Jesus*, it has not been very much concerned with the historicity (the actual "happenedness") of the miracles. The concern has been with what the gospel writers intended to say with the miracle stories as components of a larger narrative or literary unit, the gospels themselves. Such meanings are disclosed by paying meticulous attention to the relationship of a particular miracle story to the gospel in which it is found: to its use of recurrent themes or motifs which are important to the author, or to its placement within a particular gospel. Attention is also paid to the relationship between the miracle stories and the larger religious-literary tradition of which they are a part. The early Christians who put the miracle stories of Jesus into their present form did so not only in light of their post-Easter experience of the living Christ, but also as part of a rich literary-religious tradition constituted by the Jewish religion and the Hebrew Bible (which was still their sacred Scripture). Not suprisingly, they often alluded to their tradition as they told their stories about Jesus.

For example, the story of Jesus miraculously feeding five thousand people in the wilderness alludes to Israel's period in the wilderness following the exodus from Egypt under the leadership of Moses. There, where there was no food, the Israelites were nourished by God who fed them with *manna*, a mysterious bread-like substance which fell from the sky each morning like dew. The story of Jesus feeding the five thousand makes the points that Jesus was one "like unto Moses," or even greater than Moses; that his ministry was an act of deliverance parallel in significance to the event which first created Israel; and that the people of God were once again being fed by "supernatural food" in the wilderness.

The story not only points backward to the exodus but also forward to the early church's sacred meal, in which the bread of the eucharist (or Lord's Supper or communion or mass, as the meal is variously known) was understood as the "body of Christ." The bread of the eucharist is like the manna in the wilderness, the "supernatural food" whereby the people of God are nourished. Indeed, the author of John's gospel made the connection explicit. At the conclusion of John's story of the feeding of the five thousand, the Jesus of John says, "I am the bread of life," "the bread of God which comes down from heaven and gives life to the world."[2] That is, the story ends by saying that *Jesus* (and not the loaves themselves) is the bread in the wilderness, the bread of life.

The modern scholarly approach has thus led to the realization that many of the miracle stories have a *symbolic* thrust. The word "symbolic" makes some Christians uncomfortable, for they tend to hear it as a watering down of the "literal" or "historical." Moreover, there is a modern prejudice against the symbolic, as when we say about something, "It's *only* symbolic," implying that it need therefore not be taken seriously. But to say that a story has symbolic elements is to say that the language or content *points beyond itself* to a web of meanings or associations, and those associations enrich rather than impoverish the story.

Yet it is also true that at this level of interpretation, the historical question is not important. That is, one can write a powerful exposition of the feeding of the five thousand without even addressing the question of its historical actuality; for Christians, Jesus *is* the bread of life who nourishes them again and again with his body and blood, and this is true independently of whatever happened or did not happen on a particular day in the ministry. Though the recognition that a narrative is symbolic need not involve a denial that it is also historical, the historical question is not central. Indeed, within much of modern scholarship, it is often left unaddressed or declared to be unimportant.

The modern scholarly approach is based on a solid insight: the miracle stories are part of the church's story of Jesus, and the meaning of the stories is greatly enhanced by paying attention to the meanings seen by the early church and the allusions which they make. Yet the "mighty deeds" of Jesus are also part of the *history of Jesus*, and not simply part of the church's *story about Jesus*. That, is the tradition that Jesus was a "wonder-worker" is historically very firmly attested. Thus, as we move to the miracle stories themselves, we will find it most helpful to divide our treatment into two categories: the miracles as part of the *history of Jesus*, that which we can say with reasonable historical probability "really happened";

and as part of the *story of Jesus*, that about which we must say, "Perhaps it happened, but the *meaning* of the story seems to lie elsewhere."

THE MIRACLES AS PART OF THE HISTORY OF JESUS

Mediators between the two worlds of the primordial tradition often become "people of power,"or miracle-workers, especially healers. To be sure, not all do. In the history of Israel and other cultures, some were primarily mediators of the divine will as prophets and law-givers, or of "supernatural" knowledge as diviners or clairvoyants. Others were charismatic military leaders, "spirit warriors." But some became channels through which healing power flowed from the world of Spirit into the visible world. Such figures of power ("men of deeds," as they were called in Judaism) were known in first-century Palestine, both in her ancient tradition (notably, Elijah) and in charismatics contemporary with Jesus such as Hanina ben Dosa and Honi the Circle-Drawer.

JESUS AS HEALER AND EXORCIST

Jesus was one of these "men of deeds." Indeed, to his contemporaries, it was the most remarkable thing about him. During his lifetime he was known primarily as a healer and exorcist. People flocked to him, drawn by his wonder-working reputation, as the gospels report again and again: "They brought to him all who were sick or possessed with demons. And the whole city was gathered together about the door"; as a healer, "His fame spread, and great crowds followed him"; "People came to him from every quarter."[3]

His healings attracted attention in other quarters as well. In prison before his execution by King Herod Antipas, John the Baptist heard of Jesus' mighty deeds and sent messengers to inquire if Jesus might be Elijah *returned*, one of the great charismatic healers of Israel's history.[4] After John's death, Herod himself heard of Jesus' reputation as a miracle-worker and wondered if Jesus' powers might be the powers of John the Baptist "raised from the dead."[5] Not only do the gospel writers report the fame which Jesus' mighty deeds caused, but they devote substantial portions of their narratives to accounts of such deeds.[6]

Despite the difficulty which miracles pose for the modern mind, on historical grounds it is virtually indisputable that Jesus was a healer and exorcist. The reasons for this judgment are threefold. First, there is the widespread attestation in our earliest sources. Second, healings and exorcisms were relatively common in the world around Jesus, both within Judaism and the Hellenistic world. Third, even his opponents did not challenge the claim that powers of healing flowed through him; rather, as we shall see, they claimed that his powers came from the lord of the evil spirits. By admiring followers and skeptical foes alike, he was seen as a holy man with healing powers.

True, the accounts in their present form are the product of the gospel writers. Symbolic and stylistic elements are often present; many details are obviously omitted (the stories are very compact); most often, we cannot be certain that we are dealing with eyewitness reports of particular healings, even when personal names are mentioned. But the stories reflect the *kinds* of situations Jesus encountered and the *kinds* of deeds he did, even if we cannot be sure whether a particular story is a stylized "typical" picture or based fairly closely on eyewitness report of a specific event. That is, the verdict that we are dealing with generally historical material does not imply the historical accuracy of all details.

EXORCISMS

As an exorcist, Jesus drove evil spirits out of many possessed people. In addition to summaries which mention multiple exorcisms (for example, "And those who were troubled with unclean spirits were cured") and the reference to Mary Magdalene "from whom seven demons had gone out,"[7] the synoptic gospels contain several extended accounts of particular exorcisms and a number of sayings referring to the practice. The gospels consistently distinguish between exorcisms and healings; not all healings were exorcisms, and not all maladies were caused by evil spirits. The gospels also speak of exorcists other than Jesus: Pharisaic exorcists, an unnamed exorcist who expelled demons in Jesus' name even though he was not a follower of Jesus, and Jesus' own disciples.[8] Obviously well-attested, exorcisms were not uncommon, even though not everyday occurrences.

More so than extraordinary cures, exorcism is especially alien to us in the modern world. In part, this is because we do not normally see the phenomenon (though are there cases of "possession" which we call by another name?). Even more, it is because the notion of "possession" by a spirit from another level of reality does not fit into out worldview. Rather, possession and exorcism presuppose the reality of a world of spirits which can interact with the visible world; that is, they presuppose the truth of the "primordial tradition."

Cross-cultural studies of the phenomenon indicate a number of typical traits. "Possession" occurs when a person falls under the control of an evil spirit or spirits. Such people are inhabited by a presence which they (and others) experience as "other than themselves." In addition to having two or more "personalities," they exhibit bizarre behavior and are often destructive or self-destructive. Convulsions, sweating, and seizures are common. Unusual strength and uncanny knowledge are sometimes also reported.[9] Exorcism is the expulsion of the evil spirit, driving it out of the person and ending its "ownership." This can be done only with the aid of a superior spirit in order to overpower the evil spirit. Often elaborate rituals are used, involving incantations and "power objects."[10]

The synoptic gospels describe two cases of possession in considerable detail. Inhabited by a legion of demons with supernatural strength, the "Gerasene demoniac" lived howling in a graveyard on the east shore of the Sea of Galilee:

A man with an unclean spirit lived among the tombs; and no one could bind him even with a chain; for he had often been bound with fetters and chains, but the chains he wrenched apart, and the fetters he broke in pieces; and no one had the strength to subdue him. Night and day among the tombs and on the mountains he was always crying out, and bruising himself with stones. [And he said] "My name is Legion; for we are many."[11]

According to Mark's account, the demon also had nonordinary knowledge. It recognized Jesus' "status," even though no human being in Mark's gospel had yet done so: "What have you to do with me, Jesus, Son of the Most High God?"[12]

The self-destructive quality of the Gerasene demoniac is also found in Mark's picture of a demon-possessed boy. Whenever the evil spirit seized him, it dashed him to the ground, causing him to foam at the mouth, grind his teeth and become rigid, sometimes throwing him into the water or the fire in order "to destroy him."[13]

Typically, Jesus exorcised evil spirits by verbal command alone, as in Mark's report of an exorcism in the synagogue at Capernaum in Galilee.[14] In this case, nothing is said about the condition of the possessed person beyond the presence of more than one "personality" and the recognition by the unclean spirit of the identity of Jesus, as if through nonordinary knowledge. The exorcism itself was accompanied by a convulsion and loud cries. Striking, however, was the reaction of the crowd. Amazed, the people exclaimed, "What is this? A new teaching! With authority he commands even the unclean spirits!" Their exclamation suggests what they (or the gospel writer) saw as the source of Jesus' power to cast out demons: "With *authority* he commands even the unclean spirits," that is, from the mouth of the *Gevurah* (Spirit) he casts out demons.[15]

How modern medical doctors or psychiatrists might diagnose the condition of "possession" or describe the process of exorcism, were they to witness either, is difficult to say. Within the framework of the modern worldview, we are inclined to see "possession" as a primitive prescientific diagnosis of a condition which must have another explanation. Most likely, we would see it as a psychopathological condition which includes among its symptoms the delusion of believing one's self to be possessed. Perhaps a psychopathological diagnosis and explanation are possible.[16] Social conditions also seem to be a factor; there are some data from anthropology and social psychology which suggest that conditions of political oppression, social deprivation, and rapid social change (all of which characterized first-century Palestine) are correlated with increased frequency of possession.[17]

But whatever the modern explanation might be, and however much psychological or social factors might be involved, it must be stressed that Jesus and his contemporaries (along with people in most cultures) thought that people could be possessed or inhabited by a spirit or spirits from another plane. Their worldview took for granted the actual existence of such spirits.[18] Perhaps the shared convictions were in part responsible for the phenomenon. In any case, they did not simply *think* of these as cases of possession and exorcism; rather, all of the participants—possessed, exorcist, on-lookers—*experienced* the event as an exorcism of a spiritual force which had taken possession of the person.

Jesus' exorcisms not only attracted crowds but controversy. Some of his opponents charged that he performed them with the aid of evil powers: "And the scribes who came down from Jeru-salem said, 'He is possessed by Beelzebul, and by the prince of demons he casts out demons.'"[19] The accusation was "witchcraft" or "sorcery."[20] A Jewish source from a few centuries later, refer-ring to Jesus by his name in Aramaic, repeated the charge and connected it to his death: "Yeshu of Nazareth" was executed "because he *practiced sorcery* and led Israel astray."[21] The charge of sorcery is a pejorative characterization of his powers, and attributes them (like the Beelzebul accusation) to the powers of darkness. From his opponents' point of view, he was an unorthodox holy man, a "magician,"[22] but his powers were not denied.

Jesus responded to the accusation by affirming that the power which flowed through him was the Spirit of God: "If it is by *the Spirit of God* that I cast out demons, then the Kingdom of God has come upon you."[23] Indeed, Jesus saw his exorcisms as a sign that the "strong man," whom he had watched fall from heaven,[24] had been "bound" and overcome by the Spirit of God: "But no one can enter a strong man's house and plunder his goods, unless he first binds the strong man; then indeed he may plunder his house."[25] Thus Jesus' exorcisms, as well as his opponents' accusations, link him unmistakably to the thought world and experiential world of the Spirit-filled charismatic. He was one who experienced the Spirit of God flowing through him with power.

HEALINGS

Jesus was also known as a healer. In fact, according to the gospels, his healings outnumbered his exorcisms. They are often referred to in summary statements,[26] as well as in words attributed to Jesus himself. To messengers sent to him by John the Baptist, he said, "Go and tell John what you hear and see: the blind receive their sight and the lame walk, lepers are cleansed and the deaf hear, and the dead are raised up, and the poor have good news preached to them."[27]

In addition to these summaries, the synoptic gospels contain thirteen narratives of healings of particular conditions: fever, leprosy, paralysis, withered hand, bent back, hemorrhage, deafness and dumbness, blindness, dropsy, severed ear, and a sickness near death or paralysis.[28] These thirteen should not be thought of as the sum total of Jesus' healings; rather, they are narrated as "typical" or to make some point or other. Given the nature of the gospel narratives, we shall not treat the question of the precise event behind each account, but will simply note the impression the stories create. Even though we are not dealing with "newspaper account" material, we are at the very least in touch with how Jesus' very early followers, still in contact with the living oral tradition, "saw" him.

The stories create a vivid impression of a charismatic healer at work. Sometimes Jesus healed by word. He said to the man with the withered hand, "Stretch out your hand," and the hand was restored.[29] Most often touching was also involved. When a leper came to him, Jesus was "moved with pity" and touched him, and immediately the leprosy left him.[30] Sometimes he used physical means in addition to touching, as in the case of a deaf man. Jesus "put his fingers into his ears, and he spat and touched his tongue;

and looking up to heaven, he sighed, and said to him. '*Ephphatha*,' that is, 'Be opened.' And his ears were opened, his tongue was released, and he spoke plainly."[31] Of special interest here is the Aramaic word *ephphatha*, "Be opened." In context, it clearly refers to the opening of the man's ears, but may also have the connotation of *the heavens* opening up: "Looking up into heaven, he said, 'Be opened.'" Through the opening from heaven, healing power flowed.

Like the contemporary Galilean holy man Hanina ben Dosa, Jesus healed at a distance. A Roman centurion entreated Jesus to heal his servant who was lying paralyzed in the centurion's home some distance away. Seeing the centurion's faith, Jesus said, "Go; be it done for you as you have believed." The text concludes: "And the servant [at home] was healed at that very moment."[32]

To attempt to explain how these happened is beyond our purpose, and probably impossible. There is a tendency to see these as "faith healings," perhaps because doing so makes possible a psychosomatic explanation that stretches but does not break the limits of the modern worldview. But, though faith is involved in some of the stories, clearly in other cases the faith of the healed person was not involved at all.

Rather, within the thought-world of the accounts themselves, Jesus' healings were the result of "power." Indeed, the favorite word for the mighty deeds of Jesus in the synoptic gospels is, in Greek, *dunamis*, which translates as "power." It is most frequently used in the plural—the mighty deeds of Jesus were "powers." It is sometimes used in the singular to refer to one of the central qualities of God: "the *power* of God," or "the *power* of the Most High." It can even be used as a name for God: "And you will see the Son of man sitting at the right hand of *power*."[33] That is, the deeds of Jesus were understood by the gospel writers and Jesus himself as *powers* from *the Power*.

In the book of Acts, written by Luke and therefore also reflecting a synoptic point of view, this power is directly associated with the Spirit of God: "But you shall receive *power* when the Holy Spirit has come upon you."[34] Luke also makes the connection in his gospel: "And Jesus came in *the power of the Spirit* into Galilee."[35]

Thus, from the standpoint of the gospels, the mighty deeds of Jesus, exorcisms and healings alike, were the product of the power which flowed through him as a holy man. His powers were charismatic, the result of his having become a channel for the power of the other realm, that which Jesus and his contemporaries also called Spirit.

THE MIRACLES AS PART OF THE STORY OF JESUS

In addition to exorcisms and healings, the synoptic gospels report a number of other "spectacular" deeds: two resuscitations of apparently dead people; two sea miracles (stilling a storm and walking on the sea); two feeding miracles (the feeding of the five thousand and the feeding of the four thousand); a "miraculous" catch of fish; and the "cursing" and "withering" of a fig tree.[36] Are these narratives to be taken historically? Did Jesus also do these kinds of things? Two factors make it very difficult to know.

First, we simply do not know if there are limits to the powers of a charismatic mediator. For example, are resuscitations of *genuinely* dead people possible? Or, alternatively, does levitation really happen, and might walking on water be a special case of levitation? That is, the historical verdict about whether or not such events really happened will depend in part upon whether we think even a charismatic can do things like this.[37]

Second, symbolic elements abound in these narratives. The points of correspondence between these stories and the religious-literary tradition of the early church are so frequent and pronounced that perhaps the narratives as a whole (and not just details within them) are to be understood primarily or only in terms of how they point beyond themselves rather than historically at all.[38] As we have noted, doing so does not *require* a negative historical judgment; a narrative with symbolic elements can have a historical nucleus. But we will find it most illuminating to consider the stories of these "other powers" as part of the church's story about Jesus, and not primarily as part of the history of Jesus himself.

Classic among these are the feeding stories, already considered, and the stories of Jesus stilling the storm and walking on the water. In an important sense, neither of the sea stories concerns the public ministry of Jesus; rather, only his inner group of followers is present. In both stories, they are in a boat, at night, distressed and frightened; in both, Jesus comes to them, the winds cease, and the sea is calmed.

Central to these stories is "the sea," an image which reverberates with rich resonances of meaning in the Hebrew Bible. The Hebrew word for "sea," derived from the name of the evil god in the Babylonian creation story, carried connotations of evil, a mysterious and threatening force opposed to God. Accordingly, when the ancient Hebrews wanted to stress God's power and authority, they spoke of the divine mastery over the sea. The authors of the psalms exclaimed, "The sea is his, for he made it!" and "Thou dost rule the raging of the sea; when its waves rise, thou stillest them."[39] According to the book of Job, it was God who "shut in the sea with doors" and said to it, "Thus far shall you come, and no farther, and here shall your proud waves be stayed."[40]

The plight of the disciples and their cry for help echo another passage from the psalms which describes people in a storm at sea:

The stormy wind lifted up the waves of the sea. They mounted up to heaven, they went down to the depths. Their courage melted away in their evil plight; they reeled and staggered like drunken men, and were at their wits' end. Then they cried to the Lord in their trouble, and he delivered them from their distress; he made the storm be still, and the waves of the sea were hushed.[41]

These connections to language and imagery that were part of the early church's religious-literary tradition suggest that the story is to be understood within that larger framework.

Putting all of these elements together, the narrative makes several points. The picture of Jesus stilling the storm makes the claim that he shares in the power and authority of God; that which was said of God in the Old Testament is now said of Jesus. Moreover, like the Lord of the Psalm narrative, he responds to his followers' cry of distress when the forces of evil and chaos threaten to overwhelm them. Finally, a boat was one of the images for the early church, perhaps by the time Mark's narrative was written. If Mark was making use of this image, then the narrative portrays Jesus as the Lord of the church who saves his people when they turn to him for help in distress. The cry of the disciples is the church's cry, "Save, Lord; we are perishing,"[42] and the words of Jesus to the disciples are addressed to the church: "Take heart, it is I, have no fear."[43] In short, the *purpose* of the narrative may be symbolic rather than historical. Moreover, it is no less *true* for being symbolic; indeed, its truth is verified in the experience of Christians ever since, quite apart from the historical verdict about whether the story describes an actual incident one night on the Sea of Galilee.

Symbolic elements similarly point to a meaning beyond historical reporting in the other "spectacular" narratives. The most sensational of the resuscitation stories, the raising of Lazarus, is in John's gospel which, as we have noted, is viewed by scholars as not primarily historical in nature.[44] Of the two synoptic resuscitations, one seems not to have been an actual one, but a "revival" of a person mistakenly thought to be dead, a mistake relatively common prior to modern methods of diagnosis. To the wailing people gathered around the bed of Jairus's daughter, Jesus said, "Why do you make a tumult and weep? The child is *not dead but sleeping*."[45] Whatever one makes of the historicity behind these stories, the accounts have a symbolic edge; namely, the "raising of the dead" was associated with the coming of the "new age" and the Messiah. Thus the accounts may be expressing symbolically the conviction that the new age and the Messiah had come.

Finally, there is another power, rather strange, which Jesus spoke of, even though no story is told of his actually using this power: immunity to poisonous serpents. "Behold, I have given you authority *to tread upon serpents and scorpions*, and over all the power of the enemy; and nothing shall hurt you."[46]

Interestingly, the same power was reported of another Jewish holy man, Hanina ben Dosa. While he was praying, "A poisonous snake bit him, but he did not interrupt his prayer." Later, the onlookers found the snake dead at the opening of its hole and exclaimed, "Woe to the man bitten by a snake, but woe to the snake which bites Rabbi Hanina ben Dosa."[47] According to the book of Acts, the apostle Paul enjoyed a similar immunity.[48] Clearly, the "power" links Jesus once again to the charismatic stream of Judaism. But are the words about power over serpents to be understood literally or symbolically, perhaps pointing beyond themselves to power over Satan; or, given the story of the tempter in the Garden of Eden taking the form of a serpent, to power over sin?

Thus, about all of these stories of "other powers," a clear historical judgment is impossible. Moreover, one cannot overcome the historical uncertainty through an act of faith. An account cannot be made historically true by believing it to be so. For example, I may choose to believe that George Washington actually threw a silver dollar across the Potomac, but my belief has nothing to do with whether he actually did; he may or may not have.[49] The same is true with the historical question about whether Jesus actually did these things. Believing that he did so has nothing to do with whether he actually did. One cannot solve the historical question by faith or belief. In short, the mighty deeds of Jesus other than his exorcisms and healings must remain in a "historical suspense account."[50]

Though one must be uncertain about these stories as part of the history of Jesus, their meanings as part of the church's story of Jesus are clear. Using imagery rich with associations in that time, the stories affirm that the living Christ of the early church's experience was (and for Christians, still is) one who, sharing in the power of God, delivered them from peril and evil, nourished them in the wilderness, and brought life out of death.

CONCLUSION

In their historical context, the miracles of Jesus do not "prove" that he was divine. In the tradition in which he stood, including figures from its ancient past and persons contemporary with him, the healings and exorcisms reported of him were not unique. Yet though the historical study of the miracles results in the loss of their uniqueness, it produces a gain in their credibility. Contrary to the modern notion that such events are impossible, we must grant that the historical evidence that Jesus stood in the stream of Jewish charismatic healers is very strong.

He was, in terms of cultural and historical impact, the most extraordinary figure in that tradition. Not only did he come out of such a stream, but others followed in his wake. According to the gospels, he commissioned his twelve disciples to be charismatic healers.[51] His two most important first-century followers, Peter and Paul, were also charismatic holy men. Further removed in time, St. Francis of Assisi (1176–1226), often considered the most "Christlike" of subsequent Christians, was a mystic, visionary, and healer. Though foreign to our experience and way of thinking in the modern world, the world of spirits and God was, for Jesus and his predecessors and followers in the Jewish-Christian tradition, very real—not simply as an element of belief, but of experience.

NOTES

1. For an excellent introduction to the modern scholarly treatment of the miracle stories, see R. H. Fuller, *Interpreting the Miracles* (Philadelphia: Westminster, 1963). Somewhat more technical studies include D. L. Tiede, *The Charismatic Figure as Miracle Worker* (SBL Dissertation Series 1, 1972); H. C. Kee, *Miracle and the Early Christian World: A Study in Socio-Historical Method* (New Haven: Yale University Press, 1983); G. Theissen, *The Miracle Stories of the Early Christian Tradition* (Philadelphia: Fortress, 1983).
2. For the whole story, see John 6:1–59; quoted phrases are from 6:35, 48, 33.
3. Consecutively, Mark 1:32–34, Matthew 4:24, Mark 1:45.
4. Matthew 11:3 = Luke 7:19. John's question, "Are you he who is to come?" did not inquire if Jesus were the Messiah, as is sometimes thought. Instead, the phrase "he who is to come" is explicitly associated with the expectation of Elijah (see Malachi 3:1, 4:5), not the Messiah.
5. Mark 6:14–16.
6. For example, no less than two-thirds of Mark's gospel prior to the story of Jesus' last week in Jerusalem concerns the miraculous.
7. Luke 8:2.
8. Matthew 12:27 = Luke 11:19; Mark 9:38–39; Mark 6:7–13, 9:18; Matthew 10:1–8; Luke 9:1–6, 10:17.
9. For studies of possession and exorcism, see I. M. Lewis, *Ecstatic Religion: An*

Anthropological Study of Spirit Possession and Shamanism (Harmondsworth, England: Penguin, 1971).

10. See, for example, an account of a Jewish exorcist roughly contemporary with Jesus: "Eleazar put to the nose of the possessed man a ring which had under its seal one of the roots prescribed by Solomon, and then, as the man smelled it, drew out the demon through his nostrils, and, when the man at once fell down, adjured the demon never to come back into him, speaking Solomon's name and reciting the incantations which he had composed." The episode is reported by Josephus, *Jewish Antiquities* 8:46–48.

11. Mark 5:2–5, 9.

12. The story contains many details which point to a symbolic meaning as well. The picture Mark paints in his narrative is full of images of impurity or "uncleanness," which was believed to separate one from "the holy" (God). The demoniac lived in Gentile ("unclean") territory; he also lived among tombs (proximity to death was seen as one of the most powerful sources of defilement); he lived near pigs, which were an "unclean" animal; and he was possessed by an "unclean spirit." The scene is a picture of all that separated one from God within the framework of the religious beliefs of the time. The story makes the point that Jesus is one who overcomes the most potent and devastating sources of defilement and alienation, banishes the forces of evil from life, and restores its victims to both health and human community (the exorcism ends with the demoniac "clothed and in his right mind" and told to "go home").

13. Mark 9:17–18, 21–22. The description of a seizure in this episode should not lead to an equation between possession and epilepsy; they are two quite different phenomena.

14. Mark 1:23–27. The location of the story in the gospel narrative shows the importance of Jesus' exorcisms to Mark; this is the first *public event* of Jesus' ministry reported by Mark, following immediately upon Jesus' gathering of the nucleus of the disciples.

15. For *Gevurah* as the "mouth of Power" or Spirit, see chapter 3, page 46, note 34.

16. See the provocative and illuminating discussion by M. Scott Peck in *People of the Lie* (New York: Simon and Schuster, 1983), 182–211. Peck, a practicing psychiatrist, began his study of possession and exorcism believing that a clinical diagnosis within the framework of current psychological understanding would be possible. However, he and a team of professionals eventually became involved in two cases of "possession" (and exorcism) which he could not account for within a purely psychological framework.

17. See especially Lewis, *Ecstatic Religion*.

18. For a very illuminating description of the cosmology of such societies, see Mary Douglas, *Natural Symbols: Explorations in Cosmology* (New York: Pantheon, 1970), viii–ix, 103, and 107–124.

19. Mark 3:22. For the complete account, see Mark 3:22–30, Matthew 12:22–37, Luke 11:14–23. "Beelzebul" is a name for Satan; its two variants, "Beelzebul" and "Beelzebub," mean "lord of dung," "lord of flies."

20. In societies which affirm possession and exorcism, accusations of witchcraft are commonly used "to express aggression between rivals and enemies" (Lewis, *Ecstatic Religion*, 33). For the rivalry between Jesus and his opponents as involving accusations of witchcraft, see Jerome Neyrey and Bruce Malina,

Calling Jesus Names (Sonoma, CA: Polebridge Press, forthcoming), chapter one.

21. From the Babylonian Talmud, Sanhedrin 43a.

22. The word "magician" is not used in its modern sense of an entertainer who performs magical tricks. Rather, it is used in its ancient sense of one who can manipulate the powers of the spirit world. See especially the works of Morton Smith: *Jesus the Magician* (San Francisco: Harper & Row, 1978), and his earlier *Clement of Alexandria and a Secret Gospel of Mark* (Cambridge: Harvard University Press, 1973). Smith basically affirms the perspective of Jesus' opponents, amassing a great amount of evidence concerning magical practices in the ancient world as he does so. Walter Wink's critical and yet appreciative review of Smith's first volume is appropriate as an assessment of both. One senses, Wink writes, "subliminally that Smith's interest is in discrediting Christianity through a debunking of Jesus," and yet part of Smith's work is "a stunning scholarly achievement. . . . The great value of Smith's discussion of Jesus' 'magic' is that he does place Jesus' healings and exorcisms within a broader context of first century 'magical' practices hitherto largely ignored." W. Wink, "Jesus as Magician," in *Union Seminary Quarterly Review 30* (1974): 3–14; quotes from 9–10.

23. Matthew 12:28 = Luke 11:20.

24. Luke 10:18; see chapter 3, pages 00–00.

25. Mark 3:27.

26. For example, Mark 1:34: "He healed many who were sick with various diseases"; 3:9–10: "And he told his disciples to have a boat ready for him because of the crowd, lest they should crush him; for he had healed many, so that all who had diseases pressed upon him to touch him."

27. Matthew 11:4–6 = Luke 7:22. The list of *types* of healings (the blind see, deaf hear, lame walk, and so forth) is largely drawn from Old Testament passages that refer to the coming age (which is also referred to as the outpouring of the Spirit). Thus it is not clear whether the list was meant to be a citation of the categories of Jesus' actual healings, or whether it was a way of saying that the coming age (the outpouring of the Spirit) had begun.

28. Fever, Mark 1:29–31; leprosy, Mark 1:40–45, Luke 17:11–19 (ten lepers); paralysis, Mark 2:1–12; withered hand, Mark 3:1–6; bent back, Luke 13:10–17; hemorrhage, Mark 5:24b–34; deafness and dumbness, Mark 7:37; blindness, Mark 8:22–26, 10:46–52; dropsy (edema), Luke 14:1–6; severed ear, Luke 22:51; sick near death or paralysis, Luke 7:1–10 = Matthew 8:5–13.

29. Mark 3:5.

30. Mark 1:40–42.

31. Mark 7:32–35. See also Mark 8:22–26, which reports that Jesus applied spit to the eyes of a blind man.

32. Matthew 8:5–13 = Luke 7:1–10. For the story of Hanina, see chapter 2, page 3.

33. Mark 14:62.

34. Acts 1:8.

35. Luke 4:14.

36. Resuscitations: Mark 5:21–24, 35–43; Luke 7:11–17. Sea miracles: Mark 4:35–41 and 6:45–52. Feeding miracles: Mark 6:30–44 and 8:1–10. In the story of the catch of fish (Luke 5:1–11), Jesus functions as "game-finder" for his fishermen disciples, even though that is not the point of the story (the point of the story is

that the disciples are now to become "fishers of men"). One of the traditional functions of holy men in hunting and fishing societies is game-finding; that is, they use their powers for the sake of "the tribe" (their people). In agricultural societies, the parallel function is rainmaking. The story of the cursing of the fig tree (Mark 11:12–14, 20–25) is especially perplexing because it seems "out of character." Scholars have often speculated that the story may have grown out of a parable about a fig tree which Jesus told (Luke 13:6–9). In any case, Mark's placement of the fig tree narrative suggests a symbolic meaning. The story is told in two parts, with the "cleansing of the temple" separating the two halves. Mark apparently sees a connection between the fig tree (which is sometimes an image for Israel) having no fruit on it and the temple not serving the purpose for which it was intended. The "withering" of the fig tree points to the future which awaited Jerusalem and the temple.

37. This is a different question from the question, "Are there limits to the power of God?" Our question is whether the mediation of that power through human beings is limited in any way. Illustrative here is the story of a Christian saint, St. Denis, who as bishop of Paris was martyred by the Romans in the third century. After his beheading, we are told, he picked up his severed head and walked several miles to his church where, still holding his severed head under his arm, he sang the mass. Do things like that happen? "With God all things are possible," one might say; but does that mean all things are possible to or through a Spirit-filled mediator? To express historical skepticism about such accounts does not imply doubting the power of God.

38. The recognition that some of the miracle stories may be *wholly symbolic* and not historical is usually credited to David Friedrich Strauss whose two-volume *Life of Jesus* was published in 1835 when Strauss was only twenty-seven. Prior to Strauss, scholars generally agreed that the miracle stories were to be read as *historical* narratives, and differed on the question of whether a supernatural or natural explanation of the story was to be sought. An example of a "natural explanation" offered by one of Strauss's contemporaries (and which I once heard in a sermon) argues that the feeding of the five thousand is to be explained as follows. Many in the crowd actually had brought food, and the action of the boy in "sharing" his five loaves and two fishes moved the rest of the crowd to act in a similarly generous fashion. Ironically, the explanation preserves the "happenedness" of the story, but destroys the miracle. Strauss cut through this preoccupation with treating the miracle stories as historical and suggested instead that many of the miracle stories are to be understood as literary creations of the early church which draw upon the rich imagery of the Old Testament: their meaning lies in their symbolism. Strauss's book was radical in his day; a review called it the most pestilential book ever vomited out of the bowels of hell, and he was blackballed from the universities of Europe. With modification, his approach has now become the position of mainstream scholarship.

39. Psalm 95:5, 89:9.

40. Job 38:8, 11, part of the dramatic divine speech known as "the voice from the whirlwind."

41. Psalm 107:25–29. The psalm as a whole describes different categories of people who turned to God for help: those wandering in desert wastes, in prison and darkness, sick unto death, and those threatened by the sea.

42. The words are quoted from Matthew's version of the stilling of the storm: Matthew 8:25.
43. From the account of walking on the water in Mark 6:50.
44. John 11:1–44; for the nonhistorical character of John, see chapter 1, pages 00–00.
45. Mark 5:38–39.
46. Luke 10:19. The same theme appears in the longer ending to Mark's gospel added some time in the second century, which almost certainly does not report actual words of Jesus, but does report what some early Christians believed he had said to his followers: "They will pick up deadly serpents, and if they drink any deadly thing, it will not hurt them" (Mark 16:18; in the judgment of most scholars, Mark's gospel originally ended with 16:8). These verses are taken literally by a few Christians and are the scriptural basis for handling poisonous snakes in the context of Christian worship.
47. From the Jerusalem Talmud, Ber. 9a. Also reported in the Babylonian Talmud, Ber. 33a, and the Tosefta, Ber. 2.20.
48. Acts 28:1–6.
49. For an excellent discussion of the relationship between faith and historical judgment, see Van Harvey, *The Historian and the Believer* (New York: Macmillan, 1966).
50. Fuller, *Interpreting the Miracles*, 38.
51. Mark 6:7–13, Matthew 10:5–8, Luke 10:8–9.

II. JESUS AND CULTURE

5. The Social World of Jesus

Though Jesus shared much in common with other Jewish charismatics of his time, he also differed from them in a number of ways. What distinguished him most—besides the extraordinary fact that he was crucified and became the central figure of what was to become a global religion—was his deep involvement with the sociopolitical life of his own people. For the most part, other Jewish charismatics remained local figures, living in a particular locality and occasionally receiving visitors from afar. But Jesus became a national figure who undertook a mission to his own people in the midst of a cultural crisis, climaxing in a final journey to Jerusalem, the very center of their cultural life. Because his own culture was so important to him, not just as background for his mission but as its focus, we need to devote this chapter to describing Jesus' social world.

The phrase *social world* has two nuances of meaning. It refers to the total social environment of a people at a particular time in their history, including such material conditions as the type of economy, level of technology, degree of urbanization, mixture of population, isolation from or exposure to foreign cultures, and so forth. Even more importantly, "social world" refers to the socially constructed reality of a people, that nonmaterial "canopy" of shared convictions which every human community erects and within which it lives, and which is sometimes known simply as "culture." It is that world of shared ideas that makes each culture what it is. It consists of the shared beliefs, values, meanings, laws, customs, institutions, rituals, and so forth, by which the group orders and maintains its world.[1] The "social world" of Jesus thus refers to the social world of Judaism within the total social environment of first-century Palestine.[2]

That social world occupied a very small geographical space.

Jewish Palestine comprised an area of about seven thousand square miles, slightly smaller than the state of Vermont. Politically, it had become part of the Roman empire in 63 B.C. and was governed by rulers appointed by Rome. Until the death in 4 B.C. of Herod the Great, the most famous of the "client" kings who owed their kingship to Rome, it was administered as a single political unit. After Herod's death, it was divided into three units, each ruled by one of Herod's sons. One of these units, Judea (which included Jerusalem), came under direct Roman rule in A.D. 6, administered by a series of Roman governors who replaced Herod's son Archelaus.

Palestine was still a largely agricultural and rural society, composed of towns and small villages, many no larger than hamlets, inhabited largely by farmers who walked each day to their fields. Most were small landholders, though larger estates were emerging. Farming centered around grain, vegetables, fruit, wine, oil, and dates, as well as sheep, cattle, and goats. There were a number of cities, many of them established by Herod the Great and his successors. The rural areas tended to be Jewish, whereas the urban areas (with the exception of Jerusalem) had more of a mixed population because of the influx of Gentiles during the time of the Herods. The "ways" of the rural areas were old and relatively unchanged, whereas the cities were becoming increasingly more cosmopolitan because of the Gentiles and their "ways."

Most importantly, it was a social world in crisis. Indeed, before the first century was over, the crisis had resulted in a catastrophic war with the Romans, climaxing in the destruction of Jerusalem and the temple in A.D. 70. It was the worst calamity experienced by the Jewish people in ancient times, rivaled only by the Babylonian destruction of Jerusalem and the temple some six centuries earlier in 586 B.C. In order to understand the social world of Jesus, we need to examine the conventional wisdom which was at the heart of it, the crisis which convulsed it, and the politics of holiness which was the response to the crisis.

THE CONVENTIONAL WISDOM OF THE JEWISH SOCIAL WORLD

At the heart of every social construction of reality is the "conventional wisdom" of that culture. Conventional wisdom consists of the widely shared central assumptions about life which together comprise a culture's "dominant consciousness." Most essentially, it consists of a picture of reality and a picture of how to live, a "worldview," and an "ethos," or way of life.[3] Conventional wisdom is so basic to culture that one may speak of it as the fundamental component of culture, the "heart" of every culture. It is "what everybody knows," convictions and ways of behavior so taken for granted as to be basically unquestioned.[4]

As was generally the case in antiquity, much more so than now, the conventional wisdom of the first-century Jewish social world (as well as the social world itself) was grounded in sacred tradition. Its picture of reality was Israel's version of the primordial tradition. At the summit of the world of Spirit was Yahweh (the sacred Hebrew name for God), the creator of heaven and earth. Yahweh had entered into a special relationship with the people of Israel, constituted preeminently by the covenant given through Moses at Mt. Sinai, and continuing throughout their history. Their Scripture created an ethos as well. It contained regulations for individual and group behavior, provided at least the embryo of political organization, and proclaimed both warnings and hopes generated by the people's history. Its laws included not only "ritual" and "moral" laws, but also what we consider "secular" law: criminal law, civil law, household law, even tax law. Their sacred traditions constructed a comprehensive ethos or way of life.

The ethos of the first-century Jewish social world is illuminated by several characteristics which conventional wisdom has in common cross-culturally. First, speaking of the "wise" way of life, it provided practical guidance for living that life. Its focal points were the concerns of everyday life in the ancient world: family, wealth, honor, and virtue, all shaped by a religious framework. Such guidance was provided in part by "folk wisdom." Folk wisdom was typified by the book of Proverbs whose "wise sayings," generally couched in pithy and memorable forms of expression, circulated widely in a preliterate population. They provided practical advice on everyday questions such as the right way to raise children, the wise use of money, the importance of friendship, the value of a good name; and they extolled the practical value of virtues such as honesty, hard work, moderation, and self-control.

The primary source of conventional wisdom, however, was the Torah, the "law" of Israel. Most of it became part of the consciousness of individual Jews simply through the process of growing up within the culture. One learned the "way of Torah" by watching how people lived, as well as by hearing it read at synagogue services and on festivals. There also existed a special group of people who were the custodians and interpreters of the tradition. Known as "sages" ("teachers of wisdom"), they drew upon folk wisdom and, more centrally, the Torah itself.[5] Its 613 written laws were interpreted and applied by the sages in a wisdom mode, that is, as specific and practical guidance for living the wise way. Israel's conventional wisdom was thus largely "Torah wisdom."

Second, Jewish conventional wisdom (like conventional wisdom generally) saw reality as organized on the basis of rewards and punishments. Reality was "built" that way. Living the way of wisdom, the path of righteousness, brought blessing; following the way of folly or wickedness brought ruin and death. Some believed in rewards and punishments beyond this world, though there was not yet unanimity about this among the Jewish people.[6] Most also believed that the path of conventional wisdom produced rewards in this world. The righteous would flourish and be blessed with children, a good name, possessions, and a long life. "Live right and all will go well," is the message common to all systems of conventional wisdom, religious and secular, ancient and modern.[7] It also contains a cruel corollary. If life does not go well, it is because one has failed in some way.

Third, the conventional wisdom of the Jewish social world provided the primary source of identity. It did so by establishing boundaries. Its sacred tradition conferred a shared identity ("child of Abraham") which distinguished Jews from Gentiles. It also conferred more particular social identities with well-defined expectations and limitations: landowner, priest, husband, wife, father, oldest son, rich, poor, noble, peasant, man, and woman.[8] The different degrees of status associated with these categories produced a hierarchical order in the society. Moreover, these boundaries and hierarchies were quite rigid, firmly ingrained in the tradition (for example, the different roles given to men and to women, the different status accorded to oldest son and younger sons, the distinction between Jew and Gentile). Thus, to a large extent, both identity and social structure were "given" by conventional wisdom.

One very important boundary and source of identity was, however, the product of behavior: the distinction between "righteous" and "wicked." Some people, then as now, were simply more successful than others at living up to the standards of conventional wisdom. Those who were successful were the "righteous," those who fell short were the "wicked." Such achievement was usually socially visible as well as internally felt. Thus an important dimension of identity was "conditional" or "earned," dependent upon conforming to standards of conventional wisdom.[9]

The world established by Jewish conventional wisdom was not only hallowed by sacred tradition but maintained by its observance in the texture of everyday life. Indeed, the ethos created by the mixture of folk wisdom and Torah wisdom might have remained relatively stable for several more centuries except for changes in the Mediterranean world over which the Jewish people had no control.

TWO SOCIAL WORLDS IN COLLISION

By the first century, two social worlds were in collision: the social world of Judaism and the social world composed of Hellenistic culture and Roman political power. The annexation of Palestine by Rome in 63 B.C. generated both political conflict and severe economic pressure.

The Roman presence was very much felt, even while Rome ruled indirectly through client kings such as Herod the Great (37–4 B.C.). A Hellenizer and Romanizer in his policies, building projects, and resettlement of populations, Herod was generally despised by his Jewish subjects. At his death in 4 B.C., the brutal superiority of Roman military power was experienced directly when the Roman general Varus invaded the country to quell a Jewish revolt, ending with the mass crucifixion of two thousand Jewish rebels.

The governors sent out from Rome to rule Judea beginning in A.D. 6 were second-rank and often second-rate Roman colonial administrators, sometimes simply incompetent, sometimes corrupt, sometimes deliberately provocative of Jewish loyalties. Pilate, governor from A.D. 26 to 36, was particularly insensitive, and a few years later the insane emperor Caligula sought to have a statue of himself erected in the holy of holies of the Jerusalem temple. Even beyond these specific provocations (and there were many others), the Roman presence brought unintended but inevitable conflict with Jewish law.

UNDER ROME: DOUBLE TAXATION

Roman rule had direct economic consequences with an immense impact on the Jewish social world. It brought a second system of taxation, which was added to the system of "tithes" contained within the Torah. For modern Christians, "tithes" are understood as voluntary contributions to the church. In the Jewish social world, however, the tithes required by the Torah were understood as divine laws and functioned as its tax system. The tithes supported the priests, the temple and temple staff (the Levites), and the poor. Designed for an agricultural society, each tithe was a certain percentage of a farmer's production. Taken together, the various tithes added up to slightly over 20 percent per year.

To this system of taxation, the Romans added their own. The two with the greatest effect on farmers were the land tax (1 percent of its value) and crop tax (12½ percent of the produce). There were other Roman taxes as well (customs, toll, and tribute): but even without them, the combined total of Jewish and Roman taxes on farmers amounted to about 35 percent.[10] This was a crushing amount, and would be even today.[11] Moreover, the way in which the Roman taxes were collected exacerbated the problem. Rome sold the privilege of collecting taxes to "tax farmers," who paid Rome a fixed amount and whose own profit depended on the percentage they added to the taxes.[12]

The impact upon the Jewish social world was severe. The Jewish people were powerless to affect either system of taxation. One was dictated by Roman policy, over which they had no control; the other was required by divine revelation. But there was a difference between the two systems of taxation. The Roman taxes were enforced by police power, the Jewish taxes were not. One had no choice but to pay the Roman taxes, or lose one's land. Their collection was enforced by the state.

But there was no *legal* sanction if the Jewish taxes were not paid; Rome did not enforce their collection, and the Jews had no political power to compel payment. The situation confronted the Jewish population with an economic dilemma which was at the same time a test of religious loyalty. In addition to paying the Roman taxes, could one pay the tithes commanded by the Torah?

Many Jewish farmers could not without risking losing their land. Indeed, some small farmers could not pay even the Roman taxes and thus did lose their land, creating a growing number of landless day laborers, widespread emigration, and a social class of robbers and beggars. Many of the rest could save their land only by not paying the tithes commanded by the Torah. The system of double taxation was generating a large class of "nonobservant" Jews, not because of the attractiveness of Roman and Hellenistic ways, but because of economic pressure.

The situation created a severe crisis for the Jewish social world. Every social world is sustained by the commitment of the group which lives within it; without the group, the social world would not continue, just as the group could not survive without a social world.[13] A social world remains intact only so long as people affirm it. But under the pressure of the Roman occupation, one of the central sustaining mechanisms of the Jewish social world, the commitment of its people to the observance of its laws, was being undermined.

The introduction of Roman rule thus brought a crisis into all aspects of Jewish life, religious, political, and social—and, because of the economic impact, into the smallest hamlet of the Palestinian countryside. Moreover, the conflict between the Jewish social world and the Roman presence seemed incapable of resolution. Roman imperial strategy demanded her presence and power in Palestine, both as a buffer against the Parthian empire to the east and to ensure the security of Egypt, the breadbasket of the empire. To many within the Jewish social world, however, the Roman presence itself was the problem.

THE RESPONSE: THE POLITICS OF HOLINESS

In response to the threat produced by Roman occupation, the Jewish social world became dominated by the politics of holiness. Though the word "politics" is used in many different senses, most fundamentally politics concerns the organization of a human community. *Polis* is the Greek word for "city," and thus politics is concerned with the "shape" of the city, and, by extension, of any human community. Indeed, it concerns both the shaping and the shape, process as well as result. In this sense of the word, biblical religion is intrinsically political, for it is persistently concerned with the life of a community living in history.

The politics of holiness was a continuation in intensified form of a cultural dynamic that had emerged in Judaism after the exile.[14] It was expressed most succinctly in the "holiness code" whose central words affirmed, *"You shall be holy, as I the Lord your God am holy."* The cultural dynamic was thus articulated in one of the classic patterns of religious thought, an *imitatio dei* or "imitation of God."[15] God was holy, and Israel was to be holy. That was to be her ethos, her way of life. Moreover, holiness was understood in a highly specific way, namely as *separation*. To be holy meant to be separate from everything that would defile holiness.[16] The Jewish social world and its conventional wisdom became increasingly structured around the polarities of holiness as separation: clean and unclean, purity and defilement, sacred and profane, Jew and Gentile, righteous and sinner.

Holiness as the cultural dynamic shaping Israel's ethos had originated as a survival strategy during the exile and afterward as the Jewish people pondered their recent experience of destruction and suffering. They were determined to be faithful to God in order to avoid another outpouring of the divine judgment. Moreover, as a small social group—a conquered one at that, bereft of kingship and other national institutions—they were profoundly endangered by the possibility of assimilation into the surrounding cultures. Such has been the fate of most small social groups throughout history. The quest for holiness addressed both needs. It was the path of faithfulness and the path of social survival.

"Holiness" became the paradigm by which the Torah was interpreted. The portions of the law which emphasized the separateness of the Jewish people from other peoples, and which stressed separation from everything impure within Israel, became dominant. Holiness became the *Zeitgeist*, the "spirit of the age," shaping the development of the Jewish social world in the centuries leading up to the time of Jesus, providing the particular content of the Jewish ethos or way of life. Increasingly, the ethos of holiness became the politics of holiness.

JEWISH RENEWAL MOVEMENTS IN PALESTINE

The politics of holiness was intensified by Jewish renewal movements active in first-century Palestine.[17] Writing in the closing decades of the first century A.D., the Jewish historian Josephus spoke of four "philosophies" or sects within Palestinian Judaism. One, the Sadducees, was a conservative and aristocratic group, not a renewal movement. However, the other three — the Essenes, the Pharisees, and what Josephus called "the fourth philosophy" (sometimes incorrectly known as the Zealots) — were renewal movements. Each addressed the crisis facing the Jewish social world by asking the question, "What does it mean, in these circumstances, to be a faithful Jew?" All of them intensified the postexilic cultural dynamic of holiness as separation. But each had its own understanding of what this meant, and each offered its own strategy for coping with the Roman crisis.[18]

THE ESSENES

Known to us largely through the discovery of the Dead Sea Scrolls at Qumran on the western shore of the Dead Sea near the middle of this century, the Essenes[19] believed that a life of holiness within society as then constituted was impossible. Their response was to withdraw from society to the wilderness. They formed their own separate self-sufficient communities in which they lived a highly disciplined monastic style of life, holding all things in common. Calling themselves the "men of holiness" and a "house of holiness," they understood holiness to require separation from an impure society. Seeing themselves as "children of light," they viewed the Romans (and most of the Jewish people, for that matter) as "children of darkness," and looked forward to the day when God would destroy the Romans in a cataclysmic battle. Though an interesting example of Jewish monasticism, their experiment was short-lived. They did not survive the first century, but apparently perished in the war with Rome.

THE PHARISEES

Of the Jewish renewal movements, the Pharisees[20] are the best known, simply because they are frequently mentioned by name in the gospels. Because they most often appear as opponents of Jesus, they have become victims of a historically inaccurate stereotype, namely as hypocrites.[21] But if "hypocrite" means somebody who is insincere, or who says one thing and then does another, the stereotype is unfair. The Pharisees as a group seem to have been very serious about following the path as they saw it.

Like the Essenes, the Pharisees sought to counteract the threat to the Jewish social world and identity by radicalizing the Torah in the direction of holiness. Unlike the Essenes, however, they sought to accomplish this within society by transforming the Jewish people into a "kingdom of priests." Becoming a Pharisee meant undertaking that degree of holiness required of priests in the temple.

The laws regarding purity and tithing were the major focus of the Pharisaic intensification of holiness. The Pharisaic program thus addressed the greatest source of nonobservance, that created by the double system of taxation. All tithes were to be paid, and one who would be holy could not eat untithed food. Loyalty to God meant giving to God what was God's—namely, the tithes commanded by the Torah.

Like the Jewish people in general, the Pharisees had no police power to enforce the payment of the tithes. Their sanctions were of another kind. Though some of them appear to have boycotted the produce of nonobservant Jews, the effect of the boycott could not have been great, for their numbers were small. They had some influence upon the priests, for they would give their tithes only to priests who followed Pharisaic rules of purity. But their major sanction was social and religious ostracism. From the Pharisaic point of view, the most offensive of the nonobservant were said to have lost all civil and religious rights; they were deprived of the right to sit on local councils and lost their place as children of Abraham in the life of the age to come. They became "as Gentiles." The major vehicle of social and religious ostracism was the refusal of table fellowship. To share a meal with a person was an expression of acceptance; to refuse to share a meal symbolized disapproval and rejection. Accordingly, Pharisees would not share a meal with the nonobservant.

As the only major renewal movement operating publicly within society, the Pharisees were the most visible manifestation of the politics of holiness. They sought to preserve and shape the Jewish social world by intensifying the Torah precisely in the area in which the temptation to nonobservance was the greatest. Their accomplishment was that they provided a way of being faithful to God and the Torah even under foreign rule, without leaving society. With regard to Rome, it appears that most tolerated the payment of the Roman taxes. Those who did not would have been sympathizers with the resistance movement, as some clearly were. But toward Rome most probably adopted an attitude of resigned acceptance, protesting only when Roman practices flagrantly violated the Torah. Remembering that one's first loyalty was to God permitted other loyalties as well, so long as the Torah was not violated.

Our focus on that which distinguished the Pharisees within first-century Judaism leaves the picture of them incomplete. They also were devoted to all that was common to Judaism: absolute loyalty to God, love of neighbor, the joy of the Sabbath, the richness of the Jewish festivals, and religious disciplines such as prayer and fasting. Pharisaic circles produced some of the noblest saints in Judaism. In the first century, there was the peaceable and lovable Hillel; some years later, Yohanan ben Zakkai wrested from the ruins of the war with Rome the fundamental form of Jewish piety that remains to this day. In the second century A.D., Rabbi Akiba put loyalty to Torah above life, and in his nineties was flayed alive by the Romans. His last words as the flesh was stripped from his bones were, "Hear O Israel, the Lord is our God, the Lord is One; and thou shalt love the Lord thy God with all thy heart, and with all thy soul, and with all thy might."[22]

THE RESISTANCE

The century between the beginning of Herod the Great's reign in 37 B.C. and the outbreak of the great war of rebellion against Rome in 66 A.D. was marked by frequent incidents of guerilla warfare as well as more massive attempts to overthrow the rule of Rome and her client kings and governors. However, we do not know whether there actually existed a continuing well-defined resistance group, analogous to the Essenes and Pharisees, or whether the episodes of armed resistance were more or less spontaneous outbursts participated in by diverse elements of the population. Josephus speaks of the "fourth philosophy" as if it were a group parallel to the Essenes and Pharisees (though he does not give it a name), but our sources do not provide enough data for us to know. Perhaps we should speak of a *current* of resistance rather than a *movement*.[23]

In any case, the point of view of those who were motivated by religion to take up arms against Rome was clear. Holiness could be achieved only by expelling Rome, the impure and idolatrous Gentile occupier. Implicitly, the resistance fighters radicalized the first commandment: "You shall have no other lords besides God." Only God is Lord, not Caesar. It was the rallying cry of the founders of the "fourth philosophy" in A.D. 6, and the explicit motivation for the mass suicide of the last resistance fighters at Masada in A.D. 74. Their position on taxation was also clear. One's only loyalty was to God and the Torah; therefore, one was not to pay taxes to Rome.

Thus, with their different strategies, all of the renewal movements sought to preserve the Jewish social world by shaping it increasingly in accord with the politics of holiness. But the politics of holiness also informed the large number of Jews who were not "members" of any of these groups. The majority continued to practice the form of Judaism passed down by "the elders," the conventional Torah wisdom which enshrined the ethos of holiness. They would have been aware of the movements, and many of the more devout and earnest among them would have been attracted to one or another. But all of them—the renewal movements as well as the people not identified with any movement—were committed to the politics of holiness, for that was not the monopoly of any particular movement, but the cultural dynamic shaping the society as a whole.

Ironically, the attempt to preserve the Jewish social world through the politics of holiness further fragmented it. The result of the radicalizations of Torah taught by the various renewal groups was greater division. There was competition among the groups themselves, as well as a division between each group and the rest of the population. Each group in a sense generated its opposite; the more intense the demands of holiness became (however defined), the greater the number of people who did not meet them. Thus the intention to produce a sharper division between Jew and Gentile led to greater divisions among the Jewish people themselves.[24]

"SINNERS" AND "OUTCASTS"

In particular, the emphasis upon the politics of holiness, combined with the economic pressure toward nonobservance, produced a large group of "sinners" and "outcasts." The term "sinners" referred to an identifiable social group, just as the term "righteous" did: those who did not follow the ways of the fathers as spelled out by the Torah wisdom of the sages. The worst of the nonobservant were the outcasts. We do not know the exact extent of the class, though it included the notoriously "wicked" (murderers, extortioners, prostitutes, and the like), as well as members of certain occupational groups, membership in which made one as a "non-Jew."[25]

The outcasts were virtually untouchables, not very different from the lowest caste of the Hindu system, though the status of outcast was not hereditary in Judaism. Teachers in the Jewish tradition disagreed about whether repentance was even possible for them. Next to them were the impoverished landless, whose economic status put them outside the world of family and property presupposed by conventional wisdom, and thus outside the world of respectability. The distinction between a starkly poor person, living on a mixture of begging and day labor, and an outcast must have been almost imperceptible. The status of a small farmer who did not pay his tithes would have been somewhat better, for he and his family could live more in accord with conventional wisdom, but still they would be among the nonobservant.

THE POLITICS OF HOLINESS AND THE CONFLICT WITH ROME

The politics of holiness also intensified the conflict with Rome. Members of all of the movements, as well as much of the population in general, shared varying degrees of antipathy toward Rome, whose control of the land was primarily responsible for the crisis. The spirit of hostility and resistance to Rome was widespread, as the many episodes of massive nonviolent resistance demonstrate. The memory of the heroic and successful struggle of the Maccabees against a powerful occupying Gentile nation some two centuries earlier was alive not only among the resistance fighters, but in the population as a whole.

The generation in which Jesus lived was heading toward war, not because it was a particularly warlike generation or because it

was dominated by "men of violence." Rather, the most fundamental causes were twofold. There was the perception of real
injustice—Roman rule was chronically oppressive and could be
brutal. And there was loyalty to a deeply ingrained way of life,
namely to the ethos of holiness understood as separation from all
that was impure. To a large extent, the politics of holiness, coupled
with the insensitivity of Roman imperial power, was responsible
for the conflict. Though the politics of holiness was a survival
strategy, in fact it was a path of catastrophe, leading to the war of
A.D. 66–70 with its enormous suffering and destruction of the
temple·and Jerusalem.

In the setting of this crisis facing his social world, Jesus carried
out his ministry and mission. In a time when several renewal
movements competed for the loyalty of the Jewish people, he
founded a renewal movement whose purpose was to embody what
Israel was meant to be. In a time when the politics of holiness was
generating a disastrous direction, Jesus as a prophet called his
people to change. Foundational for the movement which he created
and for the prophetic criticism which he mounted were his perception and teaching as a sage. To that we now turn.

NOTES

1. The sources for my understanding of culture and social world are numerous.
   Three, however, have been most important: Peter Berger, *The Sacred Canopy*
   (Garden City, New York: Doubleday, 1967); Clifford Geertz, *The Interpretation
   of Cultures: Selected Essays* (New York: Basic Books, 1973); and Hans Mol,
   Identity and the Sacred (New York: Free Press, 1976). Within New Testament
   studies, see especially Wayne Meeks, *The First Urban Christians: The Social
   World of the Apostle Paul* (New Haven: Yale University Press, 1983), who
   similarly speaks of "social world" as having a double meaning, referring both to
   the total social environment as well as "the world *as they perceived it* and to
   which *they gave form and significance through their special language*" (8, italics
   added). See also John Gager, *Kingdom and Community: The Social World of Early
   Christianity* (Englewood Cliffs, New Jersey: Prentice Hall, 1975), 9–11, who
   applies the notion to the construction of a new social world by the early
   Christians in the midst of an established social world.
2. For introductions to the Jewish social world at the time of Jesus, see especially
   Gerd Theissen, *Sociology of Early Palestinian Christianity* (Philadelphia: Fortress,
   1978; published in German in 1977); B. Reicke, *The New Testament Era*
   (Philadelphia: Fortress, 1980); B. Malina, *The New Testament World: Insights*

from Cultural Anthropology (Atlanta: John Knox, 1981); and J. E. Stambaugh and D. L. Balch, *The New Testament in Its Social Environment* (Philadelphia: Westminster, 1986). For more detailed treatments, see E. Schürer, *A History of the Jewish People in the Time of Jesus*, 2 volumes, rev. ed., G. Vermes and F. Millar (Edinburgh: T. and T. Clark, 1973–79); *Compendia Rerum Iudaicarum ad Novum Testamentum*, sect. 1: *The Jewish People in the First Century*, 2 volumes, edited by S. Safrai and M. Stern (Philadelphia: Fortress Press; Assen: Van Gorcum, 1974–76). For Roman rule in Palestine, see especially E. Mary Smallwood, *The Jews Under Roman Rule from Pompey to Diocletian* (Leiden: E. J. Brill, 1976). For the impact of Hellenism upon Judaism, see especially M. Hengel, *Judaism and Hellenism*, 2 volumes, translated by J. Bowden (Philadelphia: Fortress Press, 1974).

3. See Geertz's use of the terms "ethos" and "worldview" as the two central elements of culture. He defines the "ethos" of a people as "the tone, character, and quality of their life, its moral and aesthetic style and mood"; and "worldview" as "the picture they have of the way things in sheer actuality are, their most comprehensive ideas of order" (Geertz, *The Interpretation of Cultures*, 89 and 126–141).

4. To illustrate this with the contemporary culture of the United States: though our culture is pluralistic, some widely shared assumptions constitute our "conventional wisdom"—an essentially material understanding of reality, and an ethos that stresses achievement and satisfaction within this world. See, for example, Robert Bellah *et al.*, *Habits of the Heart* (Berkeley: University of California Press, 1985), which describes the "conventional wisdom" of the American middle class.

5. The decisive role played by sages in traditional cultures is difficult to imagine in the modern world. In premodern cultures, written material was not generally accessible to ordinary people, so "independent study" of sacred tradition was simply impossible. Access was possible only through worship, folk wisdom, and the sages themselves.

6. Throughout much of her history, ancient Israel apparently did not affirm an afterlife, and thus the rewards and punishments in much of the Old Testament are understood in this-worldly terms. These traditions remained current in the time of Jesus. The belief in an afterlife emerged clearly only in the late postexilic period (ca. 200 B.C.), in part because of the *suffering* of the righteous in this life, sometimes precisely because they were faithful (the belief in an afterlife appears around the time when the righteous within Judaism were being persecuted and even martyred). By the first century, perhaps most of the Jewish people had embraced the notion of an afterlife, though the Sadducees (an aristocratic group which included the high-priestly circles) still did not (see Mark 12:18–27, Acts 23:6–8).

7. The notion of reward for following the "authorized path" and of punishment for deviating seems almost to be a "cultural universal." It is found in Eastern notions of *karma*, in traditional Western notions of a last judgment, and in modern secular forms as well. Obviously, it is the basis of all systems of law. But it is also, for example, the basis of popular culture in the United States: if one follows the central values of the American way of life, one will reap the fruits of the American dream. To say that the notion of rewards and punishments is universal does not mean that every individual subscribes to it, but that it is part of virtually every established "social world."

8. Some of these may seem to be *biological* "identities," such as man, woman, oldest son. But the *value* and *role* ascribed to these biological facts is the product of conventional wisdom.

9. Such is also the case in secular cultures. In our culture our sense of identity ("self-esteem") typically depends upon how well we measure up to our culture's standards of achievement, affluence, appearance, and so on. See Robin Scroggs, *Paul for a New Day* (Philadelphia: Fortress, 1977), especially 5–14, who speaks of this way of being as living according to "the performance principle" and as what St. Paul meant by "life under the law." Scroggs sees this way of being as cross-cultural and not peculiar to Judaism; indeed, it is found not only in contemporary American culture but also in much of "conventional" Christianity.

10. The tithes included the "wave" or "first fruits" offering, ranging from 1 to 3 percent of produce; the annual tithe of 10 percent for the support of the priests and Levites; and a second tithe of 10 percent each year which was used for different purposes in different years (every third year, for example, it was the "poor man's tithe"). See F. C. Grant, *The Economic Background of the Gospels* (London: Oxford University Press, 1926), 92–106, and his list of twelve taxes on 94–96; Safrai and Stern, *The Jewish People in the First Century*, volume 2, 818–825; and the useful notes on the tractates *Maaseroth* and *Maaser Sheni* in Danby's edition of *The Mishnah* (London: Oxford University Press, 1933), 67, 73. For Roman taxes, see F. M. Heichelbaum in T. Frank, ed., *An Economic Survey of Ancient Rome* (Patterson: Pageant Books, 1938), 231–245; Schürer-Vermes, *The History of the Jewish People*, volume 1, 372–376, 401–407; M. Stern, *The Jewish People in the First Century*, volume 1, 330–333; Grant, *The Economic Background of the Gospels*, 88–91.

11. It is significantly higher than present income tax rates in the United States. Very few (if any) pay 35% of their *total* income, *before* exemptions and deductions.

12. It is therefore not surprising that "tax farmers" and their employees the "tax collectors" were the most despised of the "outcast" class. They were chronically suspected of gouging the people; and they were also "collaborationists," working hand in glove with the occupying Gentile power. This was true even in Galilee, where the taxes went into the coffers of Herod Antipas, a client-king of Rome.

13. See Hans Mol's comments about the role of commitment in sustaining a culture's worldview, social order, and identity in *Identity and the Sacred*, 11–13, 216–232.

14. For this section, see Marcus Borg, *Conflict, Holiness and Politics in the Teaching of Jesus* (New York and Toronto: Edwin Mellen Press, 1984), 27–72.

15. Leviticus 19:2. The whole of the "holiness code" is found in Leviticus, 17–26, and as a collection is commonly viewed by scholars as an exilic or postexilic work.

16. The connection between holiness and separateness is made explicitly in the rabbinic tradition, where "separate" is actually substituted for "holy." See Borg, *Conflict, Holiness and Politics*, 52–53.

17. On the meaning of the term "renewal movement," see chapter 7, p. 126.

18. For an introduction to the movements as a whole, see especially Theissen, *Sociology of Early Palestinian Christianity*.

19. For an introduction, see G. Vermes, *The Dead Sea Scrolls: Qumran in Perspective*

(Cleveland: Collins World, 1977); for the scrolls themselves, see G. Vermes, *The Dead Sea Scrolls in English* (Baltimore: Penguin, 1968).

20. See W. D. Davies, *Introduction to Pharisaism* (Philadelphia: Fortress, 1967), and J. Neusner, *From Politics to Piety* (Englewood Cliffs, N.J.: Prentice-Hall, 1973), and *Judaism in the Beginning of Christianity* (Philadelphia: Fortress, 1984). On a more technical level, see J. Neusner, *The Traditions about the Pharisees before 70*, 3 volumes (Leiden: E. J. Brill, 1971); J. Bowker, *Jesus and the Pharisees* (Cambridge: Cambridge University Press, 1971); and E. E. Urbach, *The Sages: Their Concepts and Beliefs*, 2 volume, translated by I. Abrahams (Jerusalem: Magnes Press, 1975). For a view of the Pharisees with a different emphasis, see Ellis Rivkin, *The Hidden Revolution* (Nashville: Abingdon, 1978).

21. To a large extent, the stereotype flows out of the portrait of the Pharisees found in Matthew's gospel (see, for example, Matthew 23). Matthew was written sometime after A.D. 70, when there was considerable hostility between the early church in Palestine and the Pharisees; the conflict between the two groups is reflected in the gospel account.

22. L. Finkelstein, *Akiba: Scholar, Saint and Martyr* (New York: Atheneum, 1975; first published in 1936), 276–277.

23. See especially David Rhoads, *Israel in Rebellion: 6–74 C.E.* (Philadelphia: Fortress, 1976); W. R. Farmer, *Maccabees, Zealots, and Josephus* (New York: Columbia University Press, 1956); and Borg, *Conflict, Holiness and Politics*, 34–68. R. A. Horsley and J. S. Hanson, *Bandits, Prophets and Messiahs: Popular Movements at the Time of Jesus* (Minneapolis: Winston, 1985), argue persuasively that there was not a unified resistance movement, but a variety of peasant movements ranging from prepolitical "social bandits" to prophetic movements to armed revolutionary movements.

24. See Theissen, who handles this point masterfully, in *Sociology of Early Palestinian Christianity*, 84–85.

25. There were seven occupations included in the list of "most-despised": gamblers with dice, usurers, organizers of games of chance, dealers in the produce of the sabbatical year, shepherds, tax collectors, and revenue farmers (that is, "supervisory" tax collectors who purchased the right to collect the taxes for a given area). Deprived *de jure* of all Jewish civil and religious rights, they were viewed as "Jews who had made themselves as Gentiles." Especially noteworthy from the standpoint of the gospels is the inclusion of *shepherds* and *tax collectors* in this list. There is another list of occupations only slightly less despised: workers in the transport trades, herdsmen of all kinds, shopkeepers, physicians, butchers, goldsmiths, flaxcombers, handmill cleaners, pedlars, weavers, barbers, launderers, blood-letters, bath attendants, and tanners. These groups were deprived *de facto* of Jewish rights. For lists and commentary, see J. Jeremias, *Jerusalem in the Time of Jesus* (Philadelphia: Fortress, 1969), 303–312.

6. Jesus as Sage: Challenge to Conventional Wisdom

Jesus was a sage, a teacher of wisdom. Regularly addressed as "teacher" during his lifetime by followers, opponents, and interested inquirers alike, he has been hailed by subsequent generations of Christians as more than a teacher, as indeed he was. Nevertheless, he was not less than a teacher. But what was he a teacher of?

Some have thought that he was primarily a teacher of beliefs; or, more precisely, of what was to be believed in order to be saved, providing "correct information" in the form of divine revelation about God and Jesus' own role in salvation. Others have stressed that he was a teacher of a new moral ethic, whether understood as a new moral code consisting of highly specific commands, or as a set of more generalized ideals such as love and justice or the "golden rule" or the "brotherhood of man."

But Jesus was not primarily a teacher of either correct beliefs or right morals. Rather, he was a teacher of a *way* or *path*, specifically a *way of transformation*.[1] His teaching involved a radical criticism of the conventional wisdom that lay at the core of the first-century Jewish social world. As teacher of a way and critic of conventional wisdom, he was similar to other great sages who proclaimed a way or path sharply in tension with the culture of their time. Their number outside of Israel included Lao Tzu in sixth-century B.C. China and the Buddha in fifth-century B.C. India. Within Israel, Moses was the great sage without equal, calling his followers out of Egypt, the culture in which they lived, to a radically different way.

THE FORMS OF JESUS' TEACHING

Before turning to the content of Jesus' teaching, it is illuminating to note the typical forms which he used to communicate his alternative vision. Unlike the teachers of conventional wisdom of his day, Jesus was not a "Torah sage." His teaching ordinarily did not take the form of elaborating or commenting upon the Torah, even though he obviously knew it and sometimes referred to it. Rather than appealing to sacred text or citing opinions of earlier teachers, he most often appealed to the world of human experience or made observations about nature. As he did so, he used the typical forms of the earlier wisdom tradition.

Proverbs

Proverbs are short pithy sayings which crystalize or compel insight. The sayings of Jesus include many memorable one- or two-liners: "No one can serve two masters"; "A city set on a hill cannot be hid"; "No one lights a lamp and hides it under a bushel."[2] Some of these may have been freshly coined by Jesus himself; many may already have been traditional proverbs. In either case, to a large extent they expressed truisms; indeed, their power depended upon the immediate way in which they made sense, their evident truthfulness. What gave them their radical bite in the teaching of Jesus was, as we shall see, their *application*.

Parables

Parables are imaginative stories which may serve a number of purposes.[3] They may simply illustrate or amplify a point with a memorable story; when this is their function, the point could be made just as well without a parable, though perhaps not as artfully or entertainingly. Sometimes, however, parables have a quite different function: they invite or enable the hearers to see something that they would not have seen, or would have resisted seeing, if the point were made directly.[4] In short, parables often presuppose a difference in perception between speaker and hearer, and invite the hearer to a transformed perception.

Lessons from Nature

Like the sages of the Old Testament, Jesus often pointed to nature as a source of insight. "Consider the lilies of the field; they neither toil nor spin." The observation could take the form of a question: "Are grapes gathered from thorn bushes, or figs from thistles?" The appeal to the intelligence is clear: "Of course not," is the obvious answer. The similar saying, "A good tree bears good fruit," makes an equally common-sense observation.[5] As with most of the proverbs of Jesus, it is in the *application* of these lessons from nature that their particular power lies.

Common to all of these forms of traditional wisdom as used by Jesus was an *invitation to see differently*. He appealed to the imagination and intelligence, and not to the authority of a revealed tradition, as did the teachers of conventional wisdom. Indeed, Jesus used the forms of traditional wisdom to challenge conventional wisdom.

JESUS AS SAGE

All of Jesus' teaching was directed to his contemporaries, living in their highly particular social world. He had no other audience in mind. In this sense, there is no such thing as the "timeless' teaching of Jesus. Yet there is a timeless quality to much of what he said, simply because the alternative way which he taught not only stood in tension with his social world but also in opposition to the conventional wisdom of any time. Though he was not a systematic theologian or philosopher who divided his teaching into various topics, his sagely teaching nevertheless revolved around three great themes: an image of reality that challenged the image created by conventional wisdom; a diagnosis of the human condition; and the proclamation of a way of transformation.

JESUS' IMAGE OF REALITY

Ideas matter. Though we often think of ideas as rather flimsy constructions compared to the "real" world, our ideas profoundly shape our lives. Of the ideas that affect us, perhaps most fundamental is our idea or image of what reality itself is like. Deep within all of us is an image or picture of reality, whether consciously articulated or not, which more than anything else shapes how we live. We may "image" reality as indifferent, or as the destroyer, or as the "judge" who must be appeased, or as "friend." How we see it fundamentally affects our response to life.[6]

Of these possibilities, we who are the products of modern Western culture with its essentially "one-dimensional" understanding of reality tend to "image" reality as ultimately indifferent to us. We learn that reality is a continuum of matter and energy, of whirling atoms and their interactions, or, to use a now well-known colloquial expression, a vast "cosmic soup."[7] I do not mean that all of us without exception see it this way, or to deny that public opinion polls show that most people still affirm the existence of God. But, unless transformed by convincing experience, even religious belief in our time is most frequently simply "added on" to this more basic picture of a vast ultimately inanimate and impersonal universe which is indifferent to us, in contrast to the religious worldview which preceded modern culture.

The pervasive sense of meaninglessness in the twentieth century is to a large extent the result of this change in how we see reality.[8] The image of reality as indifferent easily shades into the images of reality as destroyer. If reality is indifferent, then it is also threatening and it is up to us to protect ourselves against that which threatens to destroy us.

Jesus saw reality very differently from both us and most of his contemporaries. In common with them and with most people in the premodern world, he saw reality as ultimately Spirit (and not ultimately material), that is, that the "final word" about reality was God. What distinguished him from most of his contemporaries as well as from us, from their conventional wisdom as well as from ours, was his vivid sense that reality was ultimately gracious and compassionate.

GOD AS GRACIOUS AND COMPASSIONATE

"Grace" is one of the central words of the Christian tradition, and not by accident. Though Jesus did not use the word "grace" itself, the picture of ultimate reality, of God's ultimate character, as gracious emerges everywhere in his teaching.

Poetic imagery drawn from nature made the point. "Look at the birds of the air," Jesus said. "They neither sow nor reap nor gather into barns, and yet your heavenly Father feeds them. Are you not of more value than they?" And again, "Consider the lilies of the field, how they grow; they neither toil nor spin; yet I tell you, even Solomon in all his glory was not arrayed like one of these."[9] On another occasion, Jesus said, "God makes his sun rise on the evil and the good, and sends rain on the just and unjust."[10] With words such as these, Jesus invited his hearers to see in nature—looked at attentively from a certain perspective—a glimpse of the divine nature. Like earlier figures in the charismatic tradition, he saw the earth "filled with the glory of God," permeated by the divine radiance.[11] Nature itself points to reality as marked by a cosmic generosity, lavish in its care.

The image of God as gracious also emerges in some of Jesus' best-known parables. The prodigal son went to a far country and squandered his father's resources in loose living; having become an "outcast," he returned in desperation and unexpectedly found an overjoyed father greeting him with a celebration.[12] Clearly, the father is an image for God: loving the prodigal from afar, welcoming him, not judging him upon his return but rejoicing with him—in short, gracious. The same picture is found in the vineyard owner who paid all of his workers a full day's wage even though many had worked only a small part of the day; when those who had worked the longest complained, the owner asked, "Do you begrudge my generosity?"[13] As an image of God, the meaning is clear—God is like that.

This image of God is implicit in one of the most striking features of Jesus' ministry, namely the meals which he shared with "sinners,"—that is, outcasts.[14] Given that sharing a meal in first-century Palestine signified acceptance of one's table companions, Jesus' behavior signified his acceptance of them. It must have been an extraordinary experience for an outcast to be invited to share a meal with a man who was rumored to be a prophet. He "spoke from the mouth of the Spirit"[15] and therefore his acceptance of them would have been perceived as a claim that they were accepted by God. Implicit in the action is an understanding of God as gracious and compassionate, embracing even the outcasts, those whose mode of life placed them outside the boundaries of respectability and acceptance established by conventional wisdom. Jesus' table fellowship with outcasts was an enacted parable of the grace of God, both expressing and mediating the divine grace.[16]

The word Jesus used most often to identify this quality of God was "compassionate."[17] It has particularly rich resonances in Hebrew and Aramaic, where it is the plural of the noun "womb."[18] Thus "compassionate" bore the connotations of "wombishness": nourishing, giving life, embracing; perhaps it also suggested feelings of tenderness.[19] God is nourishing, life-giving, "wombish."

The claim that God is gracious lies at the heart of the Old Testament. It flowed out of the charismatic stream of Jesus' own tradition: "God is in love with his people."[20] It is the heart of the exodus and exile stories. Yet the needs of conventional wisdom transformed that understanding into one in which the notion of rewards and punishments, righteous and unrighteous, deserving and undeserving, became prominent. Indeed, the voice of that conventional wisdom is heard in the protests of the workers in the vineyard and the prodigal son's older brother. They expressed the dominant consciousness of the time, as well as of all times. No wonder we can easily understand their sense of unfairness.

Jesus' image of God challenges the image of reality contained in conventional wisdom cross-culturally, including the conventional wisdom of the church and modern culture. Though speaking of the "grace of God" has virtually become a Christian cliché, Christianity as understood by many both within and outside of the church is a form of conventional wisdom in which God is imaged as the judge whose standards (whether of belief or behavior) must be met. Whenever one says that God's love depends upon having met requirements of any kind, one has abandoned grace as the dominant image of reality, no matter how much the language of grace may remain. Though without making reference to God, modern culture's ideology of the good life as flowing from measuring up to societal standards conveys the same notion of reality as compensator and judge, the reinforcer of conventional wisdom's values.

If we see reality as hostile, indifferent, or "judge," then self-preservation becomes the first law of our being. We must protect ourselves against reality and make ourselves secure in the face of its threats, whether we choose secular or religious means of doing so. But if we see reality as supportive and nourishing, then another response to life becomes possible: trust. To say that God is gracious means that the relationship with God is not dependent upon performance as measured by the standards of conventional wisdom. The relationship is prior to that. In traditional religious language, God loves and is gracious to people prior to any achievement on their part; in more religiously neutral language, reality is marked by a cosmic generosity. But we do not commonly see it that way. We typically live our lives as if reality were not gracious.

THE TWO WAYS: THE BROAD WAY AND THE NARROW WAY

The great sages typically speak of two ways or paths. There is the foolish way and the wise way, the way of death and the way of life, the broad way and the narrow way, the way of bondage and the way of liberation, the way of blindness and the way of sight, the way that most people live and the "way of the saints."[21] To use a medical metaphor, the two ways spoken of by the great sages involve a diagnosis and a cure, a description of the malady and a prescription for transformation.

Jesus spoke of two ways. There was the broad way and the narrow way, the way of destruction and the way of life: "The gate is wide and the way is easy that leads to destruction, and those who enter by it are many, but the gate is narrow and the way is hard that leads to life." There was the wise way and the narrow way: "The *wise man* built his house upon the rock, and the *foolish man* built his house upon the sand." He spoke of the two ways of "serving God" or "serving *mammon*" (riches), of "treasures on earth" and "treasures in heaven."[22]

THE BROAD WAY

Strikingly, the broad way was the ethos of conventional wisdom itself. It was not what people usually think of as "sinful," the way of the "hot sins."[23] Jesus did not indict his contemporaries for failing to live up to the moral or religious standards of the conventional wisdom of his time. Rather, he saw conventional wisdom, with its focus on the securities and identities offered by culture, even though sanctioned by Scripture and hallowed by practice, as the chief rival to centering in God.

The four central concerns of conventional wisdom in Jesus' time were family, wealth, honor, and religion. Of these, religion was most central; not only was it the legitimator of that social world, but family, wealth, and honor were all understood as blessings or rewards that flowed from being religious. Yet many of Jesus' most radical words were directed against each of these.

The family had a significance in Judaism (and most premodern cultures) which is difficult for us in the modern world to imagine. In a largely agricultural society, it was the primary economic unit. Moreover, one was identified primarily in terms of one's family; not only were genealogies kept, but one was known as "son of so-and-so." The family was thus the primary social unit, the basis of both identity and financial security.[24] Yet many of Jesus' most radical sayings call for a break with the family or familial obligations. He denied the significance of his own family.[25] He spoke of discipleship as involving "hating" one's father and mother, wife and children, brothers and sisters,[26] and of his ministry as bringing division within families.[27] To a prospective follower who said, "Master, let me first go and bury my father," Jesus responded, "Follow me, and leave the dead to bury their own dead." It is one of the most radical sayings in the teaching of Jesus, for the obligation properly to bury one's dead was among the most sacred of familial obligations within Judaism.[28]

Wealth and possessions, then as now, were a major source of security and identity. Though Judaism could speak of the "unrighteous wealthy," wealth was typically seen as a blessing from God that flowed from following the path of wisdom. Obviously, it was good to be wealthy, for wealth provided both comfort and a sign that one had lived right. Yet Jesus regularly criticized wealth. He told unfavorable stories about its pursuit, pronounced woes upon the rich and blessings upon the poor, called upon some to renounce all, and said, "How hard it will be for those who have riches to enter the Kingdom of God!"[29] He himself was apparently without possessions, and he commanded his disciples to be likewise.[30] Yet though they may have practiced a form of "holy poverty,"[31] it is not clear that Jesus opposed wealth in principle; he apparently had some wealthy followers, including some wealthy women who supported him and his disciples.[32] Nevertheless, he clearly saw wealth as one of the primary distractions and preoccupations in life, greed as one of the consuming and blinding human passions, and all of this sanctioned by conventional wisdom.

Honor was a pivotal value. To some extent the product of birth, family, and wealth, it was sustained by social recognition.[33] It was not just social status, but also the *regard* one felt entitled to in virtue of that status. Much behavior was therefore dictated by the desire to acquire, preserve, or display honor. But Jesus ridiculed its pursuit, mocking those who sought the places of honor at a banquet, the best seats in the synagogue, or salutations in the marketplace.[34] He chastised religious practices which were motivated by the desire for social recognition: "Do not sound trumpets when you give alms."[35] Honor—the community's recognition of achievement by the standards of conventional wisdom—was seen as a snare.

The final major focus of conventional wisdom was religion. If one were wise, one would be religious. Like the other themes of conventional wisdom, religion provided a culturally conferred source of identity and security. One's descent made one a child of Abraham, and thus heir to the promises of God; and one's religious behavior numbered one among the righteous or sinful children of Abraham. Within the framework of conventional wisdom, religion easily became a means of seeking both security and an honorable identity.

Yet some of the most shocking words in the gospels were directed at religious beliefs and practices. Jesus' predecessor, John the Baptist, had preached, "Do not presume to say to yourselves, 'We are children of Abraham.'"[36] For Jesus, as for the Baptist, the sacred identity conferred by conventional wisdom meant nothing.[37]

NO [

Nor was religious practice as a basis of security exempted from his critique. Especially instructive is the Parable of the Tax Collector and the Pharisee.[38] The Pharisee's prayer of thanksgiving referred to his religious behavior: "I thank thee, God, that I am not like other men; I fast twice a week, I give tithes of all that I get." It is important to note that the Pharisee was not a hypocrite in the usual sense of the word; we have no reason to think that he said one thing and did another. Instead, he was a model of what a faithful Jew should have been according to the most rigorous standards of the day. His defect was neither hypocrisy nor immodesty; rather, his fault was that he rested his security in his own genuine religious accomplishment, which had become the center of his life. Strikingly, Jesus indicted trusting in one's own "success" at doing the will of God.[39] Significantly, the Pharisee's opposite in the parable, the outcast, rested his security solely in God, laying no claim to righteousness: "God, be merciful to me a sinner."

Jesus' perception of the broad way is also disclosed by the cast of characters in his parables. They realistically portray how human beings commonly act. Indeed, it is upon the skillful portrayal of typical human behavior that the power of a parable depends—the hearers recognize themselves. The characters cover the gamut of first-century Palestinian life: laborers and elder sons and officials concerned to receive what they think they rightfully have coming to them; people preoccupied with business and family so that they refuse an invitation to a banquet; a servant fearful and anxious to preserve what he had; tenant farmers determined to seize a vineyard from its owner; rich people centered in their wealth, unmindful of death and suffering; priests and lay people alike preoccupied with their own religiosity and purity. As snapshots of typical human behavior, the parables disclose much about Jesus' diagnosis of the human condition: we often are preoccupied with our concerns, anxious about our well-being, limited in our vision, grasping in our attempts to make ourselves secure.

Jesus' analysis of the way humans typically are was also conveyed by images of blindness. Having eyes, people do not see.[40] He spoke of the conventional sages of his day as "blind" and asked, "Can a blind man lead a blind man? Will they not both fall into a pit?"[41] Something within us which likes to judge and compare keeps us from seeing clearly: "How can you say to your brother, 'Brother, let me take the speck out of your eye,' when you cannot see the log that is in your own eye?"[42] He spoke of the importance of a "sound eye," without which one lives in darkness: "The eye is the lamp of the body. So if your eye is sound, your whole body will be full of light; but if your eye is not sound, your whole body will be full of darkness."[43]

Preoccupation with the world of conventional wisdom created anxiety. Anxiety as part of the broad way is implicit in much of Jesus' teaching: he saw people as anxious to receive what they believed they deserved, anxious about holding on to what they had, anxious about social approval. It became explicit in Jesus' famous words about "the lilies of the field" and "the birds of the air."[44] Five times in that passage, in which Jesus invited his hearers to see reality as marked by a cosmic generosity, he asked, "*Why are you anxious?*" Anxiety about food, clothing, length of life, and "tomorrow" (the specific categories mentioned in the passage) was, in his view, typical.

Thus the world of concerns created by conventional wisdom—the broad way—was dominated by the quest for security. To use a word which Jesus did not use himself, Jesus saw people as profoundly "selfish"—concerned above all about the self's well-being and security, and seeking that through the means offered by culture.[45] The primary allegiances cultivated by conventional wisdom are ultimately pursued for the sake of the self in order that it might find a secure "home" in them.[46] Moreover, anxiety, self-concern and blindness go together. Anxious about securing their own well-being, whether through family, possessions, honor, or religion, people experience a narrowing of vision, become insensitive to others and blind to the glory of God all around us. God is not absent; rather, we do not see.[47]

Yet the broad way is very common, now as then. It need not be obviously sinful, at least not in the popular sense of the term; rather, it can seem very respectable, often legitimated by religion and even perceived as religious. Indeed, the path of conventional wisdom seems "obviously right," the wisdom of the elders, "what everybody knows," the dominant consciousness of both religious and secular cultures. But Jesus taught another way.

THE NARROW WAY OF TRANSFORMATION

Just as Jesus used a multiplicity of images in his diagnosis of the human condition, so he also used many different images to speak of the cure, that is, the path of transformation. Underlying this diversity is a common conceptual understanding which comes to expression most clearly in the first three images we shall treat: a *new heart, centering in God,* and *the way of death.* The images intertwine with each other, even as each works separately as well. Each expresses what the "cure" involves, even as it adds nuances of meaning that may not be captured by the other images.

A New Heart

The first of these images continues the diagnosis even as it also pictures the cure. Jesus spoke frequently of the heart—of good hearts and bad hearts, hardened hearts and pure hearts. To us, the heart is primarily a physical organ and sometimes understood metaphorically as the "home" of feelings. But within ancient Jewish psychology, it had a different meaning. The heart was the self at its deepest center, a level "below" the mind, emotions, and will. It was the ground or source of perception, thought, emotion, and behavior,[48] all of which were subject to it.

This notion of the heart as a deep level of the self and as the fundamental determinant of both being and behavior was central to the teaching of Jesus. He spoke of "the good man who produces good out of the good treasure of his *heart* and the evil man who produces evil out of the evil treasure of his *heart*," and illustrated what he meant by using the metaphor of a tree and its fruits to speak of the self and its behavior: "No good tree bears bad fruit, nor again does a bad tree bear good fruit. Figs are not gathered from thorns, nor are grapes picked from a bramble bush."[49]

As an observation about nature, the proverb is obviously true: you get figs and grapes from a fig tree and vine, not from a thorn bush or bramble bush. But when this common-sense observation was applied to the heart and its behavior, it became radical. What matters is what kind of heart you have, that is, what kind of tree you are. And you cannot change the kind of tree you are by dealing only with the fruit. That would be like trying to change a thorn bush into a fig tree by hanging figs on it.

The words not only affirm the centrality of the heart, but also subvert conventional wisdom. The latter tends to overlook this deeper level of the self by focusing on externals, on the fruit. Its concern with conventionally sanctioned belief and behavior, with a set of beliefs to be believed by the mind, and with a code of behavior to be followed, can leave the heart untouched. The mind can believe "correct doctrines" and leave the heart unaffected; a person can follow the practices and observances commanded by conventional wisdom and leave the self at its deepest level untransformed. It is not that what one believes and how one behaves are irrelevant; but the heart is not necessarily affected. Beliefs and behavior can remain "second-hand religion," religion passed on by tradition and socialization. The self can continue to be selfish even while it believes and does the proper things; indeed, conventional wisdom with its rewards and punishments subtly but powerfully encourages it to be selfish.

The tension between correctly following tradition and the importance of the inner self was a central theme in the teaching of Jesus. About some of the practitioners of tradition in his day, Jesus said, "This people honors God with their lips, but their *heart* is far from God."[50] That is, they said (and to a large extent, did) the right things, but the inner self remained far away. What mattered was what was *inside*, the heart: "The things which come *out of a person* [from the heart] are what defile him."[51] "Cleanse the *inside*," he said, "and behold everything is clean."[52] Indeed, Jesus consistently radicalized the Torah by applying it to the inner self rather than simply to behavior.[53] What was needed was a new heart.

This emphasis was not new to the Jewish tradition. The author of the fifty-first psalm petitioned God for a clean heart, in words which have been prayed and sung by Jews and Christians for centuries: "Create in me a *clean heart*, O God." Jeremiah spoke of a new covenant which would be *within, written upon the heart*.[54] Hence the struggle between Jesus and the wisdom of his time was not a struggle between a new religion (Christianity) and an old religion (Judaism), but a struggle between two ways of being religious that run throughout Judaism and Christianity alike. The conflict was between a way of being religious that depended upon observance of externals (the way of conventional wisdom) and a way of being religious that depended upon inner transformation. Indeed, this conflict is found in all of the major religions.

Thus, according to Jesus, what was needed was an inner transformation of the self at its deepest level. "Blessed are the *pure in heart*," he said, "for they shall see God."[55] The fruit of an anxious heart, concerned about its own well-being, is bitter. What is needed is a new heart, a pure heart, for such a heart produces good fruit. The central quality of a transformed heart is indicated in the next image.

Centering in the Spirit (God)

Within ancient Jewish psychology, the character of the heart depended upon its orientation, what it was pointed toward or centered in. Centered in God, in the Spirit, the heart was good and fruitful; but centered "in man," in "flesh" or the finite, the heart was bad and became "deceitful above all things."[56] Thus what mattered was the orientation of the self at its deepest level, its "center" or fundamental loyalty.

Jesus continued and radicalized this understanding. He spoke of a radical choice between two contrasting centers which competed for the loyalty of the heart. "No one can serve two masters—you cannot serve God and mammon."[57] Centering in God versus centering in the finite are contrasted in another saying: "Do not lay up for yourselves treasures on earth, but lay up for yourselves treasures in heaven, for *where your treasure is, there will your heart be also.*"[58] One may treasure the finite, that which "moth and rust consume," which "thieves break in and steal," or one may treasure God—center in Spirit above all else.

To speak of radically centering in God is central to the tradition in which Jesus stood.[59] It is the "radical monotheism" of the Old Testament, crystalized in the *Shema* which was recited twice daily by faithful Jews in the time of Jesus: "Hear, O Israel: The Lord our God is one Lord; and you shall love the Lord your God with all your heart, and with all your soul, and with all your might."[60] Indeed, Jesus himself stated that the *Shema* was the "great commandment."[61] To say that "centering in God" was the essence of the tradition was thus commonplace; but deliberately to contrast "centering in God" to the centers legitimated by conventional wisdom, indeed to conventional wisdom itself, was radical. Yet this is precisely what Jesus did. The central concerns of the conventional wisdom of his day— family, wealth, honor, and religion—were all seen as rival centers. His criticism of them was a call to center in Spirit, and not culture.

Such centering in God is the opposite of anxiety as well as the antidote to anxiety. It is what Jesus meant by the word "faith." In the passage where he five times spoke of people being anxious, he spoke of the alternative as "faith." As the opposite of anxiety, "faith" is not what is commonly meant by "belief." Obviously, people then and now could *believe* that God existed and still be anxious.[62] Rather, as the opposite of anxiety, faith must mean something more than what the mind believes, namely a radical *trust* in God, a centering in God by the self at its deepest level. Faith is thus a matter of the heart.[63]

But how does the inner transformation pointed to by the need for a new heart occur? How does the self become centered in Spirit and not in itself or culture? It cannot happen simply by an act of will, for the will is under the control of the heart, in bondage to the finite centers which capture our loyalty. It cannot happen by deciding to believe a particular way or by deciding to be "good," for that would involve trying to change the heart with the mind or will. Rather, this inner transformation and radical recentering involve the path of death.

The Way of Death

The central image of the Christian tradition is an image of death: the cross. To be sure, the cross is also an image of life because of its intrinsic connection to resurrection; Good Friday and Easter belong together.[64] Undoubtedly, the cross is so central because of the way Jesus' historical life ended. Yet what it symbolizes—death and resurrection—was also one of the central images for the path of transformation taught by Jesus himself.

In one of Jesus' best-known sayings, he spoke explicitly of the path as the way of *dying*: "If any man would come after me, let him deny himself and take up his cross and follow me."[65] Using the language of a path or way ("come after me," "follow me"), Jesus starkly identified that path as "taking up the cross." Before Jesus' death, "cross" was obviously not yet a Christian symbol but referred to a method of execution used by the Romans.[66] It was customary for the person sentenced to be crucified to carry the horizontal beam of the cross to the place of execution. Hence, "taking up one's cross" meant walking the road to death. The meaning of the saying is clear: to be a follower of Jesus was to embark upon the path of death.[67]

The same point was made with other closely related metaphors. Jesus asked his disciples, "Are you able to drink the cup that I drink, or to be baptized with the baptism with which I am baptized?" "Drinking the cup" and baptism were both images for death.[68] Similarly, Jesus said, "Whoever seeks to gain his life will lose it, but whoever loses his life will preserve it."[69]

But what kind of death was this? Clearly it was meant metaphorically and not literally. The "way of death" did not mean physical death, even though some of the early followers of Jesus were martyred. Rather, it was a metaphor for an internal process, as Luke made clear by adding the word "daily" to the saying about taking up one's cross.[70] This internal dying or death has two closely related dimensions of meaning. On the one hand, it is a dying of the self as the center of its own concern. On the other hand, it is a dying to the world as the center of security and identity. These— the self and the world—are the two great rival centers to centering in God, and the path of transformation thus involves a dying to both of them. The "world" to which one must die is the world of conventional wisdom, the world of "culture" with its preoccupying securities; and the self which must die is the self-preoccupied self. Then is born a self which is centered in God, in Spirit and not in culture.

"Dying" is a striking metaphor for this process. It points to the radicality of the change, of course; this radical recentering brings about a change so sharp that it can be described as dying to an old life and being born into a new life. "Dying" may have a further nuance as well. Because the heart which is centered in culture cannot be changed by the mind or the will (for both are slaves of the heart), a hardened heart must in a sense die in order that a new heart may be created; it cannot change itself. "Dying" is something that happens to the self as opposed to it being something that the self accomplishes. *How* this dying occurs varies greatly from person to person; for some, it may involve an inrushing of the Spirit, for others a severe life crisis, for others a long, gradual journey. But in any case, the central movement in dying is a handing over, a surrendering, a letting go, and a radical centering in God.

This transformation brought about through an internal death is at the heart of the early Christian tradition. Paul describes himself as having undergone such a death: "I have been crucified with Christ; it is no longer I who live, but Christ who lives in me."[71] It is found in John's theology: "Unless a grain of wheat falls into the earth and dies, it remains alone; but if it dies, it bears much fruit."[72] Baptism, the early church's ritual of initiation, was understood as a death of an old self and a resurrection of a new self.[73]

This widespread attestation of the motif in the tradition is to some extent due to the way Jesus' historical life ended. But it is also a continuation of what Jesus himself taught. In a quite historical sense, Jesus not only taught the way of death as the path of transformation, but his life and death became an incarnation of the way which he taught. Indeed it is this remarkable congruity between the teaching of Jesus and the way his life ended that accounts in part for the power which his figure has had over the centuries. Thus the cross is an extraordinarily rich image, pointing both to the death of Jesus and to the heart of his teaching: the path of transformation is a dying to the self and to the world.[74]

There is thus a world-denying and culture-denying quality to the teaching of Jesus. The statement needs to be guarded against three possible misinterpretations. It was not a world denial based upon a dualistic understanding of the material or natural world as evil, and the world of Spirit as good. Jesus took delight in the natural world as the creation of God. He was not an ascetic in the usual sense of the word; he was reputed to enjoy both food and drink, and was known for banqueting with outcasts. Though he spoke of abandoning the family as the center of one's loyalty and security and apparently was unmarried himself,[75] there is no reason to think that he was opposed to sexuality. Indeed, he sanctified the family more than his tradition did.[76] In short, it was not the natural world or the finite itself that was evil; consistent with the Jewish tradition, Jesus saw that as created by God and therefore good.

Second, his challenge to conventional wisdom was not a complete overthrowing or disregard of tradition. He was, in an important sense, neither anti-law nor anti-convention. He was a Jew who treasured his tradition. He quoted Scripture, explicitly affirmed the Ten Commandments, and so far as we know observed the Jewish law all his life.[77] Rather, his challenge to conventional wisdom was a challenge to what may be called "enculturated religion": religion accommodated to conventional wisdom and increasingly shaped by those who were the beneficiaries of conventional wisdom. When this happens, religion becomes a legitimator of a way of life rather than invitation to a new way of life. In short, it was the world of conventional wisdom *as the center of identity and security* that was negated.[78] In this sense, the teaching of Jesus is world denying; indeed, the world of culture *as the center of existence* comes to an end.

Third, Jesus' challenge to conventional wisdom must always be kept within the framework of his perception of reality as gracious and compassionate. His challenge must not be seen as a new *requirement*; when it is, his teaching becomes another form of conventional wisdom, sometimes a very severe one. Rather, his challenge is an *invitation* to see things as they really are—namely, at the heart of everything is a reality that is in love with us. Thus, though his way was the narrow way, "the eye of the needle," it was also somewhat paradoxically the easy way. It was hard especially for those who were secure within the framework of conventional wisdom; for them to die to the world meant letting go of a world which pronounced them "blessed." Yet his way was also the "easy yoke" for some, for those who were burdened by the world of culture: "Come to me, all who labor and are heavy-laden, and I will give you rest; for my yoke is easy and my burden is light."[79]

CONCLUSION: JESUS AS TRANSFORMATIVE SAGE

Jesus was not the first in Jewish history to criticize conventional wisdom. In the Hebrew Bible, the authors of Ecclesiastes and Job protested against the conventional wisdom represented by the book of Proverbs, that easy confidence that the righteous would prosper and the wicked wither.[80] They were *subversive* sages who challenged and subverted the popular wisdom of their day.[81]

Jesus stood in this tradition of subversive wisdom.[82] He used the *forms* of wisdom to subvert conventional ways of seeing. His proverbs and parables often reversed ordinary perception, functioning to jolt his hearers out of their present "world," their present way of seeing reality.[83] The *content* of his teaching also subverted the world of conventional wisdom, in several ways. His picture of God as gracious undermined conventional wisdom's understanding of reality. He attacked the "broad way" of conventional wisdom as an inadequate means for bringing about an internal transformation. Indeed, he saw it not only as an inadequate cure but as part of the problem. It easily became a snare, catching the self in its promise of security and identity, preoccupying the self in external matters, limiting its vision and narrowing its concern and compassion. Jesus subverted conventional wisdom at its roots, seeing it and the self-concern it fostered as the primary rival to centering in God and as the primary source of blindness to the graciousness of God.

Finally, however, his teaching involved more than a subverting of conventional wisdom. He affirmed another vision and another way. He taught an alternative way of being and an alternative consciousness shaped by the relationship to Spirit and not primarily by the dominant consciousness of culture. He was thus not only a subversive sage but a transformative sage.

There is a connection between Jesus' experience as a Spirit-filled person and the path which he taught. That path was firmly grounded in the Old Testament, at whose heart lies the notion of two ways, one the way of radical monotheism and the other the way of infidelity. Yet Jesus crystalized this understanding with such power and freshness of language, and applied it with such radical effect, that it is difficult to believe that he simply learned it from the study of tradition. It is more plausible to suppose that his intensity of perception and conviction together with the vividness of his language have their origin in Jesus' own experience as a Spirit-filled person. As a charismatic, Jesus was one who knew God; as a sage, Jesus was one who spoke about God, and we may suppose that the two facts are related. His image of reality and the path which he taught, sharply contrasting to the dominant consciousness of his day, came out of his relationship to Spirit. Standing in the charismatic stream of his own tradition, Jesus called his hearers to a life grounded in Spirit rather than one grounded in culture.

Yet he was also more than a sage. Unlike the subversive sages of the Old Testament who apparently carried out their criticism within the school of wisdom itself,[84] Jesus carried his criticism of conventional wisdom directly to the public in a mission that was national in scope. He founded a revitalization movement which sought the transformation of the historical path of his people.

NOTES

1. It is striking that the earliest name for his movement was "the Way." See Acts 9:2.

2. There are over one hundred proverbs in the sayings of Jesus. See especially Leo Perdue, "The Wisdom Sayings of Jesus," *Foundation and Facets Forum* 2.3 (1986): 3–35; Charles E. Carlston, "Proverbs, Maxims, and the Historical Jesus," *Journal of Biblical Literature* 99 (1980): 87–105; and J. D. Crossan, *In Fragments: The Aphorisms of Jesus* (San Francisco: Harper & Row, 1983).

3. Scholarly literature on the parables of Jesus is voluminous. The classic studies in twentieth century scholarship are by Joachim Jeremias, *The Parables of Jesus* (New York: Scribner's, 1972), C. H. Dodd, *The Parables of the Kingdom* (New York: Scribner's, 1961); and John Dominic Crossan, *In Parables: The Challenge of the Historical Jesus* (New York: Harper & Row, 1973). For an excellent survey of Jesus' parables, including bibliography, see Bernard Brandon Scott, "Essaying the Rock: The Authenticity of the Jesus Parable Tradition," *Foundation and Facets Forum* 2.1 (1986): 3–53. For a survey of parable research up to 1979, see W. S. Kissinger, *The Parables of Jesus: A History of Interpretation and Bibliography* (Methuen, N.J.: Scarecrow Press, 1979).

4. Classic Old Testament examples of the latter kind are found in the prophets Nathan and Isaiah. In Nathan's story about the man who had only one ewe lamb (2 Samuel 12:1–6) and Isaiah's story about the vineyard which yielded only wild grapes (Isaiah 5:1–7), both prophets elicited a verdict from their hearers about the story *before* the hearers perceived that the story applied to them.

5. Texts referred to are Matthew 6:28 = Luke 12:27; Matthew 7:16 = Luke 6:44; Luke 6:43 = Matthew 7:17 (compare Matthew 12:33).

6. For this exposition, see H. Richard Niebuhr's insightful *The Responsible Self* (New York: Harper & Row, 1963). Niebuhr argues that our view of the "ultimate context" or "total environment" in which we live (that is, our view of "ultimate reality" or God) decisively affects our response to life. He explicitly lists and analyzes the four possibilities of seeing reality as indifferent, as hostile, as requiring appeasement, and as "friend." For the notion of "imaging" reality, see also Alan Jones, *Exploring Spiritual Direction* (New York: Seabury, 1982), 83–98.

7. A phrase used by Carl Sagan in his television series and book *Cosmos* (New York: Random House, 1980).

8. The yawning sense of meaninglessness and cosmic loneliness generated by the modern worldview has been one of the central themes of twentieth-century art and literature (fiction and poetry, as well as philosophical and theological writing). Perhaps it nowhere comes to expression more clearly or humorously than in a scene from Woody Allen's movie *Annie Hall*. The main character (Allen himself) is trying to pick up a young woman who is looking at a modern painting in an art gallery. About the painting, she says: "It restates the negativeness of the universe; the hideous, lonely emptiness of existence, the nothingness; the predicament of man forced to live in a barren, godless eternity like a tiny flame flickering in an immense void with nothing but waste, horror, and degradation forming a useless bleak strait jacket in a black absurd cosmos." Granted, this is a wonderfully exaggerated caricature, but it is not going too far to say that there is a measure of this in most of us.

9. The quoted words are from Matthew 6:26, 28–29. The whole passage is found in Matthew 6:25–33 = Luke 12:22–31.

10. Matthew 5:45; compare Luke 6:35. Other relevant texts include Matthew 10:29–31 = Luke 12:6–7.

11. The quoted phrase is from Isaiah 6:3; the word "glory" is closely associated with "presence" and "radiance." Thus to say "the earth is full of the glory of God" is to say the earth is filled with the divine presence or radiance. See also many of the psalms and Job 38–41, where the magnificent display of the created world is seen as a beautiful and awesome disclosure of the divine mystery. Christians have sometimes been uneasy with the notion of God "permeating" creation, thinking it sounds like a more Eastern way of thinking. Yet it is intrinsic to the Jewish-Christian tradition to see God as *both* immanent (everywhere present) and transcendent (see chapter 2, page 28). The widespread notion of God as *only* transcendent seems to be associated with the popular image of God as a being "out there" or "beyond" the universe, and *not* "here."

12. Luke 15:11–32. The depth of his desperation and degradation is indicated by a detail of the parable: he became a *swineherd*, lower than an outcast, if such be possible. Herders of *sheep* were in the lowest class (see chapter 5, pages 91–92, and note 25); a *swineherd* was even worse, in a sense unheard of, for pigs were unclean animals. Other details in the parable also make it clear that the son had become "worse" than an outcast.

13. Matthew 20:1–15.

14. See chapter 5, pages 91–92. Norman Perrin, *Rediscovering the Teaching of Jesus* (New York: Harper & Row, 1967), 107, refers to Jesus' meals with outcasts as perhaps "*the* central feature" of Jesus' ministry (italics added).

15. See chapter 3, pages 46–47.

16. Both Perrin and Jeremias refer to it as a "parabolic action" which expressed forgiveness or the grace of God; Jeremias, *The Parables of Jesus*, 227, and Perrin, *Rediscovering the Teaching of Jesus*, 107. For the social meaning of the action, see chapter 7.

17. For example, in the parable of the prodigal, the father's response is summed up with the words, "He had compassion." In an especially important passage which summarizes a block of Jesus' teaching, Jesus is reported to have said, "Therefore be merciful [compassionate], even as your Father is merciful [compassionate]" (Luke 6:36; for further treatment of this passage, see chapter 7).

18. See Phyllis Trible, *God and the Rhetoric of Sexuality* (Philadelphia: Fortress, 1978), 31–59, especially 33, 38–53.

19. For a striking account of the prophetic notion of the *feelings* or *pathos* of God, including compassion and tenderness, see Abraham Heschel, *The Prophets*, volume 1 (New York: Harper & Row, 1962).

20. The phrase comes from Abraham Heschel, *The Prophets*, 44, who uses it to sum up the central claim of the prophets of Israel.

21. See W. T. Stace, *Religion and the Modern Mind* (Philadelphia: Lippincott, 1952), 252: according to the religious traditions, "there are two ways of life, that which most of us follow, and which consists in 'making the best of a bad job,' and the 'way of the saints. . . .'" The two ways correspond to the perception of human existence common to the religions of the world. There is the claim that there is something wrong with human life as it is most commonly lived, that it is filled with suffering, anxiety, grasping, and bondage, that it is "fallen" or "sinful,"

not what it is meant to be. The sense of something being wrong may be felt internally or seen externally in injustice and wars and all the other suffering that we inflict upon each other. Yet the religions also teach that there is a way of overcoming the dis-ease and disorder that mark existence most of the time. The centrality of these two elements is nicely summarized by William James, *The Varieties of Religious Experience* (New York: Macmillan, 1961), 393: the "common nucleus" to which the religions of the world "bear their testimony unanimously" consists of two elements: "An uneasiness" and "Its solution" (that is, the problem and its cure).

22. Matthew 7:13–14; compare Luke 13:23–24. Matthew 7:24–27. Matthew 6:24. Matthew 6:19–21 and Luke 12:33–34.

23. That is, gluttony, drunkenness, adultery, and so forth. The teaching of Jesus in this respect (as well as many others) differs markedly from the "hot" preaching of some evangelists today.

24. For a systematic contrast between the contemporary American and ancient Mediterranean understandings of the family, see B. Malina, *The New Testament World: Insights from Cultural Anthropology* (Atlanta: John Knox, 1981), 94–102.

25. Mark 3:33–35.

26. Luke 14:26 = Matthew 10:37. The passage is softened somewhat (but only somewhat) by the fact that "hate" can be an idiom in Hebrew and Aramaic meaning "love less" or "put in second place."

27. Matthew 10:34–36 = Luke 12:51–53.

28. Luke 9:59–60; see also the closely related saying in verses 61–62. Perrin perhaps overstates the case when he calls the first the *most* radical of all the sayings of Jesus (see *Rediscovering the Teaching of Jesus*, 144).

29. Mark 10:23; the passage continues with the famous line, "It is easier for a camel to go through the eye of a needle than for a rich man to enter the Kingdom of God." Attempts to water this down by speaking of a low gate called "the needle's eye" through which a camel *could* go on its knees miss the point. Not only is there no such evidence for such a gate, but the point of the saying is its radicality. Other relevant passages include Luke 6:24–26, 12:13–21, 16:19–31; Mark 10:28; Matthew 6:19–21 = Luke 12:33–34; Matthew 6:24 = Luke 16:13.

30. Mark 1:16–20, 2:13–14, 6:8–9; Luke 9:57–58 = Matthew 8:19–20.

31. The way of "holy poverty," known in many traditions including the Christian tradition (the preeminent postbiblical example is St. Francis, who embraced "lady poverty"), abolishes one of the fundamental distinctions culture imposes upon the world, the distinction between "mine" and "not-mine." About that which is mine I will be anxious, seeking to preserve it and perhaps add to it; I then easily become centered in that which is "mine." "Holy poverty" not only abolishes this distinction, but makes one radically dependent upon God.

32. Luke 8:1–3. Wealthy followers or "sympathizers" would also include Joseph of Arimathea (Mark 15:43). There is no good reason for regarding him as a literary invention. On the subject of poverty and wealth, see also chapter 7, pages 135–137.

33. On honor, see especially Malina, *The New Testament World: Insights from Cultural Anthropology*, 25–50. A person concerned about honor "constantly thinks about what he or she ought to do, about what is ideally acknowledged in the society as meaningful and valuable," and expects others to acknowledge his or her achievement of such ideals (28). Indeed, "honor is all about the tribunal

or court of public opinion and the reputation that court bestows" (36). Malina speaks of two kinds of honor: it may be one's by birth, but may also be *acquired* by "excelling over others in . . . social interaction" (29). Honor was the product of excellence as defined by the canons of conventional wisdom.

34. Luke 14:7–10, Mark 12:38–39, Luke 11:43 = Matthew 23:6–7.

35. Matthew 6:1–6, 16–18. Other practices mentioned include prayer and fasting: one is to practice both "in secret," and not for the sake of being seen.

36. Matthew 3:9 = Luke 3:8.

37. Jesus' teaching continued the emphasis sounded by the Baptist: many of his hearers (who were children of Abraham) would see *others* enjoying the banquet of the age to come with Abraham, Isaac, and Jacob, and they themselves shut out (Matthew 8:11–12 = Luke 13:28–29). Jesus also applied the notion in reverse; about the "outcasts," those who had forfeited their standing as children of Abraham, he could say, "Are these not also children of Abraham?" (see Luke 19:9 and 13:16).

38. Luke 18:9–14.

39. This is the radical meaning of self-righteousness: to rest one's standing before God in the self's fulfilment of religious requirements, whether one publicly displays that fulfilment or not. It was not simply characteristic of particular individuals in the time of Jesus, but is a perennial temptation of religious people. It is the religious form of living according to the "performance principle" (see chapter 5, page 83 and note 9).

40. See, for example, Mark 4:12, 8:18.

41. Luke 6:39 = Matthew 15:14.

42. Luke 6:41–42 = Matthew 7:3–5. See Robert Tannehill's excellent commentary on this passage in *The Sword of His Mouth* (Philadelphia: Fortress, 1975), 114–118.

43. Matthew 6:22–23 = Luke 11:34–36.

44. Matthew 6:25–34 = Luke 12:22–31. See also page 101 above.

45. This "selfishness" need not be thought of in a radically individualistic way, as if it means a concern for one's self *alone*. That is, one's "selfishness" will normally extend to a concern for the communities considered vital to one's existence (for example, the family and perhaps the nation).

46. To say that humans are "selfish" can easily become a cliché. For a powerful and persuasive description of this "root" selfishness in humans, flowing out of our anxiety and distorting both our vision and our thinking, see Langdon Gilkey's reflective account of his experience in a civilian internment camp in China during World War II: *Shantung Compound* (New York: Harper & Row, 1966).

47. The last sentence of the paragraph builds on a statement from Abraham Heschel, quoted from memory: "God is not dead; we are."

48. For a compact statement of this generally held view, see *The Interpreter's Dictionary of the Bible* (Nashville: Abingdon, 1962), II. 549b: the heart was "the psyche at its deepest level," "the innermost spring of individual life, the ultimate source of all its physical, intellectual, emotional, and volitional energies."

49. Luke 6:43–45; see also Matthew 7:16–20, 12:34–35. The combination of heart imagery with tree and fruit imagery is also found in Jeremiah 17:5–8, one of many points of contact between Jeremiah and Jesus.

50. Mark 7:6. The words are a quotation from Isaiah, suggesting that the tension between external observance (the way of conventional wisdom) and the condition of the heart runs throughout the history of Israel.

51. Mark 7:14–15; all of Mark 7 deals with the importance of the heart compared to observance of traditional practice.

52. Matthew 23:25–26 = Luke 11:37–41.

53. See Matthew 5:21–22, 27–28. See also Matthew 5:20: "If your virtue goes no *deeper* than that of the scribes and Pharisees, you will never get into the kingdom of heaven" (translation from *Jerusalem Bible*).

54. Jeremiah 31:31–34. The connection between "new covenant" and "heart" in the Jeremiah passage is striking. With his emphasis upon the heart, it is conceivable that Jesus saw himself as instrumental in bringing about the new covenant spoken of by Jeremiah. The early church clearly made this association in its understanding of Jesus' last supper with his disciples. See 1 Corinthians 11:23–25, Mark 14:24, and Matthew 26:28, all of which use the language of "covenant." Paul explicitly says "new"; in the synoptic passages, "new" is a textual variant; see also the longer text of Luke in 22:19b–20.

55. Matthew 5:8.

56. Jeremiah 17:5–10. The importance of the heart's orientation was also stressed within the rabbinic tradition, which spoke of the heart being ruled either by the "evil inclination" (*ha-yetzer ha-ra*) or "good inclination" (*ha-yetzer ha-tob*). One's actions depended upon the inclination of one's heart—if evil, then evil; if good, then good. See W. D. Davies, *Paul and Rabbinic Judaism*, 4th ed. (Philadelphia: Fortress), 20–35. See also E. E. Urbach, *The Sages* (Jerusalem: Magnes, 1975), 471–483. The great power of the evil inclination over the heart is indicated with a variety of images: it is like a king ruling the 248 parts of the body; it ensnares the self like a spider web at the beginning, but its threads soon become as thick as a ship's rope; the evil inclination begins in the heart as a visitor, then a regular guest, and finally becomes the host—that is, has taken charge.

57. Matthew 6:24 = Luke 16:13. "Mammon" literally meant "wealth," though it also had the extended meaning of finding one's security in the world.

58. Matthew 6:19–21 = Luke 12:33–34.

59. It is the way of life (contrasted to the way of death) spoken of by Moses in Deuteronomy 30:15–20, the "choose you this day" of Joshua in Joshua 24 and of Elijah in 1 Kings 18, and the consistent challenge of the prophets.

60. Deuteronomy 6:4–5.

61. Mark 12:28–31 = Matthew 22:34–40; see also Luke 10:25–28, where a "lawyer" (an expert in the Law) recites the "great commandment," which Jesus then approves. In each case, a second commandment is also added: "You shall love your neighbor as yourself."

62. The point is an important one. Religious *belief* does not necessarily relieve anxiety. Indeed, I have seen many cases (and heard of many more) in which embracing a form of Christianity has only heightened anxiety and fearfulness about whether one is *really* "in the Lord." When this happens, Christianity is no longer the antidote for anxiety but the intensifier of it. Moreover, if faith is "trusting in God," then this is not faith.

63. Strikingly, the roots of the Latin verb for faith, *credo* (with which the *creeds* of the church begin), reflect this connection to the heart. *Credo* comes from two words which together mean, "I give my heart to." See Wilfred Cantwell Smith, *Faith and Belief* (Princeton: Princeton University Press, 1979), 76–78. For an illuminating discussion of the development of the word "belief" in English, see 105–127.

64. The cross as pointing to both life and death is symbolized by the two types of

crosses found within the church: the crucifix with the dying Jesus on it, and the empty cross suggestive of the resurrection.

65. Mark 8:34 = Matthew 16:24 = Luke 9:23. See also Luke 14:27 = Matthew 10:38. The specification of the "way of Jesus" as the way of the cross or death is sometimes thought to be a post-Easter creation of the church. In all probability, the highly specific "predictions" of Jesus' own death and resurrection (see, for example, Mark 8:31, 9:31, 10:33–34) were created by the church after Easter. But the sayings in which Jesus spoke of the way of transformation as involving death are quite well-authenticated, occurring not only in Mark but also in Q.

66. Specifically, it was the penalty for rebellion or treason against Rome, and was used with great frequency in Palestine.

67. See the statement by Dietrich Bonhoeffer in *The Cost of Discipleship* (New York: Macmillan, 1963; originally published in German in 1937), 7: "When Christ calls a man, he bids him come and *die.*"

68. Mark 10:38.

69. Luke 17:33; also found in slightly varying versions in Mark 8:35 = Matthew 16:25 = Luke 9:24; see also Matthew 10:39.

70. Luke 9:23. That Jesus said "daily" is unlikely, since it is clearly Luke's redactional addition; yet the addition seems accurately to state the sense of Jesus' saying.

71. Galatians 2:20. Paul also speaks of this experience as common to all Christians. See, for example, Romans 6:1–11, especially verse 3.

72. John 12:24. Immediately thereafter, John adds: "He who loves his life loses it, and he who hates his life in this world will keep it in eternal life."

73. See Marcus Borg, *Conflict, Holiness and Politics in the Teaching of Jesus* (New York and Toronto: Edwin Mellen Press, 1984), 244. Moreover, the "way of Jesus" as the "way of death" is a major structural element in both Mark's gospel and Luke's gospel; *ibid.*, 245 and notes 52–53, 378.

74. Other images in the teaching of Jesus make the same point. *Repentance* did not mean primarily remorse or regret for sin, but a radical *turning* to God, that is, a radical centering in God. *To become as a servant* meant to become as a "slave," that is, a person who had no will of his or her own, but only the will of the master; one could be a slave of either God or "mammon." The paradoxical sayings about *humbling/exalting* (Luke 14:11, 18:14b; Matthew 18:4, 23:12) and *first/last* (Mark 10:31, Matthew 19:30 and 20:16, Luke 13:30) have a similar thrust. To be humble meant to be "empty" of internal possessions and therefore able to be filled with God; those who put themselves first shall be last, and vice-versa. Similarly, the images of *becoming as a child* and being *born anew* are frequent and natural images for the new life that flows out of the path of dying: one becomes a new person with a new heart centered in God, and not in self or culture.

75. There is some (though not much) uncertainty about the marital status of Jesus. He clearly seems to have been single during the ministry. William Phipps, *Was Jesus Married?* (New York: Harper & Row, 1970), argues that Jesus may have been married as a youth and that his wife may have died before the ministry. The basis for the argument is the normal pattern for Jewish males as they grew into adulthood. Marriage, arranged by one's parents, was so taken for granted that ancient Hebrew does not have a word for "bachelor." Clearly, however, there were exceptions, including Jeremiah in the Old Testament (Jeremiah

16:1–4). For a treatment of the nonascetic quality of Jesus' path of renunciation, see especially G. S. Sloyan, *Jesus in Focus: A Life in Its Setting* (Mystic: Twenty-Third Publications, 1983), chapters 17–18.

76. Mark 10:1–12.

77. Mark 7:19b reports that Jesus abolished the Jewish food laws. However, the parenthetical expression is clearly an addition by the evangelist and reflects the understanding of the church of his day, and not the intention of Jesus. We have no reason to think that Jesus abolished the distinction between clean ("kosher") and unclean food. Had he done so, we might have expected his opponents to have accused him of this, but there is no such record in the gospels. Moreover, the early church's struggle with that issue as reflected in Acts and the letters of Paul is inexplicable if Jesus had already resolved it. To put the point more broadly, the conflict between Jesus and his contemporaries did not concern the *validity* of the Torah, but its *interpretation*.

78. Because of the history of Jewish-Christian theological polemics, I want to stress that I am seeking to describe a characteristic of conventional wisdom generally, and not something peculiar to a Jewish way of being religious. In most periods of its history, Christianity has been as thoroughly permeated by conventional wisdom's image of God as the judge and compensator, as well as legitimator of those who "live right," as Judaism ever was. In short, over time conventional wisdom or enculturated religion intrinsically seems to distort the original view of the founders of the tradition, even as it may continue to mediate the Spirit through its preservation of tradition.

79. Matthew 11:28–30.

80. The story of Job is the story of his transformation from the viewpoint of conventional wisdom (which is represented in the book by his friends, a framework within which Job's suffering made no sense) to a wisdom based upon the experience or vision of God. See the climax of the book in 42:5: "I had heard of thee by the hearing of the ear [that is, from conventional wisdom], *but now my eye sees thee.*" The book of Ecclesiastes denies that life can be so easily ordered as conventional wisdom suggests: "Who can make straight what God has made crooked?" (1:15). Moreover, following the wise path (the way of conventional wisdom) for the sake of reward is included in the category of "vanity," a "striving after wind" (see, for example, 7:15). Thus both challenge conventional wisdom.

81. Scholars regularly divide the wisdom tradition of Israel into two categories: conventional wisdom, and skeptical or subversive wisdom. Job and Ecclesiastes comprise the latter; included in the former are the books of Proverbs and (in the apocrypha) Sirach (a second-century B.C. work sometimes known as "Ecclesiasticus" or "The Wisdom of Jesus the Son of Sirach"). For introductions to the wisdom tradition of Israel, see G. von Rad, *Wisdom in Israel* (Nashville: Abingdon, 1972); R. Murphy, *Wisdom Literature* (Grand Rapids: Eerdmans, 1981); and James Crenshaw, *Old Testament Wisdom: An Introduction* (Atlanta: John Knox, 1981).

82. Jesus is also portrayed as a teacher of wisdom in the Gospel of Thomas, a collection of sayings attributed to Jesus and discovered in Egypt in 1945. Though much in Thomas is consistent with the view sketched above, and though many scholars convincingly argue that some of the sayings in Thomas are as early as the traditions found in the synoptics, I have chosen in this book to

base my portrait on the canonical gospels. For an introduction to Thomas, see Stevan Davies, *The Gospel of Thomas and Christian Wisdom* (New York: Seabury, 1983).

83. For a description of how the forms of Jesus' teaching themselves mediated and invited end-of-world, see especially the work of John Crossan and William Beardslee, conveniently reported by Norman Perrin in *Jesus and the Language of the Kingdom* (Philadelphia: Fortress, 1976), 48–56. The notion of *subversive wisdom* is used with great effect by Crossan in his book *In Fragments: The Aphorisms of Jesus*.

84. Wisdom in ancient Israel was taught by teachers of wisdom in special schools. The very fact that Job and Ecclesiastes were put into *literary* form suggests that they were part of an internal dialogue within the wisdom tradition rather than a direct attempt to "proselytize" the public at large. By the time they were preserved in the canon, both were provided with endings that made them more in conformity with conventional wisdom (see Ecclesiastes 12:9–14 and Job 42:7–17).

7. Jesus as Revitalization Movement Founder

We are not accustomed to thinking of Jesus as a political figure. In a narrow sense, he was not. He neither held nor sought political office, was neither a military leader nor a political reformer with a detailed political-economic platform. But he was political in the more comprehensive and important sense of the word: politics as the shaping of a community living in history.[1]

In this sense his own tradition was deeply political, and so was he. His concern was not simply the individual and the individual's relationship to God, though obviously he was concerned about that. But the way of transformation he taught was not divorced from the particularities of his social world and the crisis which was convulsing it. Just as he challenged the conventional wisdom at the heart of his social world, so he also challenged the politics of holiness as the dynamic shaping his people's corporate life. We see his political concern in his roles as revitalization movement founder and prophet, and in his final appeal to Jerusalem.

JESUS AS REVITALIZATION MOVEMENT FOUNDER

We commonly think of Jesus as the founder of Christianity. But, strictly speaking, this is not historically true. Instead, his concern was the renewal of Israel. Toward this end, he created a sectarian revitalization or renewal movement within Israel, now commonly called the "Jesus movement,"[2] whose purpose was the transformation of the Jewish social world.

The relationship between a renewal or revitalization movement and a social world is one of both affirmation and advocacy of change. On the one hand, such movements profess a strong loyalty to an inherited social world or tradition (if they did not, we would speak of them as *new* movements rather than renewal or revitalization movements). On the other hand, they claim that present circumstances call for a radical response. Spawned by a perceived difference between how things are and how they ought to be, all within the framework of a tradition, they affirm a tradition, even as they seek to revitalize or transform it.[3]

The fact that Jesus did not intend to create a new religion but intended the revitalization of his own tradition does not mean that Christianity is a mistake. Rather, Christianity as a religion separate from Judaism came into existence as the result of a historical process which took several decades after his death. Two factors were most important. As a revitalization movement within Judaism after his death, the Jesus movement in an important sense *failed*. Though most of its early members were Palestinian Jews, it did not capture the allegiance of the majority of the Jewish people. The second factor leading to separation was the success of the Jesus movement in the Mediterranean world outside of Palestine. There it quickly became a mixed community of Jews and Gentiles, and the more Gentiles it attracted, the more it seemed distinct from Judaism.[4] Thus, before the end of the first century, Christianity had in effect become a "new" religion.[5] Henceforth, though Christianity continued to affirm its connection to Judaism, the connection was increasingly to the Old Testament rather than to the Jewish people themselves. In terms of its membership, it was no longer a peculiarly or predominantly Jewish movement. But this is to get ahead of our story.

CHARACTERISTICS OF THE MOVEMENT

Intended for Israel

Like the other Jewish renewal movements with which it competed for the allegiance of the Jewish people, the Jesus movement saw itself as a *way for Israel*, as a historical alternative in the crisis facing the Jewish social world. One of the most certain facts of

Jesus' ministry points to the concern with Israel: the choosing of *twelve* followers as having a special calling. "Twelve" is the number of tribes of Israel, descended from the twelve sons of Jacob, the "father" of Israel. That Jesus chose twelve rather than nine or thirteen is thus no accident; Jesus saw them as the nucleus of the "new" or "true" Israel. Moreover, they themselves were given a mission, and their mission, like his, was to Israel: "Go nowhere among the Gentiles, and enter no town of the Samaritans, but go rather to the lost sheep of the house of Israel."[6]

The most plausible explanation of the restriction to Israel is that Jesus' primary concern was the revitalization of Israel. Such is also indicated by the movement's course of action in Palestine even after his death, where it remained a Jewish revitalization movement until shortly after the destruction of the temple in A.D. 70.

A Charismatic Movement

The movement was grounded in the Spirit. Sometimes renewal movements come into existence simply through a strongly perceived difference between how things are and how they ought to be; but often the vivid spiritual experience and conviction of a particular individual is also a major factor. The Jesus movement clearly belongs in the latter category. It came into existence in part because of the crisis facing Judaism, but also because of the Spirit-filled experience of its founder.[7]

The powers of the Spirit were present in the movement, in Jesus as well as in some of his followers. The "twelve" were given powers to cast out demons and to heal.[8] After Jesus' death, the early Christian communities continued to be Spirit-filled, both in Palestine and beyond. The book of Acts reports numerous paranormal experiences, including the descent of the Spirit at Pentecost and healings and visions throughout. Paul's letters indicate that the "gifts of the Spirit" were known in his churches as well.[9] Though the movement's charismatic character is often underemphasized within both contemporary scholarship and the mainstream church, it was one of its most remarkable features.

An Itinerant Movement

During Jesus' lifetime, the core of the movement was centered around a person; wherever Jesus was, there the movement was. Thus it was not only a movement, but also literally a group on the move. Of the crowds who were attracted to Jesus, not everybody who responded to him followed him literally in the sense of joining the itinerant movement; most probably remained in their own communities as "local sympathizers." Before his death, we do not know how many sympathizers there were, but they must have numbered at least several hundreds and perhaps a few thousands.

But some did join him "on the road."[10] Though it was not unheard of in first-century Palestine for a group of people to leave their homes and follow a charismatic leader, it was striking.[11] The group's composition was also exceptional; in addition to the nucleus of Jesus and the twelve, it included outcasts and women, thus violating (as we shall see) the central norms of the culture. Though some Pharisees and well-to-do people were attracted to it, it seems to have been largely a movement of common people, including many who were poor. For the core which traveled with him, there may have been special requirements which did not apply to those who remained in local communities.[12] As an itinerant movement, it sometimes was offered local hospitality by sympathizers, but also no doubt often slept in the open air. As a group on the move, traveling through Galilee and finally to Jerusalem, it must have been a remarkable sight.

Joy in the Presence of Jesus

The movement was marked by joy, as several details in the gospels suggest. There was celebration in the meals which he shared with his followers and others. They were festive occasions, banquets as opposed to ordinary meals.[13] He had a reputation as a "glutton" and a "drunkard," and though this was an accusation by opponents, it is clear that he was not a world-denying or joy-denying ascetic.[14] His followers did not fast during the ministry, which also drew an accusation: "Why do John's disciples and the disciples of the Pharisees fast, but your disciples do not fast?" Jesus' response was significant: "Can the wedding guests fast while the bridegroom is with them?"[15] Fasting is for a time of mourning, feasting for a time of joy. The response compared being in the presence of Jesus to one of the most joyous occasions known in the ancient world: a wedding banquet.

The impression is clear: to be in the presence of Jesus was a joyous experience. This experience of joy in the presence of a remarkable religious figure has parallels in other times and places. Both within and beyond the Christian tradition, people speak of a "presence" or "zone" around a holy one which is virtually palpable, which can be "felt." Simply to be in the presence of such a person mediates the reality of which he or she speaks.[16] This joy is not to be confused with a feeling or mood of constant happiness, but goes beneath moods and feelings. To be in the presence of Jesus was experienced as being in the presence of the Spirit which flowed through him.

THE ETHOS OF THE MOVEMENT: COMPASSION

This joyous group moving through Palestine was not simply a circle of devotees gathered around a spiritual master and wonder-worker who taught a path of individual transformation. Rather, it was a movement whose life embodied a different vision of what Israel was to be, a different ethos for the people of God. The image of reality generated by Jesus' charismatic experience created a new ethos for the life of the people of God, a central paradigm or ethic in accord with which they were to live.

Compassion as the Content of the Imitatio Dei

Like the social dynamic of his culture as a whole and of the renewal movements with which his competed, Jesus expressed this ethos as an *imitatio dei*, or "imitation of God."[17] But the content of

Jesus' *imitatio dei* differed: whereas first-century Judaism spoke primarily of the holiness of God, Jesus spoke primarily of the compassion of God.

We are accustomed to thinking of compassion as a feeling. And so it is in the Bible—a feeling localized in the abdomen, perhaps in the bowels or womb, and which is a "being moved by," a "feeling with," as even the Latin roots of the word suggest. It is being moved by another's situation, at a level lower than the head or intellect.

Compassion is not only a human feeling, but also a quality of God in Scripture. The fact that the Old Testament speaks of God as compassionate indicates that the contrast between Jesus and the Judaism of his time must be understood as a matter of emphasis. First-century Judaism could also speak of the compassion of God, and Jesus never denied that God was holy. The issue was not whether God was compassionate or holy, but concerned which of these was to be the central paradigm for imaging God and for portraying the life of the faithful community.

Jesus repeatedly emphasized the compassion of God. The father of the prodigal son "had compassion," the Samaritan was the one who "showed compassion," the unmerciful servant did not act in accord with the compassion which had been shown him, the tax collector in the Parable of the Tax Collector and the Pharisee appealed to the compassion of God.[18] Aspects of Jesus' healing activity point to the same quality: consistently the motivation was *compassion*. Moreover, Jesus sometimes healed on the sabbath, a practice that typically generated criticism.[19] Within Judaism, the sabbath was "holy" and one of the most emphasized features of the quest for holiness; healing on it was permitted only when there was danger to life. But for Jesus, even when life-threatening conditions were not involved, healings—the work of the compassionate Spirit— took precedence over the demands of holiness.

The substitution of compassion for holiness is most strikingly clear in a passage which is formally an *imitatio dei* and whose structure echoes the climactic words of the holiness code: "Be *compassionate*, even as your Father is *compassionate*."[20] Just as God is compassionate or "wombish,"[21] so people who are faithful to God, who are "children of God," are to be compassionate.[22] Just as God is moved by and "feels with" the "least of these," so the Jesus movement was to participate in the *pathos* of God.[23] Indeed, the *pathos* of God *as compassion* was to be the ethos of the Jesus movement and, ideally, of Israel.

THE POLITICS OF COMPASSION

Just as the ethos of holiness had led to a politics of holiness, so also the ethos of compassion was to lead to a politics of compassion. The ethos of compassion profoundly affected the shape of the Jesus movement, both internally and in its relationship to the world. The "shape" of the alternative community or "counterculture" was visible in the constituency of its membership which stood in sharp contrast to the relatively rigid social boundaries of the Jewish social world: boundaries between righteous and outcast, men and women, rich and poor, Jew and Gentile. These boundaries, established by the politics of holiness and embodied in the culture as a whole and in varying forms in other renewal movements, were negated by the Jesus movement. The negation pointed to a much more inclusive understanding of the community of Israel.

Banqueting with Outcasts

At the center of the church's worship life throughout the centuries stands a meal, variously known as the Lord's Supper, the mass, the eucharist, or communion.[24] As a sacrament of bread and wine presupposing the death and resurrection of Jesus, it is manifestly a post-Easter development. Yet it has its roots in the ministry of Jesus.

Eating together or "table fellowship"—not yet a ritual meal, but the festive act of sharing food and drink at a table—was one of the central characteristics of his movement.[25] Many texts refer to meals, or are set in the context of one; and the meals provoked strong criticism from his opponents. Several times the gospels report the criticism, consistently the same: "So—he eats and drinks with tax collectors and sinners"; "He has gone in to be the guest of a man who is a sinner"; "This fellow welcomes sinners and eats with them"; "Look at him! A glutton and a drinker, a friend of tax-gatherers and sinners!"[26]

The charge is very simple: he eats with "sinners." To modern ears, familiar with the Christian affirmation that *all* people are sinners, the accusation that Jesus ate with "sinners" tends to brand the accusers as self-righteous people who did not realize that they, too, were sinners. But the term "sinners" had not yet been universalized and theologized; instead, it referred to a specific social group, namely the "outcasts." It identified the chronically nonobservant, and included many of the poor.[27]

Beyond the fact that these meals provoked criticism, we do not know much about them. As already noted, they were festive meals or "banquets" rather than simply routine consumption of nourishment. Sometimes Jesus was the guest of a local person, but sometimes he seems to have been the host. Perhaps his movement, with him at the center, held festive meals in the villages they passed through, either in the open air or in the house of a sympathizer. A large number of his parables defended his practice of eating with outcasts.[28] Indeed, one may speculate that many of his parables may even have been spoken in the context of these festive meals as the "table talk" of Jesus.[29]

Though we do not know many details about these meals, much can be said about their significance. We have already indicated what Jesus' table fellowship would have meant to outcasts. Eating with them would have shattered the social world which pronounced them unacceptable, and would have enabled them to see themselves as accepted by God.[30] But it also radically threatened the social world of his opponents, and was thus a cultural as well as religious challenge. For a charismatic person to say, with both his teaching and behavior, that the outcasts were accepted by God was to challenge and threaten the central ordering principle of the Jewish social world: the division between purity and impurity, holy and not-holy, righteous and wicked. The table fellowship of Jesus called into question the politics of holiness as the cultural dynamic of the society.

What was at stake, from the standpoint of Jesus' opponents, was the survival of the people of God. "Sinners" were those whose nonobservance threatened the survival of the group; tax collectors were even worse, for they were collaborators with the Gentile oppressors. It is no wonder that his table fellowship aroused criticism. Indeed, some scholars have argued that Jesus' acceptance of outcasts was the primary source of the hostility which his ministry generated.[31] It was an extraordinary action for a religious figure in the Jewish tradition.[32]

Thus the simple act of sharing a meal had exceptional religious and social significance in the social world of Jesus. It became a vehicle of cultural protest, challenging the ethos and politics of holiness, even as it also painted a different picture of what Israel was to be, an inclusive community reflecting the compassion of God.

Association with Women

One of the most remarkable features of Jesus' ministry was his relationship to women. Challenging the conventional wisdom of his time, it continues to challenge the conventional wisdom of much of the church.

Rigid boundaries between men and women marked the world in which he lived. Although perhaps intensified by the politics of holiness,[33] these boundaries were not its direct result but a perennial characteristic of conventional wisdom in most cultures: patriarchy. Conventional wisdom is typically male-dominated. Produced and written by men, it is taught by men to men and reflects a male point of view.[34] So it was in the cultures surrounding the Jewish social world and within Judaism itself.[35]

Though there are positive statements about women in both the Old Testament and postbiblical Judaism, the dominant attitude reflected in the teaching of the sages was negative.[36] A good wife was much appreciated, but women as a group were not thought well of. The synagogue prayer recited at each service included the words, "Blessed art thou, O Lord, who hast not made me a woman." In synagogues women typically were required to sit in a separate section and were not counted in the quorum of ten people needed to hold a prayer meeting. They did not teach the Torah,[37] and as a general rule were not even to be taught the Torah.[38]

Their religious disenfranchisement extended into the social sphere. Except among the poorer classes, men and women were rigidly separated in public life. Young women of the wealthier families were completely secluded until marriage; after marriage, they could go out in public only if veiled. They were not to talk to men outside of their families. Similarly, a respectable Jewish man (and especially a religious teacher) was not to talk much with women, apparently for two reasons. There was no benefit to be gained, for they were viewed as not very bright and as preoccupied with trivia. Moreover, women were considered to be seductive and sexually rapacious temptresses. Their voices, hair, and legs were felt to be especially enticing. Thus, in part because they were regarded as inferior and in part because of male perceptions (and fears) of their sexuality, women were systematically excluded from both the religious and public life of the social world.[39]

Against this background, Jesus' own behavior was extraordinary. The itinerant group of immediate followers included women, some of whom—Joanna and Susanna—supported the movement financially.[40] The sight of a sexually mixed group traveling with a Jewish holy man must have been provocative. Similarly, the occasion on which a woman who was a "sinner" washed Jesus' feet with her tears and dried them with her hair as he reclined at a banquet given by a Pharisee was shocking.[41]

Jesus was a guest in the home of two sisters named Mary and Martha. Martha played the traditional woman's role of preparing a meal, while Mary related to him as disciple to teacher. When Martha complained that she was doing all the work, Jesus endorsed Mary's behavior. In a first-century Jewish social context, it was a radical point. Jesus treated women and men as equally capable (and worthy) of dealing with sacred matters.[42] In a time when a respectable sage was not even to converse with a woman outside of his family,[43] and when women were viewed as both dangerous and inferior, the practice of Jesus was startling.

The radically transformed attitude toward women continued in the early church for the first several decades, according to both Acts and the letters of Paul, where women in many of his churches were prominent enough to be greeted by name. Paul's own position was consistent with the radicalism of the Jesus movement: "There is neither Jew nor Gentile, there is neither slave nor free, *there is neither male nor female*; for you are all one in Christ Jesus."[44]

As already noted, patriarchy is not peculiar to ancient Judaism, but characterizes most cultures, Christian ones included.[45] Indeed, the radical attitude of the Jesus movement toward women was already modified within the church before the New Testament was even completed. One of the later New Testament documents repeats the patriarchal view of the dominant culture: women are to be submissive and modest, are *not* to be teachers of men, and are even held responsible for bringing sin into the world.[46] Cultural attitudes from the Jewish and broader Mediterranean world had begun to cloud the vision generated by the Spirit.

Such attitudes have been part of the church and Western culture ever since. Yet when one sees the rejection of patriarchy by Jesus and his earliest followers and the clear historical evidence that patriarchy reentered the tradition at a later date, representing a "fall" from the radicalism of the early movement, it is almost incomprehensible that many within the church continue to teach the subordination of women. The Jesus movement as a counterculture stands in contrast to later Christian tradition even as it stood out in its own social world.

"Good News to the Poor."

Yet another dimension of Jesus' social world was addressed by the politics of compassion. According to Luke, the opening words of Jesus' public ministry announced "good news to the poor." In the passage which begins with the words, "The Spirit of the Lord is upon me," Jesus continued, "He has anointed me to preach *good news to the poor*."[47]

In what sense was Jesus' mission "good news to the poor"? Matthew understood the poor to be the "poor in spirit," and the hungry as "those who hunger for righteousness." But Luke has simply, "Blessed are you poor," and "Blessed are you that hunger now," and makes clear that he has the economically poor in mind by contrasting them explicitly to the materially wealthy: "Woe to you who are rich, for you have received your consolation."[48]

At the very least, Jesus challenged the connection between righteousness and prosperity made by conventional wisdom, with its corollary that the poor had not lived right and thus were "unworthy" children of Abraham. Moreover, because the standards of culture are internalized even in those who fail to meet those standards, the poor would have seen *themselves* as "unworthy" children of Abraham. Indeed, most of the poor were among the nonobservant. By accepting "the poor," Jesus as one in touch with the Spirit of God would have enabled the poor to see themselves differently. It is the same dynamic operative in his banqueting with outcasts.

There may be another dimension of meaning as well. According to Luke, Jesus used language associated with the Jubilee year to announce his "good news to the poor." His mission was "to proclaim release to the captives," "to set at liberty those who are oppressed," and "to proclaim the acceptable year of the Lord,"[49] all phrases tied to the Jubilee year, one of the most radical pieces of social legislation in the Old Testament. According to it, every fifty years the land was to be redistributed to the poor—that is, to those who had lost their land since the last Jubilee.[50] The intention of the Jubilee was to prevent the growth of a landless class in Israel, though it was so radical that it was rarely observed.[51] The Jubilee year was indeed good news for the poor, in effect the periodic elimination of the category "poor."

Did Jesus literally intend the redistribution of land? Since he did not seek political power, it is impossible to see it as part of a political "platform." Did he seek through persuasion to lead the wealthy to redistribute their land to the people from whom they had acquired it? Was he simply announcing how things "ought to be," without any practical plan or intention for actualizing it? Had the language of Jubilee become completely metaphorical so that it was language announcing the "time of salvation" rather than referring to the actual redistribution of land?

However one understands Jesus' relationship to the Jubilee, it is apparent that he was concerned about the economically poor and that he had harsh words for the rich. He urged his followers to give to beggars, to lend without expecting repayment, and to give alms without expecting reward.[52] He spoke of the impossibility of serving both God and mammon, and warned against laying up treasures on earth.[53] Whether Jesus objected to wealth and private ownership in principle is not clear. The "Jerusalem church," composed of Jesus' immediate followers and early converts, apparently practiced a form of common ownership, but we do not know if this was widespread among Christians in Palestine as a whole.[54]

Although much must remain uncertain about Jesus' teaching regarding rich and poor, it is clear that in a community organized around compassion, there would not be gross inequity between rich and poor. Indeed, one would imagine that there would no longer be any abject poor.

The Peace Party

The application of Jesus' teaching to his social world is also seen in the fact that his movement was the peace party within Palestine. In the same context where Jesus spoke of the *imitatio dei* as compassion, he also spoke of loving one's enemies: "You have heard that it was said, 'Love your neighbor,' but I say to you, Love your enemies."[55] The quoted words, "Love your neighbor," come from the holiness code and were understood within contemporary Judaism to mean, "Love your fellow member of the covenant," that is, your fellow Israelite or compatriot.[56] In this context, the opposite of neighbor is clearly "non-Israelite," and so loving one's enemy must mean, "Love the non-Israelite enemy," including the Gentile occupiers.

Other traditions in the gospels also indicate that the Jesus movement was the peace party. In the same immediate context as the saying about loving one's enemies, Jesus said, "If anyone strikes you, turn the other cheek" and added "If any one forces you to go one mile, go with him two miles,"[57] which referred to the right of a Roman soldier to require a civilian to carry his gear for one mile. In these sayings, the spirit of resistance was countered. Elsewhere he said, "Blessed are the peacemakers, for they shall be called children of God,"[58] and "All who live by the sword will perish by the sword,"[59] Moreover, as we shall see later, Jesus entered Jerusalem in a manner which proclaimed that his alternative was the way of peace, not the way of war.[60]

The famous passage, "Render to Caesar the things that are Caesar's, and to God the things that are God's," points in the same direction.[61] The setting is both fascinating and instructive. Some Pharisees asked Jesus a "trap" question: "Is it lawful to pay taxes to Caesar?" If Jesus had responded, "Yes," he would have discredited himself with many who resented the tax; if he had said, "No," he could have been arrested on the charge of urging nonpayment of the Roman tax.[62] Jesus responded with a "counter-trap." Requesting and receiving a coin from his interrogators, he then asked them, "Whose likeness and inscription are on the coin?" They responded, "Caesar's," thereby discrediting themselves with those in the crowd who believed that it was wrong even to carry an image of Caesar.

Their response also permitted Jesus' final reply, which basically meant, "It's Caesar's coin—go ahead and give it back to him." As an implicit approval of paying the tax, his reply constituted a rejection of one of the central convictions of the armed resistance movement. But the response did not address the larger question of what was Caesar's and what was God's. Ironically, a passage which initially undercut the path of military violence has often been used in subsequent centuries to justify military service and war. In much of the church's history, the whole realm of politics was given to Caesar, to secular authority. But the passage has no such comprehensive meaning in its context. Rather, it was an answer which the liberation movement could not have accepted, and which indicated that the real issue was not which earthly kingdom ruled the land.

As the peace party in Palestine, the Jesus movement thus rejected the path of violent resistance to Rome.[63] The people of God were not to secure their existence through force of arms or violence; faithfulness pointed to another way. With its emphasis upon compassion, the Jesus movement also undercut the connection between holiness and resistance that existed within the other renewal movements and the culture as a whole.

It is odd that many in the church throughout the centuries (including many biblical scholars and theologians in the modern period) have denied that Jesus' teaching about love of enemies had any kind of political application. Often it is claimed that his teaching applied only to personal enemies and not national enemies, or that "turning the other cheek" was meant as an impossible ideal whose purpose was to make people aware of their sinfulness.

Yet these sayings would have had an unmistakable meaning in the politically violent situation of first-century Palestine, just as they would in the Middle East or Central America or other places of armed conflict today. For a public figure to speak of loving one's enemies in such a setting would unambiguously mean to disavow the path of violence and war. Moreover, those closest to Jesus in time clearly understood his teaching to mean nonviolence. The early church for the first three hundred years of its existence was pacifist.[64] Though it is odd that the church has largely denied the political thrust of these traditions, it is also understandable. Through time the church became enculturated, and it is very difficult for enculturated religion to stand in tension with culture. For the church to have said that following Jesus meant nonviolence would have made the church into a counterculture. Only occasionally has it been willing to be so since the time of Jesus and his earliest followers.

Thus the Jesus movement visibly and radically shattered the norms of the Jewish social world. Strikingly, the *imitatio dei* as compassion transcended the cultural distinction between Jew and Roman, righteous and outcast, men and women, rich and poor.[65] The source of this radical relativizing of cultural distinctions is found in the charismatic grounding of the movement.[66] Because Jesus saw God as gracious and embracing, the "children of God" could and did embrace those whom the politics of holiness excluded. The relationship to God was primary, not whether one was outcast, female, poor, or enemy. The experience of the Spirit disclosed the relativity—in a sense, the artificiality and arbitrariness— of cultural distinctions. The intense experience of the Spirit generated a new way of seeing and being that stood in sharp contrast to the boundaries and rivalries created by culture.

Spiritualization of Central Elements

In yet one more way the Jesus movement differed from the conventional wisdom of the Jewish social world and from the renewal movements which operated within it. Key elements of Jewish teaching were spiritualized. "Spiritualization" involves the claim that what truly matters is not the external practice or reality, but the internal or spiritual reality to which the external points.

Specifically, Jesus denied that purity was primarily a matter of externals, concerning pots or pans or hands, or whether one ate food that was untithed. True purity was internal, not dependent upon the ability to measure up to standards of purity as defined by conventional wisdom and the other renewal movements. What mattered was an internal transformation, "purity of heart,"[67] which was possible even for those whom the social world placed beyond the pale. Similarly, the notion of righteousness was internalized.[68]

Jesus may have spiritualized the notion of the temple as well, though we cannot be sure. At the very least, the notion of a temple "made without hands" is a very early Christian tradition, and it may go back to Jesus himself.[69] A saying attributed to Jesus concerning whether his followers should pay the annual temple tax affirms, in effect, "There is no obligation—but go ahead and pay it."[70] He pronounced judgment against the present temple, as we shall see in the next chapter. These traditions are consistent with the notion that "temple" for Jesus had become something more or other than the Jerusalem temple, even though he remained concerned with the latter. In any case, clearly for Jesus the temple was not the sole or primary mediator of the presence of God, as it was in its role as the *axis mundi* of the social world. Rather, the Spirit or presence of God was present in the movement itself.

Jesus also spiritualized the very notion of Israel. Membership in the people of God was not determined merely by descent; Israel was not to be equated with "children of Abraham."[71] Neither was "Israel" defined by conventional wisdom's distinctions between righteous and outcast. Nor was being a "child of Abraham"—that is, an Israelite—an identity worth killing for; what mattered was being a child of God, whose fundamental trait was compassion.[72]

Yet, though the Jesus movement was concerned with the internal or spiritual meaning of core elements of the Jewish tradition, it also remained concerned with actual Israel and with actual Israel's historical life. Jesus remained deeply Jewish, even as he radicalized Judaism. He neither advocated the social world of the Gentiles, nor dissolved Judaism in the name of a more universal vision. His movement was concerned with what it meant to be Israel.

CONCLUSION: THE MOVEMENT AS ALTERNATIVE CULTURE

The traits which distinguished the Jesus movement in the social world of first-century Judaism were to a large extent rooted in the history of Israel itself. Indeed, the tension between Spirit and culture runs throughout the Old Testament. Israel had begun as a charismatic movement under the leadership of Moses and was, at its inception, a group of outcasts—slaves in Egypt who were dispossessed and marginal, led into a new life by the grace and compassion of God. The great prophets of the Old Testament consistently challenged the dominant cultural consciousness of their day in the name of a more comprehensive vision, attacking their people's reliance on arms and protesting against the treatment of the marginal.

The spiritualization which we see in the Jesus movement is also known in the Old Testament: "The sacrifice acceptable to God is a broken and contrite heart."[73] That is, the conflict between the Jesus movement and its contemporaries was not a conflict between two different religions, an old one and a new one. It was a conflict within the tradition itself, between a version of the tradition which had hardened into conventional wisdom under the pressure of historical circumstances, and an alternative version which was freshly in touch with the Spirit.

The politics of compassion addressed the two central issues generated by the crisis in the Jewish social world: the growing internal division within Jewish society, and the deepening of the conflict with Rome. Jesus' emphasis upon compassion as the ethos and politics of the people of God contravened the barriers created by Israel's social world, made up of its blend of conventional wisdom, holiness, exclusivity, and patriarchy. Historically speaking, Jesus sought to transform his social world by creating an alternative community structured around compassion, with norms that moved in the direction of inclusiveness, acceptance, love, and peace. The alternative consciousness he taught as a sage generated a "contrast society," an "alternative community with an alternative consciousness" grounded in the Spirit.[74]

Thus Jesus saw the life of the Spirit as incarnational, informing and transforming the life of culture. His mission, however, did not simply involve the creation of an alternative community. It also involved him in radical criticism of his culture's present path, warning his people of the catastrophic historical direction in which they were headed. To Jesus as prophet we turn in the next chapter.

NOTES

1. See chapter 5, page 86.
2. So far as I know, the term "Jesus movement" has come into common use recently through Gerd Theissen's *Sociology of Early Palestinian Christianity* (Philadelphia: Fortress, 1978; published in German in 1977). His focus is on the Jesus movement in the decades between Jesus' death and the destruction of Jerusalem, and not on the movement during Jesus' lifetime; but the term is now used quite widely to refer to the movement during the ministry as well. For an important critical and yet appreciative response to Theissen's work, see John H. Elliott, "Social-Scientific Criticism of the New Testament and Its Social World: More on Method and Models," in *Semeia 35* (Decatur, GA: Scholars Press, 1986), 1–33. Other works which emphasize the "Jesus movement" as seeking the renewal or restoration of Judaism include E. P. Sanders, *Jesus and Judaism*

(Philadelphia: Fortress, 1985); Gerhard Lohfink, *Jesus and Community* (New York and Philadelphia: Paulist and Fortress, 1984). A major section of Elisabeth Schüssler Fiorenza's *In Memory of Her: A Feminist Theological Reconstruction of Christian Origins* (New York: Crossroad, 1983) 68–159, treats the theme. See also C. H. Dodd, *The Founder of Christianity*, who speaks of Jesus' *purpose* as creating "a community worthy of the name of a people of God"; Jesus sought to form "the new Israel under his own leadership; he nominated its foundation members, and admitted them into the new 'covenant,' and he laid down its new law. That was his mission" (90, 102).

3. The classic anthropological study of "revitalization movements" as a cross-cultural phenomenon is by A. F. C. Wallace, "Revitalization Movements," in *Reader in Comparative Religion: An Anthropological Approach*, 3rd edition, edited by W. A. Lessa and E. Z. Vogt (New York: Harper & Row, 1972), 503–512, initially published in *American Anthropologist* 58 (1956), 264–281. I am using "renewal movement" and "revitalization movement" as synonyms, making no effort to define the type of movement more specifically. For distinctions among social movement, social movement organization, coalition, and faction, all of which move in the direction of greater refinement of types, see Bruce Malina, "Normative Dissonance and Christian Origins," in *Semeia 35*, edited by John H. Elliott (Decatur, GA: Scholars Press, 1986), 35–36.

4. For these two factors, see especially Theissen, *Sociology of Early Palestinian Christianity*, 112–114.

5. There is an interesting historical parallel to the Buddha. Like Jesus, he is best understood as a renewal movement founder. He did not see himself as the founder of a new religion, but as a reformer or purifier within Hinduism. Like Jesus, he taught a way which differed radically from the conventional wisdom or dominant consciousness of his day. Finally, like Jesus, his movement "failed" within his own culture and became a "new religion" which flourished in neighboring cultures (to this day, Buddhism is not as strong in India as it is in other Asian countries).

6. The words are from Jesus' instructions to the twelve as he sent them out on a mission in the midst of the ministry in Matthew 10:5–6; see also Matthew 15:24. The mission to the Gentiles is a historical development that began after Easter. In the synoptic gospels, this is reflected by the fact that it is the *risen* Lord who speaks of going to "all the nations" (see, for example, Matthew 28:19).

7. See A. F. C. Wallace's comment, "Revitalization Movements," 512, that revitalization movements typically come into existence through "a prophet's revelatory visions."

8. See Mark 3:14–15, 6:7, with parallels in Matthew 10:1 and Luke 9:1–2; Luke 10:17 reports that the powers were found in a larger group, "the seventy." See also Mark 9:14–29 which, though it reports a failure on the part of the disciples, presumes that they normally had the power to heal.

9. See especially 1 Corinthians 12–14.

10. After Easter, as Theissen argues in *Sociology of Early Palestinian Christianity*, the Jesus movement was composed of two "symbiotic" or interdependent groups: wandering charismatics (the twelve and some others, who were the authority figures in the movement), and communities of "local sympathizers," who remained in their own locales and gave support to the charismatics.

11. The only known parallels in first-century Judaism were a few "prophets" mentioned by Josephus who led people into the wilderness. See R. A. Horsley and J. S. Hanson, *Bandits, Prophets and Messiahs* (Minneapolis: Winston, 1985), 161–172, 257, who argue that these popular prophetic movements may provide the closest social parallel to the movement of Jesus and his followers.

12. For example, homelessness, lack of possessions. For the suggestion that the Jesus movement after the death of Jesus had two sets of ethical norms, the more radical of which applied to the "wandering charismatics," see Theissen, *Sociology of Early Palestinian Christianity*, 8–23.

13. The festive character of the meals is pointed to by a small detail: Jesus "reclined" at table (see, for example, Mark 2:15, 14:3; Luke 7:36). Ordinary meals were eaten in a sitting position, whereas festive meals or banquets involved "reclining," lying on one's side at a low table.

14. Matthew 11:18–19 = Luke 7:33–34.

15. Mark 2:18–19a. Verses 19b–20 are probably the product of the early church; they implicitly identify Jesus with the bridegroom who "has been taken away" and justify the church's practice of fasting after the death of Jesus. However, verse 19a by itself need not be seen as the creation of the early church on the grounds that it implies that Jesus is the "messianic bridegroom." It can be read parabolically or proverbally to mean, "People do not fast in a time of joy." This common-sense observation is the justification for the followers of Jesus not fasting. See especially the treatment of this passage by E. Schillebeeckx, *Jesus* (New York: Crossroad, 1981), 201–206. He comments, "Being sad in Jesus' presence [was] an existential impossibility" (201); and the text reveals "something of the enchantment and the power executed upon them by the living Jesus of Nazareth" (205).

16. Within the Buddhist tradition, people speak of a "Buddha field" which could be felt not only around the Buddha, but also around other enlightened figures who came after him. Within the Christian tradition, a similar "zone" was felt around St. Francis, as well as around other figures.

17. On this section, see Marcus Borg, *Conflict, Holiness and Politics in the Teaching of Jesus* (New York and Toronto: Edwin Mellen Press, 1984), 123–129, 133–134.

18. Luke 15:20, Luke 10:37, Matthew 18:23–35, Luke 18:13. According to Matthew 9:13 and 12:27, Jesus quoted an Old Testament passage (Hosea 6:6) contrasting compassion with the demands of holiness: "God desires mercy and not sacrifice."

19. Mark 3:1–6, Luke 13:10–17, 14:1–5; see also Matthew 12:11–12. John's gospel also reports two: 5:1–18, 9:1–17.

20. Luke 6:36. The parallel in Matthew 5:48 has "perfect" instead of "compassionate" (merciful). "Perfect" is characteristic of Matthew's redaction.

21. For compassion as "wombishness," see chapter 6, page 102.

22. See Dodd, *The Founder of Christianity*, 63–65: the heart of Jesus' ethical teaching is "Like father, like child"; that is, children of God are those who are "like God" in the quality and direction of their behavior.

23. The *pathos* of God is here used in the sense in which Abraham Heschel uses it in his book, *The Prophets* (New York: Harper & Row, 1962); it refers to the biblical affirmation that God is not the distant one, unmoved by what happens to human beings in history, but that God *feels* for and with them.

24. On this whole section, see Borg, *Conflict, Holiness and Politics*, 78–95 and notes 14–73, 306–314.

25. See chapter 6, pages 101–102.

26. Mark 2:15, Luke 19:7, Luke 15:2, Matthew 11:19 = Luke 7:34. The accusation is thus found in three of the four strands of the synoptic tradition (Mark, Q, and L).

27. The exact boundaries of the outcast class are not clear. Though larger than the lists of despised occupations (see chapter 5, note 25), it is not to be thought of as comprising a majority of the population. Tax collectors were particularly offensive, in part because of resentment against an oppressive tax system and their own questionable practices, but also because they were seen as collaborators with the occupying power, as traitors or "quislings."

28. Three of his most famous parables—the Lost Sheep, Lost Coin, and Lost (Prodigal) Son—are said by Luke to have been Jesus' response to the charge that he ate with sinners (Luke 15:1–32); scholars tend to agree that Luke's setting may well be historically correct. Each climaxes with a *celebration* that "the lost" has been found. Implicitly, the festive meals of Jesus are that celebration. Other parables also implicitly or explicitly defend his association with outcasts: Workers in the Vineyard (Matthew 20:1–15), the Two Sons (Matthew 21:28–32), the Unmerciful Servant (Matthew 18:23–35), and the Great Supper (Luke 14:15–24 = Matthew 22:1–10).

29. Presumably *something* happened at these meals; a likely possibility is that "the master" would speak.

30. See chapter 6 above, pages 101–102.

31. Some have claimed that it was the primary cause of Jesus' being handed over to the Romans for crucifixion by some leaders within Judaism. See, for example, Norman Perrin, *Rediscovering the Teaching of Jesus* (New York: Harper & Row, 1967), 103; and W. R. Farmer, "An Historical Essay on the Humanity of Jesus Christ," in *Christian History and Interpretation*, edited by Farmer *et al.* (Cambridge: Cambridge University Press, 1967), 103.

32. See the comment of the Jewish scholar Geza Vermes in *Jesus the Jew* (New York: Macmillan, 1973), 224: Jesus' association with outcasts was the factor which differentiated him *"more than any other"* (italics added) from "both his contemporaries and even his prophetic predecessors"; Jesus "took his stand among the pariahs of his world, those despised by the respectable. Sinners were his table-companions and the ostracized tax collectors and prostitutes his friends."

33. Restrictive attitudes toward women in Judaism seem to have intensified after the exile, in part as the building of the "in-group/out-group defenses" that characterized the quest for holiness. See Leonard Swidler, *Biblical Affirmation of Women* (Philadelphia: Westminster, 1979), 158–159.

34. For a treatment of the theme in the religions of the world, see Denise Carmody, *Women and World Religions* (Nashville: Abingdon, 1979). The male monopoly on conventional wisdom may not always have been so. There is some reason to believe that women may have been seen as equal (or primary) sources of wisdom in the stone ages, when many cultures imaged deity as primarily female. In both Hebrew and Greek, the word for "wisdom" is feminine, perhaps reflecting this ancient connection. When male images of deity began to

become dominant, religious authority figures became male as well.

35. For a striking collection of negative statements about women in ancient Greek and Latin authors, see C. E. Carlston, "Proverbs, Maxims, and the Historical Jesus," *Journal of Biblical Literature* 99 (1980): 95–96. In the Old Testament, the book of Proverbs illustrates well the male domination of conventional wisdom. Most likely it was an "instruction manual" used in "wisdom schools," which educated young men of the upper classes (women were excluded from such education). The teachers in these schools were men, and the point of view was male. For example, though there are many statements about a "contentious" or "fretful" wife, there are no corresponding statements about troublesome or difficult husbands. Noteworthy, however, is the very positive picture of the ideal wife in Proverbs 31.

36. See especially the work of Leonard Swidler. His *Women in Judaism: The Status of Women in Formative Judaism* (Methuen, N.J.: Scarecrow Press, 1976), treats the period from the second century B.C. to the fifth century A.D. His *Biblical Affirmations of Women* surveys both positive and negative attitudes toward women up to the postapostolic period.

37. The "exception that proves the rule" is a woman sage named Beruria in the second century A.D.; see Swidler, *Women in Judaism*, 97–104.

38. See the first-century A.D. statement: "If any man teach his daughter Torah, it is as though he taught her lechery" (Mishnah Sotah 3.4).

39. Images for God in the Old Testament are generally (though not universally) masculine (for example, king, shepherd, father). It is tempting to speculate about the correlation between masculine images for God and a patriarchal social order. Do masculine images of God intrinsically go with patriarchal understandings of society? If so, then what is at stake in gender imagery for God is the ordering of social reality.

40. Luke 8:1–3. Presumably, the women at the tomb (see Mark 16:1–8 and parallels) were among the group which followed him during the ministry.

41. Luke 7:36–50. Described as a "sinner" and "a woman of the city," she *may* have been a prostitute. That she unveiled and unplaited her hair in public is also striking. There is another story of a woman devotedly anointing Jesus with ointment in Mark 14:1–9.

42. Luke 10:38–42.

43. As part of John's gospel, the story of Jesus and the woman at the well in John 4:7–30 is difficult to assess historically. However, it reflects the ethos of the time: the woman is surprised that Jesus converses with her, as are the disciples.

44. Galatians 3:28. See also note 46 below.

45. See the important comments of Schüssler Fiorenza, *In Memory of Her*, 106–107, who correctly insists that the patriarchal attitudes of early and subsequent Christianity should be emphasized as strongly as the patriarchal attitudes of first-century Judaism. That is, the antipatriarchal practice of Jesus was not directed against Judaism itself, as if patriarchy were something intrinsic or peculiar to Judaism; rather, "his movement is best understood as an inner-Jewish renewal movement that presented an *alternative* option to the dominant patriarchal structures rather than an oppositional formation rejecting the values and praxis of Judaism" (107).

46. 1 Timothy 2:8–15. Though attributed to Paul, most scholars believe that it (along with the other two "pastoral letters," 2 Timothy and Titus) was written

by a second-generation follower of Paul near the end of the first century. It was common practice in the ancient world to attribute documents to an earlier master. The only passage in letters written by Paul himself which clearly subordinates women is 1 Corinthians 14:34–36, and this may be an editorial addition by somebody later than Paul. See especially Robin Scroggs, *Paul for a New Day* (Philadelphia: Fortress, 1977), 45–48.

47. Luke 4:18, quoted from Isaiah 61:1–2. Luke obviously sees them to be a fitting crystalization of Jesus' mission.

48. Matthew 5:3, 5:6; Luke 6:20–21, 24–25. Matthew's interpretation has often been preferred to Luke's in the history of the church, including the modern church, due in part to the socioeconomic position of the interpreters of Scripture over the centuries. That is, how we "see" Scripture is to a considerable extent shaped by our own position in society. Once the church became the "established religion" of most Western cultures, the interpreters of Scripture generally interpreted Jesus' words about the poor and rich in such a way so as not to call into question the political and economic structures of those cultures. "Liberation theology" is reminding us how different Scripture looks when viewed "from below," that is, from a vantage point which does not take the existing socioeconomic order for granted. For a good introduction to liberation theology's way of seeing Scripture, see Robert McAfee Brown, *Theology in a New Key* (Philadelphia: Westminster, 1978), especially 75–100.

49. Luke 4:18–19.

50. For the Jubilee regulations, see Leviticus 25:8–17, 23–55; 27:16–25. The Jubilee also required that all "slaves" or indentured servants be released. For scholarly treatments of the possible relationship between Jesus and the Jubilee year, see John Yoder, *The Politics of Jesus* (Grand Rapids: Eerdmans, 1972); and Sharon Ringe, *Jesus, Liberation, and the Biblical Jubilee* (Philadelphia: Fortress, 1985). More generally on the question of Jesus and the poor, see Walter Pilgrim, *Good News to the Poor: Wealth and Poverty in Luke-Acts* (Minneapolis: Augsburg, 1981); and Luise Schottroff and Wolfgang Stegemann, *Jesus and the Hope of the Poor* (Maryknoll, NY: Orbis, 1986).

51. For an occasion when it was observed, see Nehemiah 5.

52. Luke 6:30 = Matthew 5:42, Luke 6:34–35, Matthew 6:1–4, Mark 10:21. See also the petition in the Lord's prayer, which may refer to actual debts: Matthew 6:12 = Luke 11:4.

53. Matthew 6:24 = Luke 16:13, Matthew 6:19–21 = Luke 12:33–34. See also chapter 6, pages 104–105.

54. Acts 2:44–45, 4:32–35. The churches of Paul, all outside of Palestine, apparently did not practice common ownership.

55. Matthew 5:43–44 = Luke 6:27.

56. Leviticus 19:18b. Thus the words are found in the same chapter as the central affirmation of the quest for holiness (Leviticus 19:2). Consistent with the emphasis upon holiness as separation, "neighbor" was understood to mean "fellow Israelite" (note that it is parallel to "sons of your own people" in the first half of Leviticus 19:18). The command later in the chapter (verse 34) to love the "sojourner" (that is, the foreigner in the land), was understood by the first century to mean "proselyte" or "convert"—that is, Gentiles who had become Jews. Thus neither command applied to non-Jews. On this whole section, see Borg, *Conflict, Holiness and Politics in the Teaching of Jesus*, 129–133.

57. Matthew 5:41.

58. Matthew 5:9; the phrase "children of God" connects the passage explicitly to the notion of the *imitatio dei*; to be children of God is to be like God. Both Matthew 5:45 and Luke 6:35 connect this behavior to being "children of God."

59. Matthew 26:52. Like the previous saying, this is found in Matthew alone. A version of it is found in Revelation 13:10b, which suggests that the saying was widespread in the early Christian communities and not simply the creation of Matthew. It may well come from Jesus himself, and in any case is consistent with what we know of Jesus.

60. See chapter 9, pages 173–174.

61. Mark 12:13–17.

62. Luke 23:2 reports that his opponents did accuse him of this as they brought him before Pilate: "We found this man perverting our nation, and forbidding us to give tribute to Caesar." Luke apparently regards the charge as false.

63. See also Theissen, *Sociology of Early Palestinian Christianity*, who stresses that the Jesus movement was the "peace party" among the renewal movements operating within Palestine (see 64–65, as well as 99–110, where he speaks of strategies within the movement for overcoming and containing aggression). Within an evangelical framework, Ronald Sider and Richard Taylor also argue for a "pacifist" Jesus deeply involved with issues of war and peace in his own time; see their *Nuclear Holocaust and Christian Hope* (New York: Paulist, 1982), 95–134. See also William Klassen, *Love of Enemies* (Philadelphia: Fortress, 1984); Stanley Hauerwas, *The Peaceable Kingdom* (Notre Dame: University of Notre Dame Press, 1983), especially 72–95; and the works of John Yoder, especially *The Original Revolution* (Scottsdale, PA: Herald Press, 1971), *The Politics of Jesus* (Grand Rapids: Eerdmans, 1972), and *Christian Witness to the State* (Newton, KS: Faith and Life Press, 1977).

64. See the classic study by Roland Bainton, *Christian Attitudes Toward War and Peace* (New York: Abingdon, 1960). Bainton also reports the process whereby the church moved from pacifism to the "just war" theory following the conversion of the Roman emperor Constantine to Christianity in the fourth century. Ironically, since the time of Constantine the church has typically been more concerned to legitimate war than to advocate peace.

65. Striking also is the attitude toward Samaritans, who from the Jewish point of view were heretical and of mixed ancestry. Hostility between Jews and Samaritans was deep. Though we do not know that any Samaritans were part of the Jesus movement during Jesus' lifetime, stories in the gospels portray them in a favorable light. According to Luke, of ten lepers healed by Jesus, the one grateful one was a Samaritan (17:11–19). Even more strikingly, the "hero" of one of Jesus' most famous parables was a Samaritan, deliberately contrasted to a Jewish priest and Levite (Luke 10:29–37). The portrait of a Samaritan as "good" put together an impossible combination of words in the Jewish social world of the day. Yet the movement during Jesus' lifetime may not have been directed to Samaritans; see Matthew 10:5–6, Luke 9:52–53. Clearly, however, it included Samaria soon after Jesus' death; see Acts 8.

66. It is difficult to imagine any other satisfactory explanation. The culture-shattering quality of the Jesus movement does not seem to flow out of an ideology arrived at through a process of deductive reasoning; moreover, the criticism of cultural norms by revitalization movements in other cultures seems

to flow out of the intense religious experience of their founders. Granted, charismatic experience is not a sufficient explanation all by itself, for there are charismatics who affirm very rigid cultural boundaries (including the classic in-group/out-group distinction). Perhaps one must speak of incomplete or culturally contaminated experiences of the Spirit.

67. See chapter 6, pages 108–110.

68. See Matthew 5:20 in the translation of the Jerusalem Bible: the righteousness of Jesus' followers is to "go deeper" than that of the scribes and Pharisees.

69. Part of the accusation brought against Jesus in Mark 14:56–58, and though characterized as "false," it may have had some basis in the teaching of Jesus. In any case, it is clearly present in early Christianity; see the use of the notion in John 2:19–22 and 4:20–24, and in Hebrews 9:11, 24.

70. Matthew 17:24–27; found only in Matthew, the authenticity of the saying is indeterminate. Minimally, it indicates what the community of Matthew thought, usually understood as an extension of the Jesus movement in a Jewish environment.

71. See the preaching of John the Baptist: "Do not presume to say to yourselves, 'We have Abraham as our father,' for God is able from these stones to raise up children to Abraham" (Matthew 3:9 = Luke 3:8).

72. See Luke 6:35 ("children of the Most High") = Matthew 5:45 ("children of your father"), in the context of the *imitatio dei* as compassion. See also Mark 3:31–35: the family of Jesus consists of those who do the will of God.

73. Psalm 51:17.

74. Quoted phrases from Lohfink, *Jesus and Community*, and Walter Brueggemann, *The Prophetic Imagination* (Philadelphia: Fortress, 1978), 80, 96. Brueggemann sees the tension between "alternative community" an dominant culture running throughout the Bible.

8. Jesus as Prophet: Social World in Crisis

Of all the figures in his tradition, Jesus was most like the classical prophets of Israel.[1] Active from about 750 B.C. to 400 B.C., they are among the most remarkable people who ever lived. Sharing the feature which defines the figure of prophet as known in many cultures, they were "verbal mediators" or messengers between the two worlds of the primordial tradition. Indeed, the name of the last of them, Malachi, means simply "my messenger."

Their role as messengers of God flowed out of the intensity of their experiences of the Spirit, among the most vivid in the Spirit-filled tradition of Israel.[2] As mediators of the Spirit, they spoke "the Word of the Lord," and the "I" of the prophetic speeches is most often the divine "I." Moreover, their language was vivid, compact, and poetic, surging with extraordinary energy.

Especially characteristic of them was their passionate and critical involvement in the historical life of their people in their own day. Speaking in times of historical crisis, they radically criticized their culture in the name of God and became voices of an alternative consciousness challenging their culture's dominant consciousness.

CLEARING AWAY A MISCONCEPTION

To modern ears the word "prophecy" suggests predicting the distant future on the basis of special knowledge unavailable to "ordinary" people. It implies that the future is already fixed or predetermined and that it can be known by specially gifted people who can see into it and disclose coming events to others. "Prophecy" and "prediction" have become virtual synonyms.

To some extent, the church is responsible for this stereotype, for

Christians have commonly seen the prophets of the Old Testament as "foretellers" of the Messiah, predicting the coming of Jesus. Popular works of Christian apologetics[3] often point to the numerous correlations between passages in the Old Testament and events reported in the New Testament, and then argue that those correlations *prove* that Jesus was the Messiah and that Scripture is supernatural in its origin. Though the argument is well-intended, it treats the truth of Christianity as if it were a fact to be demonstrated by tight rational argument. Moreover, it fails to recognize the literary conventions followed by the New Testament authors as well as the intent of Old Testament prophecy itself. The correlations between the two testaments stem from the fact that the authors of the New Testament were deeply versed in the Old Testament (it was, after all, their Scripture). In common with ancient authors generally, they took it for granted that present events of great importance were "prefigured" in texts that were ancient in their day. Thus the New Testament authors often allude to or quote from the Old Testament, even though the correlations most often had nothing to do with the *intention* of the Old Testament author.[4]

Indeed, some Christians continue to see prophecy's primary significance to be predictive, as if its purpose were to disclose the signs of the end preceding the *second* coming of Christ.[5] But the *distant* future—whether the first or second coming of Christ—was not central to the prophets of Israel. Instead, they were concerned with the *immediate* present of their people and of the *immediate* future that flowed out of that present.

THE PROPHETS AND HISTORICAL CRISIS

Strikingly, the classical prophets are concentrated in two periods of cultural crisis when Israel's social world faced destruction by a foreign power. The first cluster appeared in the decades prior to the destruction of the northern kingdom by Assyria in 722 B.C.[6] Somewhat over a hundred years later, a second cluster of prophets spoke in the decades surrounding the destruction of Jerusalem and the temple by the Babylonians in 586 B.C.[7] It is no coincidence that we do not find a significant Jewish prophet in a quiet time. Rather, these Spirit-filled persons were called forth by crisis and addressed their people in the midst of crisis.

INDICTMENT, THREAT, AND CALL TO CHANGE

The prophetic urgency can be seen in the threefold pattern marking the message of the prophets who spoke before the destruction of the two kingdoms: indictment, threat, and call to change. As messengers of God the prophets charged Israel with violations of the covenant (the indictment), warned that the future would be filled with destruction (the threat), and called their people to change before it was too late. The pattern not only characterized the most common form of their speech, the "threat oracle,"[8] but also their mission as a whole: Israel faced historical destruction because of her present path unless she returned to the "way of the Lord."

The Indictment

The prophets indicted the ruling elites of power, wealth, and religion who were responsible for the shape and direction of the nation's historical life.[9] In particular, they indicted the wealthy and powerful for the exploitation of the marginal and powerless within Israel. The established classes of religion, wealth, and power, they cried, had become calloused and hardened, insensitive to suffering. No longer mindful that their ancestors were once victims of oppression in Egypt, Israel's elite, grown "fat," had now become oppressors themselves.

The prophets also charged that Israel's relationship to God had become distorted. Though Israel's religion was organized around the God of Israel, and though priests and prophets and religious practice flourished, those in charge of Israel's religious and political life no longer knew God: "There is no *knowledge of God* in the land."[10] Knowledge *of* God did not mean knowledge *about* God; Israel, we may suppose, had plenty of that. Rather, knowledge *of* God referred to *knowing* God, a relationship of intimacy and trust, and not simply believing what one had heard about God. The latter was religion accommodated to conventional wisdom, an enculturated religion which legitimated the dominant consciousness of the time. For the prophets, such religion amounted to infidelity, vividly spoken of as "adultery." Israel's corporate life showed that she no longer was faithful to God, but had gone whoring after other securities. Not knowing God, she had become blind, her heart had become hardened; she was arrogant and insecure at the same time, "silly and without sense."[11] The ruling elites in Israel had come to trust in their own wealth and power, in kings and the established order, in arms and military alliances, rather than in God.

The Threat

The predestruction prophets warned their society of imminent judgment by God. Importantly, it was not the last judgment or end of the world, but the threatened end of their social world through historical catastrophe. Specifically, they warned of impending military conquest and destruction, understood not just as a political event but as the judging activity of God.

Amos and Hosea warned the northern kingdom that it would be destroyed by Assyria as God's judgment upon them unless they changed.[12] The same message sounded over one hundred years later when Jeremiah and Ezekiel warned that Jerusalem and the temple would be destroyed by Babylon if the society continued its present direction. Infidelity to God and absence of compassion in the society's life meant the collapse and destruction of their social world.

Call to Change

The prophets called Israel to *repent*, which meant to *turn* or *return*, and which referred primarily to a change in Israel's *collective* life, and not simply to a change in individual lives.[13] Indeed, such change was the purpose of the threats and indictments the prophets issued. They sought to transform their social world so that the future would be different: "Seek the Lord and live! Seek good, and not evil, that you may live!"[14] The contingent nature of the future (as distinct from a foreordained future) was the presupposition of the prophetic message. Ironically, to the extent that a prophet was successful, the future of which he spoke would *not* come to pass.[15] The purpose of the prophets was not to *reveal* the future, but to *change* it.

The crisis announced by the predestruction prophets thus had both present and future dimensions. The future crisis was the threatened end of their society, and the present crisis was the need to change the state of affairs that was leading to the catastrophe before it was too late. This connection between the immediate present and immediate future gave the prophetic message its urgency.

Prophetic Acts

Occasionally, the prophets acted out their message by performing symbolic or bizarre actions. Such actions are associated especially with the two major prophets in the years before the destruction of Jerusalem and the temple in 586 B.C. Jeremiah dashed a potter's flask to the ground in front of the city's leaders and declared that God would destroy the city in like fashion. On another occasion he wore a wooden yoke around his neck to a military conference in order to proclaim that those present should not resist Babylon, but instead should wear the yoke of Babylon.[16] In the public square of Jerusalem, Ezekiel built a model of the city and laid siege to it with a toy army; he was ordered by God to lie on his left side for 390 days and then on his right side for 40 days to symbolize the number of years of captivity for the two kingdoms; and he ate starvation rations to symbolize the starvation that would come with the siege of Jerusalem.[17]

Sometimes the meaning of a prophetic act was virtually transparent and required little or no interpretation. At other times the action may have been performed to provoke the question, "Why are you doing *that*?"[18] Jesus, as we shall see, continued this dramatic tradition.

THE PROPHETS AS CULTURAL CRITICS

The predestruction prophets were thus charismatics who were also radical cultural critics. Their twofold focus was Spirit and culture, God and their social world. As the voice of an alternative consciousness, they protested against the victimizing of the powerless, and challenged the dominant consciousness of their day. They were iconoclasts who shattered their society's most cherished beliefs, especially the ideology that legitimated power, wealth, and privilege with an enculturated religion which spoke of God only as the endorser of society and not as its judge.[19] God would not defend Jerusalem and the temple, but would fight on the side of Babylon; faithfulness to God did not mean defense of one's country, but meant deserting to the enemy. Israel's status as the chosen people did not mean that Israel was first in line for blessing, but first in line for judgment; though the ruling classes within Israel practiced the religion commanded by tradition, they did not know God—indeed, God despised their worship.

Not surprisingly, these critics of the culture's dominant consciousness were unpopular. Those in power did not like what they had to say. Often deeply alienated from their compatriots, they got in trouble. Amos was ordered to leave the country.[20] Jeremiah was threatened with death, beaten several times, put into the stocks, accused of treason, imprisoned, and finally lowered into a muddy cistern to die.[21] They must sometimes have envied the official prophets who prophesied what the powerful wanted to hear, crying "Peace, peace," when there was no peace.[22]

Their passion about their people's life in history had as its primary source their communion with God. Their relationship to the Spirit led them to see things from a perspective very different from the dominant consciousness. Moreover, they did not simply *see* differently; they also *felt* deeply. They not only knew God, but *felt* the *feelings* of God: the divine compassion for the victims of suffering, the anger of God at the oppressing classes, the divine grief about the suffering that would soon come upon victimizer and victim alike.[23] What happened in history—war, oppression, injustice, the institutionalization of greed—is one of the greatest sources of human suffering, and therefore one of the greatest sources of divine concern. For the prophets, God cared about what happened in history, and not simply about what happened within individuals.

The concern of these God-intoxicated individuals was thus political in the sense in which we have used the term. That is, their concern was the *shape* of the human community in which they lived. They criticized their culture's central loyalties and values and called their culture to change at a very fundamental level. As critics of culture and advocates of another way, they were concerned with their people's collective life, both its present state and its historical direction. Their concern was the intersection between Spirit and culture, God and history.

JESUS AS PROPHET

Jesus identified with his prophetic predecessors. Not only did some of his contemporaries perceive him as such, but he spoke of himself as one.[24] Like the prophets, his twofold focus was God and the cultural life of his people in a time of crisis. Like them, the pattern of threat, indictment, and call to change ran throughout his ministry. Indeed, his passion for the historical life of his people ultimately cost him his own life.

CRISIS: THE THREAT TO SOCIAL WORLD

The mission of Jesus was dominated by a sense of urgency and crisis. He charged his contemporaries with knowing how to interpret the signs of the weather, but not knowing how to interpret the present time. Their situation, he said, was like that of an insolvent debtor being dragged to court with only a small amount of time left in which to avert his fate, or like that of an unfruitful fig tree in a vineyard which had only one more year in which to bear fruit.[25] Images and parables of judgment and crisis abound: the axe laid at the root of the tree, the fire licking the chaff; servants suddenly being called to account, maidens asleep and without oil for their lamps, people finding themselves shut out of a banquet because they didn't respond. He warned his generation that they *in particular* faced a crisis: "The blood of the prophets, shed from the foundation of the world, will come upon this generation!" "This generation" faces a crisis like the people of Nineveh in the time of an earlier prophet, Jonah.[26]

But what was the crisis? According to the image of Jesus which dominated scholarship throughout much of this century, the crisis facing his generation was the imminent end of the world and the last judgment.[27] But, though Jesus did speak of a last judgment, there is no reason to believe that he thought it was imminent.[28] Instead, like the predestruction prophets before him, the crisis he announced was the threat of historical catastrophe for his society.[29]

CULTURAL CRITICISM: INDICTMENT OF THE POLITICS OF HOLINESS

Jesus' role as revitalization movement founder and prophet overlap. As founder of a renewal movement, he pointed to an alternative path; as prophet, he explicitly indicted his people's present path. The issue was not individual sinfulness, but allegiance to a cultural dynamic that was leading to historical catastrophe. Advocating the politics of compassion, Jesus criticized the politics of holiness.

The politics of holiness had made Israel unfruitful and unfaithful. Like the prophets, Jesus used the image of a vineyard to speak of Israel's relationship to God. Israel (or its leadership) was like the tenants who refused to give the vineyard's produce to its owner, like the unfruitful fig tree given one more year to bear fruit.[30] He also used the imagery of Israel as the servant of God. Israel had become like the servant who was not acting mercifully, like the cautious servant who buried his talent in the ground in an effort to preserve it, like an unfaithful servant.[31] He used other images of things not performing their proper function: salt had lost its salinity, light was not giving light but had been hidden.[32] The Israel of his generation, living by the ethos of holiness, was no longer what it was meant to be—the vineyard of God yielding fruit, the faithful servant of God, the light to the nations.

Jesus indicted those responsible for his people's present direction. He characterized the teachers of his day as "blind" and warned of the consequences of following a blind guide: "Will they not both fall into a pit?"[33] He accused the scholars of the Torah—the sages—of having "taken away the key of knowledge," rather than unlocking the meaning of Israel's traditions.[34] He charged them with honoring the prophets whom "their fathers killed," although they would have done the same thing.[35] He found many in his generation to be preoccupied with "business as usual," blind to the crisis (and opportunity) that faced them.[36]

Yet there is no reason to think that his generation was particularly "wicked." They were no more wicked than many other generations before or since, and in their devotion and sincerity were perhaps better than most.[37] We can see this especially in Jesus' relationship to the Pharisees. Despite the modern stereotype of them as "hypocrites" (and worse),[38] the issue was not "hypocrisy"—if by that is meant people putting on an outward show in order to pretend a devotion they do not feel.[39] The Pharisees were good, devout people; the issue was not their sincerity or lack of it, but *what they were sincere about*: the ethos and politics of holiness to which they were committed.

Jesus attacked the Pharisees' concern about purity and tithing, two of the issues most central to the ethos of holiness. Purity, Jesus claimed, was not a matter of externals, but of the heart,[40] and the emphasis upon separation of pure and impure created division within society. Similarly, in the Pharisees' meticulous concern with tithing, the politics of holiness had led to a neglect of what was most central: "Woe to you Pharisees! For you tithe mint and rue and every herb, and neglect justice and the love of God."[41]

Though the politics of holiness was intended to make Israel "pure," Jesus ironically and dramatically described the Pharisaic influence upon Israel as having the opposite effect, namely as *defiling* and not hallowing. "Woe to you Pharisees! For you are like graves which are not seen, and men walk over them without knowing it." Because contact with death was one of the greatest sources of defilement within Judaism, graves were whitewashed so that people could see them and avoid stepping on them. But according to Jesus, the Pharisees were like graves which had *not* been whitewashed; people did not realize that the Pharisees' path of holiness was actually defiling.[42] The same point was made in his characterization of the Pharisees as "leaven." Leaven was unclean, and just as it spread through the dough which it leavened, so the influence of the Pharisees was seen as contagious and defiling.[43] What Jesus criticized in the Pharisees was the same dynamic operative in the culture as a whole, only in intensified form. We miss the point if we think of the Pharisees as "bad" people. Rather, Jesus' indictment of them was a criticism of a way of organizing life that was pervasive in his time, and, in different forms, in many times since.[44]

Indictment of the politics of holiness also underlies one of Jesus' most famous parables, the Good Samaritan.[45] The story is very familiar. A man attacked by robbers was left "half-dead" on the road; a priest and Levite passed by, and then a Samaritan stopped to help. The parable ended with Jesus asking a question: "Which of these three proved to be a neighbor to the man who fell among robbers?"

Though the parable has a timeless relevance with its characterization of what it means to *be* a neighbor,[46] in its original setting it sharply criticized the dominant social dynamic of the day. The priest and Levite passed by out of concern for the standards of holiness, for in that situation they could have been ritually defiled in a number of ways through proximity to death. In passing by and avoiding such contact, they actually followed the demands of holiness. Like the Pharisees, they were not "bad" people, but acted in accord with the logic of a social world organized around the politics of holiness. Thus Jesus was not criticizing two particularly insensitive individuals, but was indicting the ethos of holiness itself.[47] The Samaritan, on the other hand, was commended specifically for his *compassion*.

Jesus also indicted those who benefitted from the politics of holiness. He ridiculed those who derived their self-esteem from the honor achieved in their culture: "Beware of the scribes, who like to go about in long robes, to have salutations in the market places, the best seats in the synagogues and the places of honor at feasts."[48] For the righteous, he had especially harsh words: "Tax collectors and harlots are entering the Kingdom of God before you."[49] He indicted the rich; and though, as we have noted, it is difficult to discern an economic program in the teaching of Jesus, it is safe to say that he saw a social order organized around affluence and its legitimation to be a violation of the politics of compassion.[50]

Oftentimes Jesus' criticism of his social world is seen as an indictment of Judaism itself. But it was not. Not only does such an attitude affect one's assessment of Judaism today, but it also ignores the fact that Jesus (like his prophetic predecessors) was the voice of an alternative consciousness *within* Judaism calling his Jewish hearers to a transformed understanding of their own tradition. It was not Judaism itself which he saw as unfruitful, any more than the prophets of the Old Testament were "anti-Jewish." Rather, it was the current direction of his social world that he saw as blind and misguided. The conflict between Jesus and his contemporaries was not about the adequacy of Judaism or the Torah, or about the importance of being "good" rather than "bad," but was about two different visions of what it meant to be a people centered in God. Both visions flowed out of the Torah: a people living by the ethos and politics of holiness, or a people living by the ethos and politics of compassion.

The conflict thus concerned the proper *interpretation* of the Torah: whether the Torah was to be interpreted according to the paradigm of holiness or the paradigm of compassion. It was thus, if the language is not too theological, a *hermeneutical* battle. "Hermeneutics," from the Greek word meaning "interpretation," is that branch of theology concerned with the *interpretation* of Scripture, both individual texts and Scripture as a whole. The "lens" through which one views Scripture very much affects what one sees. In that time, when religion constituted the very structure of the social world, the hermeneutical struggle had decisive historical and cultural consequences.[51]

THREAT: HISTORICAL CATASTROPHE

Thus Jesus indicted the politics of holiness, that way of organizing a social world shaped by the ethos of holiness and hardened into a quite rigid ideology under the pressure of conflict. Indeed, Jesus saw the conventional wisdom of his time, with its division of the world into pure and impure, righteous and outcast, rich and poor, neighbor and enemy, to be leading to catastrophe and judgment. Like the prophets before him, he warned that Jerusalem and the temple would be destroyed by military conquest unless the culture radically changed its direction. In order to see the full significance of these threats, we need first to describe the role Jerusalem and the temple played in the Jewish social world.

Jerusalem and the Temple

Jerusalem drew its significance primarily from the fact that the temple was there. As already noted, it was believed that God dwelt there; the temple was the place linking the two worlds of the primordial tradition. Because it was God's dwelling place, many believed that the temple and Jerusalem were secure, their protection guaranteed by God. Such a belief reached far back into Israel's history. Jeremiah sarcastically quoted the refrain of those who rested their security in the temple: "This is the temple of the Lord, the temple of the Lord, the temple of the Lord!"[52] The belief also existed in the time of Jesus. The temple had become the center of an ideology of resistance to Rome; it was believed that God would defend the divine dwelling place against all enemies.[53] Like many cultures before and since, they believed that God would protect their nation.

The ideology was reinforced by the evidence of the senses. As was the case with most cities in antiquity, Jerusalem had massive defensive walls, making the city itself a fortress. But the temple area at its center was an even more formidable fortress. Rebuilt by Herod the Great in the decades before Jesus' birth, it stood on a large raised platform, the height of whose walls ranged from ninety-eight feet on the west to over three hundred feet at the southeast corner where the mountain on which the temple was built sloped down into the Kidron Valley. Some of the stones in the walls were immense, measuring over thirty-five feet long and weighing more than seventy tons. Herod's building project had made the temple look both glorious and impregnable.

But like Jeremiah and Ezekiel some six centuries earlier, Jesus warned that Jerusalem and the temple faced the threat of destruction. Like them, he proclaimed that the divine presence had left the temple. Using the "divine I" of prophetic speech, he said:

O Jerusalem, Jerusalem, killing the prophets and stoning those who are sent to you! How often would I have gathered your children together as a hen gathers her brood under her wings, and you would not. Behold, *your house [the temple] is abandoned!*[54]

Bereft of the divine presence, Jerusalem faced the possibility of destruction.

Jesus warned that the days were coming when there would be "great distress in the land" for Jerusalem would be "surrounded by armies":

But when you see Jerusalem surrounded by armies, then know that its desolation has come near. For great distress shall be upon the earth and wrath upon this people; they will fall by the edge of the sword, and be led captive among all nations; and Jerusalem will be trodden down by the Gentiles.[55]

On another occasion Jesus warned that invaders would build a "siege wall" around Jerusalem and destroy her.[56] When his disciples marveled at the size of the stones in the temple, Jesus said, "There will not be left here one stone upon another that will not be thrown down."[57]

Like Jeremiah, he told his hearers not to join in Jerusalem's defense. Rather than entering or remaining in Jerusalem (the normal response in time of war, when one would flee to the walled city, either for protection or to join the defenders), he urged them to flee to the mountains.[58] The future held the threat of invasion and war; the crisis facing Jesus' contemporaries was the destruction of their social world and all the suffering that would accompany it.[59]

The message of indictment and threat which Jesus spoke required courage. Like the prophets before him, he was an iconoclast, attacking the central images and convictions by which his contemporaries lived. Holiness is what God wants, they believed; the rich are blessed, the righteous are better than the outcasts, the faithful life is the life of conventional wisdom, Jerusalem is safe because God is there, God will defend us.

Just as he and the prophets were not intimidated by the most cherished beliefs of their time, so also he was neither threatened by nor servile toward human authority. He called King Herod a "fox," a contemptuous term meaning not simply "sly" or "clever," but roughly the equivalent of "skunk" or "rodent."[60] He criticized the behavior of the "kings of the Gentiles," with their concern with power, as an object lesson of how *not* to behave.[61] Uncooperative in his interrogation before both Pilate and the Jewish authorities, he gave either equivocal answers or none at all, behavior exasperating to an inquiring magistrate in any time.[62]

Both his courage and perception flowed out of that same grounding in the Spirit reported of his predecessors and promised to his followers.[63] Yet his message was not exhausted by his warning of historical catastrophe. Like the prophets before him, he also offered hope.

THE CALL TO CHANGE

By the time the gospels were written, the destruction of Jerusalem was in the past. To the gospel writers it thus seemed to be the inevitable result of the rejection of the Jesus movement by the dominant consciousness of the day.[64] But for Jesus himself, some forty years before, the destruction was still a threat, not a foreordained future. There was still time to change, and the possibility of change was the presupposition and purpose of his mission.

In a sense, the whole of Jesus' ministry was a call to change. At the center of it, Mark tells us in his advance summary of Jesus' mission and message, was the call to repent, that radical turning which was also a returning to God: "The time is fulfilled, the Kingdom of God is at hand, therefore *repent*." The Greek word used here for "time," *kairos*, is different from chronological time or "ordinary" time. It refers to a time that is "momentous," "filled" with extraordinary import. The text speaks of Jesus' time as a pregnant and momentous time—"therefore repent!"[65] Though Jesus used the word "repent" itself relatively infrequently, the notion is everywhere in his teaching. He called his hearers to a turning to God, to Spirit, that was at the same time a turning away from the present path of their culture.

Indeed, the call to change was at the heart of his various roles. As founder of a revitalization movement, he created an alternative community grounded in the Spirit, whose purpose was to provide an alternative cultural path to the politics of holiness. Much of his teaching was concerned with that movement, describing its "shape" as the community of compassion, and defending its shape in the face of questioning and opposition from others.

Similarly, the way of transformation which he taught as sage was part of his call to repentance. It was a call to be in relationship to the Spirit and not primarily to the religious beliefs and cultural convictions of the time. It was an invitation to the individual to change his or her orientation toward life by moving from the taken-for-granted world of conventional wisdom with its distinctions and apparent securities to a relationship with God as the heart of reality. Out of this relationship flowed a new ethos, and with it the politics of compassion instead of the politics of holiness.

The call to repentance was not simply individual but collective. Though all of his teaching was in a sense directed to individuals (indeed, to whom else can one address teaching?), his concern as he did so was Israel. That is, Jesus was concerned not only with individuals and their relationship with God, but also with the collective course of his people. Israel itself was being called to change in the face of a future that was still contingent.[66]

A Time of Opportunity

The call to change indicates that Jesus saw his time not only as a time when disaster threatened, but also as a time of opportunity. Though the possibility of judgment runs through his warnings, the overall tone of his ministry was not judgment but joy. His words and activities indicate that he saw his time as a time when God was visiting and redeeming his people through him and the movement centered around him.

Alongside the warnings and threats are "oracles of salvation," passages using imagery drawn from the Old Testament to affirm that his time was also one of redemption. To the messengers sent to him by John the Baptist, he said, "Go and tell John what you see and hear: The blind receive their sight and the lame walk, lepers are cleansed and the deaf hear, and the dead are raised up, and the poor have good news preached to them."[67] The phrases are from Isaiah,[68] where they refer to a deliverance soon to come to the people. There, their meaning seems metaphorical—that is, Isaiah does not seem to be anticipating *healings* of people who were actually blind, deaf, and lame, but uses these images to speak of a time of deliverance. Though Jesus actually performed healings, these words seem to refer to more than healings; his use of them identifies his time as a time of deliverance.

Thus his movement and message were a call to a new way of life marked already by joy even while the shadows were lengthening on the social world of his day. Two paths lay before the people to whom Jesus spoke, the broad way of conventional wisdom and its loyalties, and the narrow way of transformation to an alternative way of being. The broad way led to destruction, the narrow way to life. The message of the two ways led Jesus, as prophet, sage, and renewal movement founder, to make his final and climactic journey to Jerusalem, the center of his people's life.

NOTES

1. The "classical prophets" are those who have books named after them: three "major" prophets (Isaiah, Jeremiah, and Ezekiel) and twelve "minor" prophets. For introductions, see especially Abraham Heschel, *The Prophets* (New York: Harper & Row, 1962) and Walter Brueggemann, *The Prophetic Imagination* (Philadelphia: Fortress Press, 1978). See also J. A. Blenkinsopp, *A History of Prophecy in Israel* (Philadelphia: Westminster, 1983); G. von Rad, *Old Testament Theology*, volume 2 (New York: Harper & Row, 1965); and R. R. Wilson, *Prophecy and*

Society in Ancient Israel (Philadelphia: Fortress, 1980). For prophecy in the New Testament, see David E. Aune, *Prophecy in Early Christianity and the Ancient Mediterranean World* (Grand Rapids: Eerdmans, 1983).

2. The classical prophets and their predecessors were "seized" by the Spirit. The notion is expressed in many ways: the Spirit of God "rested on them" or "clothed itself" with them; the "hand of the Lord" grasped them. See, for example, Numbers 11:25–26, Judges 6:34, 1 Samuel 10:6, 1 Kings 18:46, 2 Kings 3:15, Jeremiah 15:7, Ezekiel 1:3, Isaiah 61:1.

3. "Apologetics" is a genre of religious writing which seeks to defend the truth of religion. It can be done rather well or rather crudely.

4. See, for example, the use of Hosea 11:1 in Matthew 2:15; in its original context, Hosea 11:1 obviously did not refer *forward* to Jesus' time, but *backward* to the Exodus. See also the numerous references to Psalm 22 in the story of Jesus' death in Mark 15:22–37; this psalm as part of the devotional life of ancient Israel was obviously not "predictive". The point is very simple: the prophets (and the Old Testament generally) need to be understood in terms of what their words would have meant to the communities which they addressed.

5. The book of Daniel, though thought of as "prophecy" in some Christian circles, is not included among the prophets in the Hebrew Bible, but is in the "writings" and is a "persecution book" most likely written in the time of Antiochus Epiphanes and the Maccabees (ca. 165 B.C.).

6. In the north, Amos and Hosea; in the south, Micah and Isaiah of Jerusalem (the prophet whose words are preserved in the first part of the book of Isaiah, chapters 1–39).

7. Speaking mostly of the coming destruction were Jeremiah, Ezekiel, Zephaniah, and Habakkuk. Speaking to the community during or immediately after the exile which followed the destruction were Haggai, Zechariah, and Isaiah of Babylon (sometimes called "Second Isaiah" or "Deutero-Isaiah" to distinguish him from the eighth-century B.C. Isaiah of Jerusalem; his words are found in the second half of the book of Isaiah, beginning with chapter 40).

8. The "threat oracle" is part of what scholars sometimes speak of as a "covenant lawsuit" brought against Israel by the prophets on behalf of God. Sometimes the legal imagery in a "threat oracle" extends beyond indictment and threat and even includes a "summons to the accused." See, for example, Micah 3:9–12, which includes a "summons" in verse 9a, a list of indictments in 9b–11, and the threat in verse 12. Amos 4:1–3 is another classic threat oracle: summons = "cows of Bashan" (the wealthy women of Samaria, whom Amos calls "hunks of prime beef"); indictment = you oppress the poor and crush the needy; threat = you will be carried off as prisoners of war. The image of the prophets as "prosecuting attorneys" bringing a lawsuit against Israel is illuminating so long as they are not simply reduced to that image.

9. This is an important point; though the prophets were concerned with Israel's *collective* life, they did not indict Israel *as a whole*, as if every person in Israel were equally guilty. As defenders of the poor, they did not hold the poor responsible for their own plight or for their nation's direction; they saw them as victims.

10. Hosea 4:1, and frequently elsewhere in the prophets. See especially Heschel's exposition of "knowledge of God" (*daath elohim* in Hebrew) in *The Prophets*, volume 1, 57–60.

11. Hosea 7:11. The prophets frequently charged Israel with seeking security in kings

and princes, military alliances and arms, and saw this as a clear sign of Israel's lack of trust in God—that is, as idolatry. See, for example, Hosea 5:13, 8:9–10, 10:13, 13:10; Isaiah 31:1; Micah 5:10–11.

12. See, for example, the "threats" in Amos 1:4–5, 7–8, 10, 12, 14–15; 2:2–3, 5, 13–15; 3:11; 4:2–3; 5:27; 6:7, 14; 7:17; 8:2–3; 9:1, 8. Though they make use of varied imagery, including fire, it is clear that a historical judgment through military conquest is being talked about.

13. The prophetic understanding of "repent" is somewhat different from popular Christian usage, where it often is understood individualistically as sorrow or contrition for sin. As "turn" or "return," it has the double connotation of a radical turn in Israel's direction, which involves a *collective* returning to God. This does not imply that "saving" individuals is unimportant; the point, rather, is that this was not the central concern of the prophets.

14. Amos 5:6, 14–15.

15. In this sense, none of the predestruction prophets was "successful." Somewhat ironically, the only "successful" prophet was Jonah, and his mission was to the hated Assyrians, not to Israel. Nineveh (the capital of Assyria) repented, and the threatened destruction was withheld. The book of Jonah, however, is best understood as a postexilic work protesting against the increasing exclusivism of the quest for holiness, and its character is more parabolic than historical (note in 3:6–9 that even the *cattle* of the Assyrians fast and put on sackcloth!).

16. Jeremiah 19, Jeremiah 27–28. Another prophet by the name of Hananiah, apparently an "official" prophet supported by the court or temple, broke Jeremiah's yoke in order to symbolize the opposite message: God would break the yoke of Babylon. Though momentarily "defeated," Jeremiah soon returned with an iron yoke. The episode is fascinating because of its drama and also because of the conflict it reveals between two prophets. As one of the "official" prophets, Hananiah legitimated the present order and spoke what the powerful wanted to hear. It must have been bewildering to those present—to whom should one listen? Then, as now, one perhaps heard what one wanted to hear.

17. Ezekiel 4. Major cities in the ancient world were surrounded by massive defensive walls. In time of siege, the enemy would encircle the city, thereby cutting off all food supplies and eventually producing starvation.

18. Other prophetic acts include the symbolic naming of children (Hosea 1:4–9, Isaiah 7:3, 7:14, 8:1–4), Isaiah walking naked for three years (Isaiah 20), Jeremiah's episode with the loincloth (Jeremiah 13) and his purchase of a field (Jeremiah 32:1–16), and Ezekiel's cutting of his hair (Ezekiel 5).

19. For the contrast between the alternative consciousness of the prophets and their culture's dominant consciousness, see especially Brueggemann, *The Prophetic Imagination*, 28–43. He speaks of the latter as the "royal consciousness," composed of the economics of affluence and the politics of oppression, and legitimated by "an official religion of optimism." Brueggemann sees this "royal consciousness" running throughout modern society and the church as well.

20. See Amos 7:10–17, one of the classic confrontations between a prophet and the established order.

21. Jeremiah 20, 26, 37–38, plus the numerous references made by Jeremiah to people seeking his life.

22. Jeremiah 6:14; see also Micah 3:5.

23. That the prophets *felt* the *feelings* of God is one of the central emphases of

Heschel's *The Prophets*, especially 23–26. The fundamental content of the prophetic experience was *sympathy* with the *pathos* (feelings) of God.

24. See chapter 3, page 48.

25. These specific examples all come from Luke 12:54–13:9. The section as a whole is very illuminating, including the episode reported in 13:1–5; see note 66 below.

26. Luke 11:50; cf. Matthew 23:35–36. Luke 11:29–32; cf. Matthew 12:38–42. "This generation" has its natural temporal meaning of "contemporaries" and not "offspring of this race," as is sometimes suggested.

27. See chapter 1, pages 11–13.

28. For last judgment texts, see Mark 9:43–48; Matthew 25:31–46; Luke 10:12–15 = Matthew 10:15, 11:21–23; Luke 11:31–32 = Matthew 12:41–42. In none of these cases is it said that the judgment is imminent. The element of *imminent* judgment is found in some of the "coming Son of man" sayings (Luke 12:8–9 = Matthew 10:32–33, Mark 8:38, Luke 12:39–40 = Matthew 24:43–44; Luke 17:23–24, 37 = Matthew 24:26–28). A near consensus of contemporary scholarship affirms that these do not go back to Jesus himself. See also Marcus Borg, "A Temperate Case for a Non-Eschatological Jesus," *Foundations and Facets Forum*, volume 2, number 3 (September 1986: 81–102) and "An Orthodoxy Re-Considered: The 'End-of-the-World Jesus,'" in *The Glory of Christ in the New Testament* (Oxford: Oxford University Press, 1987), 207–217.

29. For a detailed technical study of the synoptic threat tradition, see Marcus Borg, *Conflict, Holiness and Politics in the Teaching of Jesus* (New York and Toronto: Edwin Mellen Press, 1984), 201–221 and tables on 265–276. The threats fall into three roughly equal categories: threats of historical destruction, threats of the last judgment, and threats of unidentifiable content (that is, the threat is left in the imagery of the parable or proverb in which it is found, and its referent is not identified). Peculiar to Matthew's redaction is an emphasis on eternal judgment for individual acts of wrongdoing (see especially 203–204, and 266–268). When once it is seen that the *imminent* crisis was not the last judgment, then it becomes clear that the crisis of the ministry was the historical threat to Israel's social world and the urgent call to change in the midst of that crisis.

30. Mark 12:1–9, Luke 13:6–9. The best known Old Testament passage speaking of Israel as the unfruitful vineyard of God is Isaiah 5:1–7, whose language is echoed in the "parable of the wicked tenants" in Mark 12:1–9. Often seen as inauthentic because of its possible reference to Jesus' crucifixion as "the son," the core of the Marcan parable without an explicit reference to Jesus' death or "sonship" may well go back to Jesus.

31. Matthew 18:23–35, Matthew 25:14–30 = Luke 19:11–27, Luke 12:42–46 = Matthew 24:45–51. The two versions of the parable of the cautious servant in Matthew 25:14–30 and Luke 19:11–27 are closest in the "reckoning scene" with the third servant, which suggests that that was where the original emphasis was placed. For the "cautious servant" who provided no return on his master's "investment" as then-contemporary Israel or its leadership, see C. H. Dodd, *The Parables of the Kingdom* (New York: Scribner's, 1961), 114–121, and Joachim Jeremias, *The Parables of Jesus* (New York: Scribner's, 1972), 55–63.

32. Matthew 5:13, Luke 14:34–35, Mark 9:50; Matthew 5:15, Luke 11:33, Mark 4:21.

33. Luke 6:39 = Matthew 15:14.

34. Luke 11:52 = Matthew 23:13. The term "lawyers" (Luke) refers to those skilled in the Law (Torah) and is thus equivalent to "Torah sages." See chapter 5, page 82.

35. Luke 11:47–48 = Matthew 23:29–31.

36. See, for example, Luke 14:15–24 = Matthew 22:1–10; Luke 17:26–30.

37. Jacob Neusner, *A Life of Yohanan ben Zakkai*, 2d ed. (Leiden: Brill, 1970), 11, comments correctly about the generation living before the war of A.D. 66–70: "It was not a sinning generation, but one deeply faithful to the covenant and the Scripture that set forth its terms, perhaps more so than many who have since condemned it."

38. See chapter 5, page 88. Because Matthew heightens the conflict with the Pharisees, I have not made use of material *peculiar* to Matthew, but only that shared by Luke or Mark.

39. The word "hypocrite" meant an actor, a person who performed behind a mask. It has two quite different nuances of meaning. If one is conscious of the mask, then "hypocrisy" refers to "pretense," a contrast between external appearance and internal state; for example, a "pretended" righteousness. In this sense, the Pharisees were not hypocrites. For the most part, they practiced what they preached. However, one may also be unconscious of the fact that one is wearing a mask or playing a role. In this sense, "hypocrisy" has nothing to do with lack of sincerity, but consists of playing a role (often with great sincerity) which includes professing a religious loyalty which much of the rest of one's life belies. In this sense, the Pharisees (and many others, before and since) may be "hypocrites."

40. Mark 7, Luke 11:38–41 = Matthew 23:25–26; see also chapter 6, pages 109–100.

41. Luke 11:42; according to Matthew 23:23, the emphasis on fastidious tithing led to the neglect of "justice, mercy and faith." The two versions have essentially the same meaning.

42. The comparison of the Pharisees to graves or tombs is found in two different versions in Luke 11:44 and Matthew 23:27; I have followed Luke. In Matthew the Pharisees were compared to tombs which *had* been whitewashed: they were beautiful on the outside, but inside were full of rot. Matthew's version missed the point of whitewashing (it was *not* to make tombs beautiful) and also changed the criticism of the Pharisees into a contrast between outward appearance and internal state. Luke's version more closely reflects the setting of Jesus' ministry: the criticism was of the Pharisaic *path*, not of Pharisaic "pretense."

43. For the Pharisees as leaven, see Luke 12:1, Mark 8:15, and Matthew 16:6, 11–12.

44. If we turn all of Jesus' opponents into "bad" people, we trivialize and distort his message, as if it were primarily about being "good" instead of "bad." The point is that his opponents were for the most part "good" people who were sincere and earnest about their convictions.

45. Luke 10:29–37. For details of exegesis, see Borg, *Conflict, Holiness and Politics*, 103–106.

46. Note that it does not answer the question, "*Who* is my neighbor," but instead portrays the Samaritan as one who *acted* as a neighbor. Thus the parable shifts the focus from the question, "Who is to be included among those I am to love?" to the affirmation, "*Be* a neighbor."

47. The parable provides a good example of a wisdom *genre* (a parable) being used in a prophetic way.

48. Mark 12:38–40. Luke 6:26, 14:7–14; Matthew 6:1–8, 16–18.

49. Matthew 21:31.

50. See chapter 7, pages 135–137.

51. The struggle continues in the modern church. If one interprets Scripture through the "lens" supplied by contemporary conventional wisdom, Scripture will appear to be in basic harmony with it. To use another example, whether Christians interpret Scripture as a set of requirements for salvation or as the story of God's compassion makes a large difference in one's vision of the Christian life.

52. Jeremiah 7:4.

53. For this section and development of the "ideology of resistance" surrounding the temple, see Borg, *Conflict, Holiness and Politics*, 163–170.

54. Luke 13:34–35 = Matthew 23:37–39. Jeremiah used virtually the same language; see Jeremiah 12:7. Ezekiel had a vision of the divine presence leaving the temple (11:22–23); thus, to those who would say, "God dwells on Zion; Zion and Jerusalem shall be safe," Ezekiel could say, "But I saw God *leave*."

55. Luke 21:20, 23b–24. For the scholarly debate regarding the authenticity of this and similar passages, see Borg, *Conflict, Holiness and Politics*, 184–190.

56. Luke 19:42–44. See also chapter 9, page 173. The phrase "cast up a bank about you" refers to the typical military strategy for laying siege to a walled city. To keep supplies out of the city and to provide protection for itself, the attacking army would build its own wall around the city.

57. Mark 13:1–2; see also Luke 19:44. The phrase provides the title for Lloyd Gaston's excellent technical study of the "political" dimension of Jesus' ministry: *No Stone on Another* (Leiden: Brill, 1970).

58. Luke 21:21; see also Mark 13:14.

59. Other texts referring to the destruction of Jerusalem or the imminence of war in addition to ones already cited include Luke 17:31–36 (invasion; the instructions to flee with haste make little sense if one interprets these verses as referring to the end of the world); Luke 23:28–31 (warning about what will happen when the country is filled with rebellion); Luke 13:1–5 (see note 66 below); Mark 13:14–18 (desecration of the temple); Matthew 26:52 (those who take the sword will perish by it; though applied to an individual in its Matthean context, it may also have had a collective application); and, as we shall see in chapter 9, Mark 11:15–17 (the "cleansing" of the temple). See also the accusation that Jesus said he would destroy the temple and build another (Mark 14:58, 15:29; cf. John 2:19, Acts 6:14). See Borg, *Conflict, Holiness and Politics*, 177–195.

60. Luke 13:32. The Herod referred to here is Herod Antipas, son of Herod the Great and ruler of Galilee. On "fox" as a term of contempt, see H. W. Hoehner, *Herod Antipas* (Cambridge: Cambridge University Press, 1972), 220–221, 343–347.

61. Mark 10:42–43; compare Luke 22:25–26.

62. See, for example, Mark 14:61, Matthew 26:64, Luke 22:67; Mark 15:2, 5; Luke 23:9.

63. Mark 13:11; Matthew 10:19–20, Luke 12:11–12 and 21:12–15.

64. The only possible exception is Mark, which may have been written as early as A.D. 65 (the war began in A.D. 66).

65. Mark 1:15. As Mark's advance summary of Jesus' mission it indicates what Mark thought was most central. The usual translation ("The time is *fulfilled*") perhaps suggests too much of a *prediction-fulfillment* understanding, as if it meant "This is the time when the 'predictions' of the Old Testament are being fulfilled."

66. See Luke 13:1–5, one of the few times when Jesus is reported to have used the word "repent." Some people brought news of a Roman atrocity to Jesus: Pilate had killed some Galileans while they were sacrificing in Jerusalem. Jesus responded, "Unless you *repent*, you will all likewise perish," added a story of people killed in Jerusalem by a falling tower, perhaps in an act of resistance against the Romans. The text, part of a sequence beginning with the urgency of the present time and concluding with the unfruitful fig tree (Luke 12:54–13:9), suggests that the threat was *contingent* and the call to repentance *collective*: the whole country, Galilee and Jerusalem, was headed for destruction by the Romans *unless* they repented. See Borg, *Conflict, Holiness and Politics*, 191–193.

67. Matthew 11:5 = Luke 7:22.

68. Isaiah 29:18–19, and 35:5–6.

9. Jesus as Challenge: Jerusalem and Death

In the spring of A.D. 30 at the season of Passover, Jesus deliberately "set his face to go to Jerusalem," a resolve that led to his death.[1] The miracle-worker who drew crowds, the teacher who challenged the conventional wisdom of his day and taught an alternative path of transformation, the prophet and revitalization movement founder who indicted his people's corporate path, took his message and his itinerant group of followers to Jerusalem.

Why did he make that final journey? Some have thought that he did so *in order to die*; that is, that his own death was the outcome he intended. Such is implied by the popular image of Jesus. As one whose purpose was to die for the sins of the world, he went to Jerusalem deliberately to offer his life as a sacrifice for sin, a position that has also occasionally been affirmed within the scholarly world.[2] But, though many of the texts are filled with a foreboding that the likely result of his sojourn in Jerusalem would be death,[3] the *outcome* was not the *purpose* of the journey.

Rather, as the climax of his prophetic mission and call to renewal, he went there to make a final appeal to his people at the center of their national and religious life. As he journeyed there, he is reported to have said, "Can it be that a prophet should perish outside of Jerusalem?"[4] Indeed, Jesus identified himself with that line of prophetic voices sent by God to gather the inhabitants of Jerusalem like a hen gathering her brood:

O Jerusalem, Jerusalem, killing the prophets and stoning those who are sent to you! How often would I have gathered your children together as a hen gathers her brood under her wings, and you would not.[5]

Jesus became one more of those "sent" to Jerusalem. At precisely the time of year when the city was most filled with Jewish pilgrims, when his people were most comprehensively represented at the center of their social world, he went there to issue the call to change.

THE MESSAGE TO JERUSALEM

The final week of Jesus' life was filled with a series of dramatic actions, confrontations, and events, all flowing from his involvement in his people's direction and future.

The Approach to Jerusalem

Luke movingly depicts Jesus' concern about Jerusalem and the future of the nation in his portrait of Jesus and his followers arriving on the ridge of the Mount of Olives which overlooks Jerusalem from the east. There, we are told, Jesus looked out over the city and grieved for its inhabitants because of what he could see about their future and they could not: the threat of war, their city surrounded by enemies, then conquered and destroyed.

The days shall come upon you, when your enemies will cast up a bank about you and surround you, and hem you in on every side, and dash you to the ground, you and your children within you, and they will not leave one stone upon another in you.

Like Jeremiah before him, he wept about his people's future, feeling the grief of God about what would happen because of their blindness. "Would that even today you knew the things that make for peace," he exclaimed; "But they are hid from your eyes."[6] Not knowing the things that made for peace, they faced a future of destruction.

The Entry into the City

In the time of Jesus, Jerusalem had a population estimated between forty thousand and seventy thousand. The most Jewish of cities in first-century Palestine, it was also occupied by a garrison of Roman troops reinforced at the major festivals to cope with the throngs of Jewish pilgrims. Thus, at the season of Passover, Roman troops arrived at Jerusalem from the west in a procession led by the Roman governor, accompanied by all the trappings of imperial power.

Jesus and his followers arrived from the east, possibly on the same day. As they entered the city, also in a procession, Jesus performed the first of two prophetic acts. According to the gospels he deliberately made arrangements to enter the city on a donkey's colt, cheered by followers and sympathizers.[7] The meaning of the act becomes clear when we realize that he was intentionally enacting a passage from the prophet Zechariah which spoke of a *king of peace* riding "on a colt, the foal of an ass."[8] He was not mechanically fulfilling a prophecy; rather, he chose a known symbol from his tradition in order to say that the kingdom of which he spoke was a kingdom of peace, not war.[9] If the language is not too modern, his entry was a planned political demonstration, an appeal to Jerusalem to follow the path of peace, even as it proclaimed that his movement was the peace party in a generation headed for war. It also implied that the alternative of peace was still open.

The Prophetic Act in the Temple

Soon afterward, Jesus entered the temple area or "temple mount," a large flat platform of about thirty-five acres.[10] On it were various courts and buildings, including the main temple building (the sanctuary) itself. Relatively small, it (like most temples in the ancient world) was not really a public building but was understood as "the house of the god," a residence for the divine.[11] Public worship took place in the courts surrounding the sanctuary: the priests' court, the court of Israel (for Jewish males only), and the court of the women. Beyond these courts were other courts, including one where sacrificial animals were sold and the image-bearing coins of pilgrims were exchanged for "holy" coins, that is, coins without images. Access to the temple area was strictly limited for Gentiles, who were not permitted beyond a certain point under penalty of death.[12]

It was in one of these outer courts that Jesus performed a second and even more dramatic prophetic act. In what has been called his "greatest public deed,"[13] he expelled the moneychangers and sellers of sacrificial birds. It was a provocative action and must have created somewhat of a stir if not an uproar. Yet also quite clearly it was not intended as a takeover or occupation of the temple area.[14] Had it been so, it is inexplicable why the Romans, whose garrison overlooked the temple courts, did not immediately intervene. Rather, it was a prophetic act, limited in area, intent, and duration, done for the sake of the message it conveyed. As often with prophetic acts, the action was accompanied by a pronouncement which interpreted its meaning: "Is it not written, 'My house shall be called a house of prayer for all the nations'? But you have made it 'a den of robbers.'"[15]

Both the action itself and the words of interpretation point to the act as an attack upon the politics of holiness and a warning of its consequences. The moneychangers and sellers of sacrificial birds were there in service of the ethos of holiness. The annual temple tax had to be paid in "holy" coinage, and not with "pagan" or "profane" coins bearing images. Similarly, the merchants sold sacrificial birds to pilgrims who could not be expected to carry ritually pure sacrifices tens or even hundreds of miles. The activity of these "ecclesiastical merchants" manifested the clear-cut distinction between sacred and profane, pure and impure, holy nation and impure nation, that marked the ethos and politics of holiness. They were servants of the sacred order of separation.

In his words of interpretation, Jesus quoted two passages from the prophets. The first stated the purpose of the temple: "My house shall be called a house of prayer for all the nations."[16] Here, as most often in Scripture, *nations* means "Gentiles." The purpose of the temple, Jesus said, was universal. It was not to be the private possession of a particular group, not even of the holy people. The second quote stated what the temple had become: "You have made it a den of violent ones." The common translation, "den of robbers," obscures the meaning, as if the issue were dishonest business practices or the gouging of pilgrims.[17] Rather, the phrase quotes Jeremiah; there "violent ones" referred to those who believed that the temple provided security in spite of their violations of the covenant.[18]

We should probably not be too precise about the meaning of "den of violent ones" as part of Jesus' pronouncement. The phrase could have pointed to the temple as the scene of actual violence between the Romans and Jews, which it had sometimes been, or to the temple's role in the ideology of resistance, or to the temper of the time. In any case, having become a "den of violent ones," the temple now faced the same threat as in Jeremiah's generation: destruction. Jesus' act was both a threat and an indictment. Because the temple had become a center of violence, it faced judgment.[19] The act challenged the politics of holiness, even as it was also an invitation to another way.

The last week of Jesus' life thus began with two dramatic actions which carried his message of indictment, threat, and call to change to Jerusalem itself. Both were bold actions. To ride into Jerusalem at the head of a procession on an animal which symbolized kingship (even if of a rather strange kind) could not help but excite the curiosity of many and the attention of those charged with keeping order. The prophetic act in the temple was even more provocative. Indeed, immediately afterward some of the temple leadership came to Jesus and interrogated him, "By what authority are you doing these things?" Though he avoided giving a direct answer and made his interrogators look a bit foolish, implicitly his answer was, "From the Spirit."[20] The answer, however, did not deter them; according to Mark, it was the act in the temple that led the authorities to take action against him.[21] It took a few days to work out the details.

Conflict and Opposition

During those days, according to the gospels, Jesus continued his mission at the center of the Jewish social world.[22] He taught regularly in the courtyards of the temple, public places in the open air accessible to large numbers of people. Not only were there thousands of pilgrims there for Passover, but the temple mount and its courtyards were a public thoroughfare for traveling from one part of the city to another. We may imagine sympathizers gathered around him as he taught, while curious bystanders came and went.

Critics and opponents also appeared, engaging him in questioning. In his temple debates, he is portrayed as in conflict with the other major religious options of his day: the devout Pharisees, the aristocratic Sadduccees, and, with his answer to the question about tribute to Caesar, with the resistance movement.[23] He indicted the rich (perhaps more visible in Jerusalem with its urban aristocracy than in the villages of the countryside), especially those who justified their acts of acquisition with religious legitimation, the experts in the law who "devoured widows' houses."[24]

To the leaders of the people, he told the story of a lord who had let out a vineyard to tenants, and who had repeatedly sent messengers to gather the fruit of the vineyard, only to have the messengers mistreated and rejected. What would the owner of such a vineyard do?[25] The implication could not have been missed, even if it was not accepted: it was an indictment of Israel's leadership, the ruling elites responsible for her current state. It also was a warning. Finally, not surprisingly, he continued to speak explicitly of Jerusalem's impending destruction.[26]

Thus, in his last week in Jerusalem, Jesus was primarily a prophet and radical teacher calling his people to change. No healings are reported, either because there were none, or because the evangelists thought more such stories were unnecessary. In any case, his "mighty deeds" were apparently not central to his Jerusalem ministry. Rather, as the voice of an alternative consciousness, he called the enculturated consciousness of the day to return to God, even as it became more apparent that the outcome would be his death.

As the week drew on, he arranged to eat what turned out to be a final meal with his followers. According to the gospels, during the meal he spoke of his impending death as the seal of the "new covenant" spoken of by Jeremiah, a covenant written on the heart and not in external laws.[27] Afterwards, in the night, he and his followers left the city and went into the valley of the Kidron just east of the city walls, to a garden called Gethsemane, and there he was arrested. He had been betrayed by one of his own.[28]

THE DEATH OF JESUS

The stories of Jesus' death are probably the earliest portion of the gospels to be put into narrative form. Though they differ somewhat in their details, they share a basic plot line. Jesus was arrested by Jewish authorities and tried before a Jewish court, where the issue was blasphemy. Finding him guilty, they then took him to the Roman governor Pilate, who initially found no fault in him; however, the Jewish leaders cajoled the reluctant Pilate into pronouncing the death sentence. Taken away to the place of execution, beaten and stripped, Jesus was crucified between two members of the resistance movement on the Roman charge of "treason."

Yet though the stories of Jesus' death took shape very early, they have also been affected by the faith of the church to such a degree that it is difficult to separate historical happening from theological interpretation. For the early church, looking back on the death of Jesus in the light of what happened afterward, it seemed clear that his death was foreordained, part of the "plan of God" from the beginning. For them, the death of Jesus was the death of the righteous sufferer, of the Servant of God who gave his life for the many, of God's only son who had been sent into the world for this purpose. Accordingly, the accounts of his death were interwoven with echoes and citations of the Old Testament which helped to make the point.[29]

Moreover, for the early Christians looking back on the story, the cause of Jesus' death was ultimately the Jewish leadership's refusal to recognize him as the Son of God. So the story of his "trial" before the Jewish high priest is told. Thus, despite the fact that Jesus' mode of death reflects a Roman execution, the stories of his death emphasized Jewish responsibility. Indeed, this emphasis led to a progressive shifting of responsibility from the Romans to the Jews, a tendency perhaps intensified by the early church's concern to claim that they were not a rebellious group within the empire, despite their founder's having been executed by the Romans as a rebel.[30] Nevertheless, granted that the passion narratives cannot be treated as straightforward historical accounts, we can in broad outline construct a reasonably probable historical scenario.[31]

To begin with what is most certain, both the mode of execution and the charge posted on the cross ("King of the Jews"—that is, a king rival to Caesar) indicate that he was sentenced to death by Pilate on the charge of treason or insurrection and executed by the Romans. The most certain fact about the historical Jesus is his execution as a political rebel. In one sense, he was not guilty; he was not a "Zealot" or Zealot-sympathizer, using "Zealot" here in its popular though inaccurate meaning. We have no reason to think of him as sympathetic to violent resistance against Rome and much to indicate exactly the opposite. Indeed, one may say that he died for a crime of which he was innocent, and of which many of his compatriots were guilty. In another sense, he was guilty, for he did not give his ultimate allegiance to Rome or to any other kingdom of the world.

From what we know about Roman policy in Palestine and Pilate's character in particular, it is completely conceivable that the Romans alone were responsible for the entire scenario of arrest, trial, and execution. Rome was chronically suspicious of indigenous movements within her occupied territories, and Palestine had a reputation for being more troublesome than most. Pilate himself was reputed to be ruthless; appointed by an anti-Semite, his ten years in office were particularly harsh.[32] The portrait of him vacillating during the trial and finally giving in to the Jewish authorities is out of character. Though it *may* reflect actual history, it may equally be the product of the early church's tendency to shift the blame away from Rome. Its effect is to say, "Rome found nothing wrong with this person." But it is easy to imagine that Pilate would take action against a Jewish charismatic leader who had attracted a considerable following and become a major center of attention in Jerusalem at the volatile season of Passover.

Thus it is historically possible that Pilate and the Romans alone were involved. Yet it seems historically unlikely. In all probability, there was collaboration on the part of a small circle of Jewish leaders centered around the high priest. As the official religious leader of the community, the high priest also played a domestic political function. Appointed by Rome and accountable to the Roman governor, he was responsible for maintaining order in Palestine; upon his success at that task, his position depended. Caiaphas, the high priest at the time of Jesus, held his position for the unusually long period of eighteen years, including the entire ten years of Pilate's governorship, suggesting that he was very good at working with the Romans.[33] To assist him in his responsibility, the high priest appointed his own "privy council" who functioned as his political advisors, and who, like him, came from the aristocracy and high priestly families. The story of the "Jewish trial" of Jesus was probably a preliminary hearing before this "political Sanhedrin" rather than a formal trial before the religious council.[34] It is likely that they were alarmed at Jesus' dramatic actions that week in Jerusalem, took the steps which culminated in his arrest, and then handed him over to Pilate for trial as a political claimant.[35]

It is easy to think of them as especially villainous, given our perception of Jesus' innocence, goodness, and identity. Yet they were not, or at least there is no reason to think so. They were the established order of their society, standing at the top of their social world politically, economically, and religiously. Their place in society not only gave them the responsibility for maintaining order, but also affected how they saw things. Given that responsibility and perception, there were a number of issues in the immediate historical situation which help us to understand their action.

First, Jesus was a charismatic leader who had attracted a large following. In the tension-ridden first-century Palestinian political situation, that was enough to get a person in trouble, as the fate of John the Baptist a few years earlier demonstrated. John had been executed by Herod Antipas (ruler of Galilee and son of Herod the Great) because Herod feared John's influence with the people.[36] Simply to have been a charismatic healer and "local teacher" who remained in his own village and did not begin a movement would not have been enough to incite a fatal hostility; but Jesus was seen as a threat to the established order because, like John, he was a public figure *with a following*.[37]

Second, Jesus had warned of the fall of Jerusalem, an action which also got one in trouble in first-century Palestine. We know of only one other contemporary Jewish figure who warned the city of impending judgment. In the decade before the war an otherwise unknown Jesus ben Ananias roamed through Jerusalem crying "Woe," for which he was judged insane and beaten.[38] That God would judge and destroy Jerusalem, the center of their social world, was in a sense unthinkable to the high priest and his council. It was also a direct insult and affront to them as leaders of Jerusalem, for it was their stewardship that was being indicted as blind and worthy of God's judgment.

Finally, from their point of view at the pinnacle of their social world, Jesus was clearly wrong. Jesus had indicted the present social order and advocated another; but they were not particularly interested in the transformation of society, both because of their place in society and the ideology which legitimated the present social order. The way of peace might have been acceptable to the collaborationist circle around the high priest, who naturally wished the preservation of the present arrangement with Rome; but Jesus also spoke of a way of life in which righteousness, purity, honor, and position did not matter, which meant blessing to the poor and woe to the rich, which loosened the ties of loyalty to cultural ways, in which outcasts were accepted—all of this challenging the conventional wisdom of the time. That conventional wisdom, from their point of view, was grounded in holy Scripture and hallowed by tradition. Thus, from their vantage point, Jesus was not only a threat to public order, but profoundly wrong.

Indeed, it was the obvious mistakenness of Jesus' teaching that enabled them to conclude that he was a "false charismatic," that is, a false teacher in touch with "another spirit." The test of a true charismatic was not the ability to perform wonders, but the content of the charismatic's teaching. If it led people astray, then the charismatic was a false prophet, and the "mighty deeds" did not come from God, but from Satan. Indeed, such a charge had been made against Jesus earlier in the ministry,[39] and though the stories of his interrogation and trial make no explicit reference to the charge, the issue could not have been far from the surface.

Thus good and prudent people could conclude that Jesus was a threat to the social order and a "false teacher." To the established classes, his teaching spoke of a social transformation that was threatening, and his movement risked inciting intervention by the Romans. Both were unacceptable to those responsible for maintaining order. The words attributed to Caiaphas in John's gospel, whether historical or not, are historically credible. After members of his council expressed fear that the movement of Jesus might lead to unrest and Roman intervention, Caiaphas said, "It is expedient that one man die rather than the whole nation perish."[40] From his (and their) point of view, the preservation of their social world was worth the death of a misguided teacher rumored to be in league with Beelzebul.

In short, those who decided that Jesus must die need not have been "bad" people. Historically, the opponents of Jesus were very much like us and our contemporaries—people trying to do the best they could in light of how they saw and what they believed. They could do little else because they could see little else from their position at the pinnacle of their social world.[41]

Thus the death of Jesus was in all likelihood the result of cooperation between the Roman governor and the circle of Jewish religious figures and aristocracy who mediated between Roman imperial rule and the Jewish population. But it is illuminating to move beyond the immediate situation surrounding his death to the broader question of *what* was responsible for the death of Jesus—from the question "*Who* killed Jesus" (and what we may imagine about "why") to "*What* killed Jesus?"[42]

To a large extent, it was the conventional wisdom of the time—the "dominant consciousness" of the day—that was responsible for the death of Jesus. The high priest and his circle were both the servants and guardians of the dominant consciousness. Shaped by it and in a sense subservient to it, they were also concerned to preserve it. With its "laws" of moderation and self-preservation, and its attempt to make reality "safe" by domesticating it in a net of beliefs and rules, the dominant consciousness of conventional wisdom is threatened by the voice of an alternative consciousness.

Religious traditions as well as secular cultures have often been uncomfortable with the voice of an alternative consciousness in their midst, especially if that voice begins to attract a following. It threatens a culture at its most fundamental level, calling into question both its view of reality and its ethos, as well as the social structure which institutionalizes those bedrock notions. In Jesus, the voice of the Spirit challenged the dominant consciousness.

The politics of holiness also played a role. It accounted for much of the resistance to his message and movement. The Pharisees, the embodiment of the politics of holiness in an intensified form, were the most vocal verbal critics during the ministry, though they do not seem to have been involved in the arrest and trial of Jesus. But the politics of holiness was in the culture as a whole, not just in the Pharisees. In this less intense form, it shaped the lives of ordinary people (even the outcasts) as well as the lives of the accommodationist ruling class.

With its emphasis upon survival through greater differentiation between Jew and Gentile, righteous and outcast, the politics of holiness found the politics of compassion both unorthodox and threatening. For the politics of holiness, the purpose of religion (and culture) was to some extent to preserve itself. Yet the "way" which Jesus taught threatened to undermine both religious tradition and society. The way of Spirit was threatening to a society based upon conventional wisdom, the way of inclusion threatening to a society concerned about righteousness, performance, and distinctions, and the way of peace threatening to a society facing war. Thus the alternative consciousness of Jesus collided with the dominant consciousness of his culture—it was wrong from the standpoint of those who devoutly pursued holiness, and destabilizing to those with a stake in preserving the present order.

But finally, we must speak not only of the forces operative in Jesus' opponents but also of Jesus' own intention. He was not simply a victim, but one who provocatively challenged the ethos of his day. He was killed because he sought, in the name and power of the Spirit, the transformation of his own culture. He issued a call for a relationship with God that would lead to a new ethos and thus a new politics. For that goal he gave his life, even though his death was not his primary intention.

The conflict between him and his opponents was between two ways of being that run throughout the history of Israel, and through human history generally, including the church and modern culture. One way organizes life around the security of the self and its world; the essential ingredients of conventional wisdom and a politics of holiness (even if in a transformed and secular form) are still very much with us. That which killed Jesus is thus still alive in human history. The other way of being organizes life around God. Ultimately, it was the conflict between a life grounded in Spirit and one grounded in culture, and Jesus' own concern to transform his culture in the name of the Spirit, that caused his death. As the voice of an alternative consciousness shaped by the Spirit, he called his people to another way.

Though Jesus was more than a prophet, it was his prophetic call to change that caused his death. He was also, as we have argued, a charismatic healer, unconventional sage, and founder of an alternative community. But even these categories do not finally do him complete justice as a historical figure. Indeed, as the Jewish scholar Martin Buber once powerfully wrote, there is something about Jesus that transcends the categories of Judaism.[43] On historical grounds alone, without any Christian presuppositions shaping the verdict, he is clearly one of the most remarkable figures who ever lived.

EPILOGUE: EASTER AND THE BIRTH OF THE LIVING CHRIST

Though the story of the historical Jesus ends with his death on a Friday in A.D. 30, the story of Jesus does not end there. According to his followers, death could not hold him, and he appeared to them in a new way beginning on Easter Sunday. Indeed, he has continued to be known by Christians ever since as a living reality.

We cannot know exactly what happened. According to the earliest accounts of Easter reported by his followers, Jesus "appeared to them" and they knew that it was the same person they had known during the ministry. We do not know what form those appearances took. Sometimes the language used to describe them seems to speak of a visionary experience; sometimes Jesus is described in quite corporeal form. We can say that the resurrection was not the resuscitation of a corpse. That is, resuscitation and resurrection are quite different from each other; the former involves a once-dead person coming back to life and resuming the conditions of ordinary existence until he or she dies again. Whatever the resurrection involved, it was clearly not that. Instead, resurrection means entry into another mode of being, not restoration to a previous mode of being. In Jesus' case, to use the language of the church, it meant being "raised to God's right hand."

Did Easter nevertheless involve *something* happening to the corpse of Jesus? On historical grounds, we cannot say.[44] What we *can* say, however, is from the standpoint of Christian faith most crucial: Jesus' followers continued to experience him as a living reality, and *in a new way*, namely as having the qualities of God. Now he could be known anywhere, and not just in a particular place; now he was the presence which abided with them, "Immanuel" (which means "God with us"); now he was "seated at the right hand of God," participating in the power and authority of God; now they knew him as both Lord and Christ. But the story of the living Christ and his lordship over the lives of Christians goes beyond the purpose of this book. Suffice it to say that he who was put to death because of his passion to transform culture in the name of the Spirit was not swallowed up by either death or culture. Indeed, Spirit triumphed over culture.

NOTES

1. The phrase is from Luke 9:51. Though the exact year of Jesus' death is uncertain, 30 is most likely; next most likely is 33. Given that he was probably born shortly before 4 B.C., he was in his mid-thirties.
2. Most notably by Albert Schweitzer in his two books about Jesus at the beginning of this century (see chapter 1, pages 11–12). According to Schweitzer, Jesus believed that his mission was to bear the woes of the end-time (the

"messianic woes") *on behalf of the many*; that is, he would suffer *instead* of others. Thus Jesus went to Jerusalem in order to get killed, and much of his activity in the final week of his life deliberately provoked the authorities to take action against him. Though Schweitzer's account sounds bizarre, it is not that different from what is implied by those who assume that the whole purpose of Jesus' mission was to die on the cross: for them also, Jesus went to Jerusalem *in order to be killed*. He went there not only knowing that his death would be the result, but his death was also his *purpose* for going there.

3. This "foreboding" is actually expressed as a *certainty* in the passages known as "predictions of the passion" (see Mark 8:31, 9:31, 10:33–34), but these are generally seen by scholars as creations of the church after Easter; from that vantage point, the *outcome* of Jesus' journey to Jerusalem was seen as its providential foreordained *purpose*. However, even without the passion predictions, there is reason to believe that Jesus anticipated that the likely result of his final appeal would be death, and that he went to Jerusalem in full awareness of that likelihood; see Luke 13:31–33.

4. Luke 13:33.

5. Luke 13:34. The "I" of this passage is the divine "I"; that is, as in the case of the classical prophets of Israel, Jesus here speaks in the name of God.

6. Luke 19:41–44.

7. Mark 11:1–10; parallels in Matthew 21:1–9, Luke 19:28–38; John reports the episode somewhat differently in 12:12–19.

8. Zechariah 9:9–10. Verse nine speaks of the king of peace mounted on a donkey, and verse 10 of the banishing of the war horse and other instruments of war from Jerusalem. The connection to Zechariah is implicit in Mark and explicit in Matthew 21:4–5 (also in John 12:15). Interestingly, Matthew apparently misread the passage in Zechariah as referring to two animals and thus added a second animal to the account, creating the rather improbable picture of Jesus riding two animals at the same time (see Matthew 21:7, plus the references to two animals throughout his narrative).

9. Did Jesus also intend with this act to make a veiled or implicit claim *to be the king of peace*, thus approaching making a messianic claim? We cannot rule out the possibility; however, there is no clear evidence that Jesus applied the metaphor of "king" to himself in other texts generally accepted as authentic.

10. It consisted of the "raised platform" built by Herod, an irregular rectangle of approximately 1500 feet by 1000 feet.

11. Its interior dimensions were approximately 105 feet long, 35 feet wide, and 52 feet high. The interior was divided into two main parts, the most sacred "holy of holies" (a perfect cube of 35 feet), plus a larger area for priests and Levites. That the temple building itself with its "holy of holies" was a residence for the divine and not a place of public worship is indicated by its most common name: "The *house* of the Lord." Worship did not occur in it, but around it.

12. Scholars sometimes refer to the "court of the Gentiles," but the designation is modern, not ancient. Though Gentiles were permitted in some areas of the temple platform, there was no court specially designated or named for them.

13. See Joseph Klausner, *Jesus of Nazareth* (New York: Macmillan, 1929), 312. Klausner's book, now sixty years old, is still very valuable. E. F. Scott calls the temple incident *the crisis* in the life of Jesus in his book bearing the same title: *The Crisis in the Life of Jesus* (New York: 1952).

14. As, for example, S. G. F. Brandon depicts it in his portrait of Jesus as a sympathizer with the liberation movement; see his *Jesus and the Zealots*, 331–334. Other scholars have occasionally argued the same point.

15. Mark 11:15–17, with parallels in Matthew 21:12–13 and Luke 19:45–46; see also John 2:13–22. Mark (along with Matthew and Luke) places the incident in the last week of Jesus' life; John places it near the beginning of the ministry. The synoptic placement is historically much more likely. For the whole incident and a more detailed interpretation, see Borg, *Conflict, Holiness and Politics in the Teaching of Jesus* (New York and Toronto: Edwin Mellen Press, 1984), 171–176.

16. Isaiah 56:7.

17. Not only were the merchants providing a necessary service, given the ethos of the time, but profits were rigidly controlled and did not go into private purses but into the temple fund. See Borg, *Conflict, Holiness and Politics*, 174, 176, and 348, note 62.

18. Jeremiah 7:11, in the context of Jeremiah's "temple sermon," where he ridiculed those who said, "This is the temple of the Lord, the temple of the Lord, the temple of the Lord."

19. Mark "surrounds" his account of the action in the temple with the puzzling story of the cursing of the fig tree (Mark 11:12–14, 20–25). If we take it as a *historical* narrative reporting something Jesus actually did, there are a number of problems. It seems out of character for Jesus; we are told that it was not the season for figs; and there is the question of whether *any* person can cause a fig tree to wither and die by cursing it. However, setting aside the historical question, *as a narrative* the account makes sense as a prophetic act: that is, the withering of the unfruitful fig tree symbolized what was happening to Jerusalem.

20. Mark 11:27–33; see also chapter 3, page 47.

21. Mark 11:18; so also, apparently, Luke 19:47.

22. In what follows, I have basically followed Mark's account without supposing that Mark's primary purpose was historical reporting. Certainly, Mark is not *comprehensive* in his account of Jesus' final week; no doubt Jesus said much more than reported in Mark's relatively few stories. What Mark *does* report seems wholly appropriate; it is what we would expect on grounds of historical probability. It is difficult to know whether this appropriateness stems from Mark's fine sense of narrative judgment, or from fairly accurate (even if stylized and condensed) historical memory.

23. Mark 12:13–27, see also chapter 7, page 138. Note that opposition by the Pharisees was not unanimous; see the story of the appreciative Pharisee who was "not far from the Kingdom of God" in Mark 12:28–34.

24. Mark 12:38–40. The reference to *scribes* who devour widows' houses implies a process of legal (that is, legitimated by the Torah) appropriation of property. See also the subsequent passage about the poor widow (12:41–44).

25. Mark 12:1–9; see also chapter 8, page 157.

26. Many of the threats to Jerusalem are located by the gospel writers in the last week of Jesus' life; besides Luke 19:41–44, see the implicit threat in Mark 12:9, and explicit threats in Mark 13:2, 13:14, and Luke 21:20–24.

27. Mark 14:22–25, with parallels in Matthew 26:26–29 and Luke 22:17–19 (or 20); the earliest reference is in 1 Corinthians 11:23–26. For the "new covenant" of Jeremiah, see Jeremiah 31:31–34. It is difficult to make any historical judgment

about the details of the "last supper," including the words actually spoken by Jesus, simply because the remembrance and celebration of it were so central in the worship of the early church. Thus the details of the story have been affected by the liturgical practice of the church. That Jesus held such a final meal does seem historically likely, however.

28. Mark 14:32–52, Matthew 26:36–56, and Luke 22:40–53.

29. See, for example, the use of Psalm 22 (the psalm of "the righteous sufferer") in Mark 15:24, 29, and 34; for the darkness at midday in Mark 15:33, see Amos 8:9, Jeremiah 15:9, Isaiah 50:3; the tearing of the temple curtain in Mark 15:38 is to be understood as the opening up of access to the holy of holies (the presence of God) through the death of Jesus.

30. The diminishing of Roman responsibility and the heightening of Jewish responsibility can be seen especially in Matthew. Found only in Matthew are Pilate's wife's dream, which disclosed to her that Jesus was a "righteous man" (27:19); Pilate's washing his hands of "this man's blood" (27:24); and the cry of *all* the people (the Jewish crowd), "His blood be on us *and our children!*" (27:25). Tragically, Matthew's effort to save the early Christians from the charge of being a seditious group within the Roman Empire had the unwitting and unintended effect of providing a "proof text" justifying Christian persecution of Jews throughout much of Western history. It is one of the terrible ironies of history that Jews have been regularly persecuted in the name of a Jew whose primary concern was their well-being. Blindness was not the special prerogative of Jesus' historical opponents.

31. The following account is dependent upon the scholarly work of many others, even though it does not directly reflect any single scholarly reconstruction. Though it is my own assessment of historical probability, it does not deviate from what may fairly be called a scholarly consensus, however tenuous the consensus is at some points.

32. For summary statements of the harshness of his rule, see the first century Jewish author Philo, *Legatio* 302, and modern authors W. R. Wilson, *The Execution of Jesus* (New York: Scribner, 1970), 18–22; and H. Cohn, *The Trial and Death of Jesus* (New York: Harper & Row, 1971), 7–17.

33. According to Jewish law, the high priest was to serve for life. However, the Romans took over the right of appointment and replaced high priests whenever they chose (the criterion presumably being their ability to cooperate with the Romans). In the fifty-two years from A.D. 15 to the outbreak of the great war, there were seventeen different high priests; fifteen of them served a total of twenty-two years. The other two served thirty years, with Caiaphas's eighteen years being the longest. Presumably he had learned how to work very well with the Romans.

34. Mark 14:53–64, with parallels in Matthew 26:57–66 and Luke 22:66–71. For the distinction between the "religious council" (the *bet din* or *boule*) and the "political Sanhedrin," and the latter as the private circle of advisers of the high priest, see especially Ellis Rivkin, *What Crucified Jesus?* (Nashville: Abingdon, 1984).

35. See the account of the charges brought before Pilate in Luke 23:2: leading the nation astray, forbidding payment of tribute to Caesar, and claiming to be a messianic king. There is reason to think that Luke had an independent source for this material rather than freely creating it himself.

36. According to Josephus, *Antiquities* 18:116–119. According to Mark, John was executed because of conniving among the women of Herod's household (Mark 6:17–29); the two stories do not necessarily conflict. For the importance of John's fate for understanding the arrest and execution of Jesus, see especially Rivkin, *What Crucified Jesus?*

37. "Local charismatics" like Hanina ben Dosa and Honi the Righteous were suspected by the conventional sages of not paying enough attention to the law, but action was not taken against them (though it should be noted that Honi was executed because he refused to take the "right side" in a political dispute).

38. Josephus, *The Jewish War*, 6.300–309.

39. See chapter 4, page 64.

40. John 11:47–53. For the fascinating suggestion that the account reflects a meeting of the council at which a death verdict was passed some time before Jesus' final visit to Jerusalem, preserved with some accuracy by John even though overlaid with his own theology, see E. Bammel, "*Ex illa itaque die consilium fecerunt . . .,*" in *The Trial of Jesus*, edited by Bammel (London: SCM, 1970), 11–40.

41. This is not to argue for a rigid social determinism, as if people's perception is absolutely conditioned by social class; there were apparently at least two exceptions in the established class of Jesus' day. The names of Joseph of Arimathea and Nicodemus, both members of the "council"—probably the religious council rather than the privy council of the high priest—are fairly well-grounded in the gospel tradition. Rather, I am making the rather obvious point that for most people most of the time, one's place in the social world affects one's perception.

42. The contrast between the question of *who* killed Jesus versus *what* killed Jesus is the basis for the title of Rivkin's book, *What Crucified Jesus?*

43. Buber's statement is very striking: "From my youth onwards I have found in Jesus my great brother. That Christianity has regarded and does regard him as God and Saviour has always appeared to me a fact of the highest importance which, for his sake and my own, I must endeavour to understand . . . My own fraternally open relationship to him has grown ever stronger and clearer, and today I see him more strongly and clearly than ever before. I am more than ever certain that a great place belongs to him in Israel's history of faith and that this place cannot be described by any of the usual categories." *Two Types of Faith* (New York: Macmillan, 1952), 12–13.

44. The story of the empty tomb, which suggests that something happened to the corpse of Jesus, is first found in Mark 16:1–8, and there it is described as if it were not generally known about: the women find the tomb empty, but then tell *nobody anything about it*. It is difficult to know whether or not to press this detail to imply that the story of the empty tomb entered the tradition at a rather late date; in any case, Mark's account is odd. Moreover, it is important to remember that the truth of the resurrection is not dependent upon an empty tomb or a vanished corpse. Rather, the truth of the resurrection is grounded in the experience of Christ as a living reality beyond his death.

10. *Conclusion*
The New Vision of Jesus: His Significance for Our Time

What Jesus was like is as much of a challenge to both church and culture in the late twentieth century as it was in his own time. The "new vision" of Jesus—an image of what can be known about him, as well as his own vision of life—radically calls into question our most common way of being and invites us to see differently.

For both Christians and non-Christians, what can be known about Jesus is a vivid witness to the reality of the Spirit. Most generations have not needed to hear this, simply because most generations took the reality of Spirit for granted. We do not, even to a large extent within the church itself, because of the pervasive effect of the modern image of reality upon the psyches of believers and unbelievers alike. For many, faith becomes the struggle to believe the church's teaching despite the fact that it does not make very good sense to us. As a set of beliefs to be believed, Christianity (and all religions which affirm "another world") is radically challenged by the image of reality that has shaped the modern mind.

In precisely this situation, the historical Jesus as a Spirit-filled figure in the charismatic stream of Judaism can address us. Jesus' *experience* of a world of Spirit challenges the modern worldview in a way that a rival belief system cannot. What he was like reminds us that there have been figures in every culture who experienced the "other world," and that it is only we in the modern period who have grown to doubt its reality. The intense experiential relationship with the Spirit reported of him invites us to consider that reality might really be other than we in the modern world image it to be. His life powerfully suggests that the Spirit is "real."

Even as the historical Jesus is a testimony to the reality of the Spirit, he also provides a vivid picture of what life in the Spirit is like. It is an impressive picture. There are, of course, the spectacular powers of the Spirit flowing through him in his mighty deeds. But we should not think only of the spectacular; the historical records about him suggest other exceptional qualities. He was a remarkably free person.[1] Free from fear and anxious preoccupation, he was free to see clearly and to love. His freedom was grounded in the Spirit, from which flowed the other central qualities of his life: courage, insight, joy, and above all compassion. All are products of the Spirit—"fruits of the Spirit," as St. Paul called them. Thus what we can know about Jesus invites us to see "life in the Spirit" as a striking alternative to the way we typically live our lives.

For Christians in particular, what Jesus was like as a historical figure is significant because of the special status which he has in the tradition of the church. Within that tradition, two things have consistently been said about him: he was "true God" and "true man," the incarnation of the truly divine and the truly human. As "true God," even during his historical life, Jesus was an *epiphany of God*, a "disclosure" or "revelation" of God (as the word "epiphany" itself means).[2] As "true man," he is a *model for human life*, specifically for the life of discipleship. This twofold status of Jesus within the tradition of orthodox Christian theology enables us to see his significance for those who would be his followers in this time.

THE HISTORICAL JESUS AS EPIPHANY OF GOD

As an epiphany of God, Jesus was a "disclosure" or "revelation" of God. He did not reveal God only in his teaching (as if revelation consisted primarily of *information*), but in his very way of being.[3] The epiphany was *Jesus*—his "person" as well as his message. As such, he was an "image" of God,[4] an "icon" of God, revealing and mediating the divine reality.[5] What he was like therefore discloses what God is like.

In traditional language, Jesus was a revelation of the love of God. For Christians, as the "Word made flesh" he was the love of God incarnate. His life thus provides particular content to what the love of God is like, giving concreteness to what otherwise can be an abstraction.

The particular quality of that love is seen above all in the compassion which we see in the historical Jesus. It is the compassion which moved him to touch lepers, to heal on the sabbath, to see in the ostracized members of the human community "children of God," and to risk his life for the sake of saving his people from a future which he could see and they could not.

There is a social dimension as well as an individual dimension to the compassion of God as we see it in Jesus. For him, as for the prophets before him,[6] the divine compassion included grief and anger about the blindness, injustice, and idolatry that caused human suffering. It included warnings of judgment, as a threat and deterrent, and as an actuality. Persistent blindness and heedlessness have their consequences. As an image of God, Jesus mirrors the care of God for what happens to humans in the world of history itself. The life of culture matters to God.

As an epiphany of God, Jesus discloses that at the center of everything is a reality that is in love with us and wills our well-being, both as individuals and as individuals within society. As an image of God, Jesus challenges the most widespread image of reality in both the ancient and modern world, countering conventional wisdom's understanding of God as one with demands that must be met by the anxious self in search of its own security. In its place is an image of God as the compassionate one who invites people into a relationship which is the source of transformation of human life in both its individual and social aspects.

JESUS AS A MODEL FOR DISCIPLESHIP

Jesus is also a model for the Christian life. The notion is expressed in the gospels with the image of discipleship. To be a disciple of Jesus meant something more than being a student of a teacher. To be a disciple meant "to follow after." Whoever would be my disciple, Jesus said, "Let him *follow me*." What does it mean to be a follower of Jesus?[7] It means to take seriously what he took seriously, to be *like him* in some sense. It is what St. Paul meant when he said, "Be imitators of Christ."[8] What Jesus was like as a figure of history becomes a model for discipleship, illuminating and incarnating the vision of life to which he called his followers.[9]

That vision is a life lived on the boundary of Spirit and culture, participating in both worlds. It has three core elements. First, its *source* is a "birth" in the Spirit. The birth involves that "dying to self" of which Jesus spoke and which he himself experienced: "If anyone would come after me, let him deny himself and take up his cross and follow me."[10] Bonhoeffer's epigram caught its meaning: "When Christ calls a man he bids him come and die."[11] The death leads to a new life, a rebirth out of the world of conventional wisdom and the preoccupation with the self and its securities which it sustains, to a new way of being. Being "born of the Spirit" creates a radically new identity, one no longer conferred by culture. It is an awakening to that "place" where one may address God as *Abba*, the intimate one.[12]

The second core element of life in the Spirit is its dominant *quality*: compassion. So it was for Jesus. As the "wombishness" which he both taught and lived, compassion is both a feeling and a way of being. One *feels* compassion and *is* compassionate. Not simply a feeling of benevolent goodwill, it is a tenderness and "embracingness" which make empathy possible—a *feeling with* others and a capacity to be *moved* by their situation. As a feeling, it becomes a motive for deeds. As a way of being, it is a persistent trait or quality of character, a "virtue," to use an old-fashioned word. One is to "be compassionate."

Compassion is a grace, not an achievement. Its constancy does not ultimately depend upon an effort of will, but upon the relationship to the Spirit. It is the child of the radical centering in God that we see in Jesus; empty of self, one can be filled with the Spirit of God the compassionate one. To change the metaphor, it is the primary "fruit of the Spirit." If we take Jesus seriously as a disclosure of life in the Spirit, then growth in the Christian life is essentially growth in compassion.

The third core element of life in the Spirit is a dialectical *relationship to culture*. The new life is simultaneously less involved and more involved in culture. As the movement to a life grounded in the Spirit of God, it is a movement away from the many securities offered by culture, whether goods, status, identity, nation, success, or righteousness. The distinctions generated by the world of conventional wisdom are seen as just that: socially created products that provide no abiding home. The vision of life lived and taught by Jesus means, as it did for the first disciples, leaving the "home" of conventional wisdom, whether religious or secular.

Life in the Spirit, however, does not simply draw one away from culture. Not an individualistic vision, it creates a new community, an alternative community or alternative culture.[13] So it was for Jesus and his followers, both during his lifetime and afterwards. The new life produced a new social reality, initially the "movement" and then the "church." Indeed, the word church itself means a community which has been "called out." In the Jewish world in which it was born and in the Roman world in which it soon lived, it stood out sharply as an alternative community with an alternative vision and values.

As an alternative culture where the Spirit is known, the church exists in part to nurture the new life through its shared perceptions, values, and worship, confirming and sustaining the new way of seeing and being. But the new community is also meant to embody the new way of being. In its own life, it is to live the alternative values generated by life in the Spirit and become a witness to compassion by incarnating the ethos of compassion. There is a radicalism to the alternative community of Jesus, and only if it incarnates that radicalism can it be "the city set on a hill whose light cannot be hid."[14] It can do this only by being a community grounded in the Spirit.

Taking the vision of Jesus seriously calls the church to be an alternative culture in our time. Though there may have been periods in the history of the West when its "official" values roughly coincided with the central values of the Christian tradition, that time is no more. In the modern period, a yawning gap has opened. The dominant values of contemporary American life—affluence, achievement, appearance, power, competition, consumption, individualism—are vastly different from anything recognizably Christian. As individuals and as a culture, with our securities and values centered in "this world," in "the finite," our existence has become massively idolatrous.

We live in a modern Babylon, one largely unrecognized as such and all the more seductive because of its mostly benign and benevolent face.[15] Indeed, to a large extent, Babylon also lives within the church, so thoroughly has it (through us) been infected with the "spirit of this age." Modern culture functions as a rival lord in our lives, conferring values and identity and demanding obedience, all in conformity to its vision of reality. If the church were to take seriously the double movement of withdrawal from culture and entry into an alternative culture, it would increasingly see itself as a community which knows that its Lord is different from the lord of culture, its loyalties and values very different from the dominant consciousness of our culture. It would live the life referred to in John's description of Jesus' followers as *in* the world, but "not *of* the world," grounded not in the world but *in* God.[16]

There is yet another dimension to life lived on the boundary of Spirit and culture, namely the relationship between the church as community of the Spirit and the larger culture in which it lives. In the church's history, that relationship has been seen in four broadly different ways.[17] Some Christians have sought to reject culture, regarding it either with indifference or hostility. Culture is simply "the world of darkness," and the Christian life entails rejection of that world and no further concern with it. Often described as the "sectarian" response, it can take a quite gentle form, as among the Amish, or a very militant form, as among those for whom the Christian message consists primarily of pronouncing judgment upon the world, a judgment from which they are usually exempt.

More commonly, Christians have followed two other options, both of which domesticate the radicalism of the alternative vision.

Often Christians have basically legitimated culture with their religious beliefs, seeing Christianity as the endorser of their culture's central values. This is the essence of "Christian nationalism" in both its virulent and more benign forms, of "enculturated religion" in which it is assumed that there is a basic harmony between one's culture's values and the values of one's religion. It is then inconceivable that there could be any fundamental tension between the values of culture and the Christian tradition. The radicalism of the alternative community of the Spirit is also lost by another common response, namely a sharp separation between life in the Spirit and life in culture, a division of life into two realms, one religious and one secular, each with its own norms. Life in the Spirit is domesticated by being restricted only to private life, perhaps only to "internal" life.

There has also been a fourth response: the conviction that culture is to be transformed by the power of the Spirit. Though less common, it has sometimes surfaced dramatically in the history of the church, and no doubt has been present in some individuals in all generations. It is what we see in the historical Jesus. Compassion, the fruit of the Spirit and the ethos of the alternative community, was to be realized within the larger culture as well. The "politics of compassion" did not lead Jesus to withdraw from culture, but to a passionate mission to transform the culture of his day. Because he saw God as caring about what happened to human beings in history, he saw culture as something to be transformed, not simply rejected or legitimated.

Taking the vision of Jesus seriously thus entails seeking to structure the life of society in accord with the politics of compassion. Though not to be identified with any specific economic or political program, its general direction is clear.[18] A society organized around the politics of compassion would look very different from one organized around other norms. Indeed, it would look very different from our culture, which to a large extent is organized around the politics of a radicalized economic individualism. In many ways, we live within a secularized form of the "politics of holiness," with only the standards of righteousness changed. Achievement and reward are its driving energies.

A politics of compassion is organized around the nourishment of human life, not around rewards for culturally prized achievement. A politics of compassion does not emphasize differences, dividing the world into deserving and undeserving, friend and enemy. Rather, a politics of compassion stresses our commonality. It is inclusive rather than exclusive. Such a politics would look sharply different from the way we presently order our national and international life.

What this means in the lives of Christians legitimately varies from culture to culture and individual to individual. In some cultures, Christians have been such a minuscule minority as to have little or no possibility of affecting their culture's life. Moreover, not every individual Christian is called to a life of political activism. There are, as St. Paul put it, diverse gifts. But in our culture, even those whose gifts take them far away from direct involvement in political life nevertheless have a voice in shaping culture through their political attitudes. Taking the politics of compassion seriously would make a difference in the kind of "politics" Christians would support.

The politics of compassion as a way of organizing human social life is an ideal and yet relevant to human history. Like "freedom," it is an ideal to be approximated, even though it cannot be perfectly realized.[19] Moreover, the degree to which it can be realized does not depend upon what a "politics of realism" might imagine, but upon an openness to the power of the Spirit to transform culture. Life in the Spirit not only mandates a concern for culture, but also becomes a channel for the power of the Spirit. The Spirit is the basis for courage, confidence and hope.

LIFE IN THE SPIRIT AND THE KINGDOM OF GOD

One of the characteristic ways Jesus spoke about the power of the Spirit and the life engendered by it was with the richly symbolic phrase "the Kingdom of God."[20] As a "linguistic symbol" with its home in the Jewish tradition, the phrase evoked the web of meanings associated with the image of God as "king."[21]

The image of God's kingship was one of Israel's classic ways of speaking about the relationship between the other world and this one. To speak of God as king was to speak of the "power" of the other world active in this one: at creation, in decisive moments within history (such as the Exodus and return from exile), and at the "end of time." The kingship of God also created a kingdom, both in the present and at the end of history. In the present, the kingdom was made up of those who put themselves under the divine sovereignty, taking upon themselves the "yoke of the kingdom." At the end would come the everlasting kingdom of peace and justice, banqueting and joy. The story of God's kingship thus related the two worlds of the primordial tradition at the beginning (creation), in history, and at the end (consummation). It was one of Israel's ways of telling the story of the Spirit and the Spirit's relationship to this world.

Jesus used the image of God's kingship and kingdom to speak about what was happening in his ministry. As an exorcist he spoke of the Kingdom of God as the power of the Spirit which flowed through him: "If it is by the Spirit of God that I cast out demons, then the Kingdom of God has come upon you."[22] He identified his time as a time when the kingly power of God was active: "The Kingdom of God has come, is near."[23] He spoke of the kingdom as a present community, as something that could be "entered" now, and as something that could be prayed for: "Thy Kingdom come." And, like his tradition, he also spoke of it as the final kingdom to which many would come from east and west to banquet with Abraham, Isaac, and Jacob.[24]

For Jesus, the language of the kingdom was a way of speaking of the power of the Spirit and the new life which it created. The coming of the kingdom is the coming of the Spirit, both into individual lives and into history itself. Entering the Kingdom is entering the life of the Spirit, being drawn into the "way" which Jesus taught and was. That Kingdom has an existence within history as the alternative community of Jesus, that community which lives the life of the Spirit.[25] That Kingdom is also something to be hoped for, to be brought about by the power or Spirit of God. Life in the Spirit is thus life lived in relationship to the kingly power of God. Indeed, life in the Spirit is life in the Kingdom of God.[26]

The vision of Jesus thus provides the content for three central images of the Christian life: life in the Spirit, the life of discipleship, and life in the Kingdom of God. Each image points to a life centered in God rather than in the lords and kingdoms of this world, in Spirit and not in culture, and yet seeking to transform those kingdoms through the power of the Spirit. In the historical Jesus and the revitalization movement he founded, two elements that are commonly separated are strikingly linked: Spirit and culture, religion and politics.

A CHALLENGING VISION

The image of Jesus sketched in this book confronts us at many points. As a charismatic, Jesus is a vivid challenge to our notion of reality, the "practical atheism"[27] of much of our culture and church. As a sage, he calls us to leave the life of conventional wisdom, whether secular or religious, American or Christian. He is, in a sense, an "undomesticated Jesus" who has not yet become part of a culture's conventional wisdom but who challenges all systems of conventional wisdom. As a renewal movement founder and prophet, he points us to human community and history, to an alternative culture which seeks to make the world more compassionate.

These are potent themes for our own times. They invite us to take seriously the two central presuppositions of the Jewish-Christian tradition. First, there is a dimension of reality beyond the visible world of our ordinary experience, a dimension charged with power, whose ultimate quality is compassion. Second, the fruits of a life lived in accord with the Spirit are to be embodied not only in individuals, but also in the life of the faithful community.

These themes are also threatening to us. They threaten our sense of normalcy. What if it is true that the world of our ordinary experience is but one level of reality, and that we are at all times surrounded by other dimensions of reality which we do not commonly experience? The claim that there really is a realm of Spirit is both exciting and oddly disconcerting. What if reality is other than we ever dreamed it could be?

The themes also threaten our comfort within contemporary culture. The historical Jesus, with his call to a counter-community with a counter-consciousness (including consciousness of another realm and lord), challenges the central values of contemporary American culture. Our quest for fulfilment seeks satisfaction through greater achievement, consumption, and enjoyment; our security rests in nuclear weapons; and our blindness and idolatry are visible in our stated willingness to blow up the world, if need be, to preserve our way of life. We as Christians are called to become the church in a culture whose values are largely alien to the Christian message, to be once again the church of the catacombs.

Images of Jesus give content to what loyalty to him means. The popular picture of Jesus as one whose purpose was to proclaim truths *about himself* most often construes loyalty to him as insistence on the truth of those claims. Loyalty becomes *belief* in the historical truthfulness of all the statements in the gospels. Discipleship is then easily confused with dogmatism or doctrinal orthodoxy.

The absence of an image—the most common fruit of biblical scholarship in this century—leaves us with no clear notion of what it means to take Jesus seriously, no notion of what loyalty might entail, no direction for the life of discipleship. But the vision of Jesus as a person of Spirit, deeply involved in the historical crisis of his own time, can shape the church's discipleship today. For us, as for the world in which he lived, he can be the light in our darkness.

NOTES

1. I first encountered this insight in the arresting phrase with which Paul Van Buren encapsulized the historical Jesus: he was "a remarkably free man." See his *The Secular Meaning of the Gospel* (New York: Macmillan, 1963).

2. Exploring the nuances of meaning of this affirmation goes far beyond the limits and purpose of this concluding chapter. I am simply pointing out that the orthodox mainstream of Christian theology has consistently affirmed that Jesus *even during his historical life* was a "revelation" of God. His "divinity" is not to be assigned simply to his post-Easter risen life and his humanity to his historical life, as if he were "simply" human during the ministry and divine only afterward (as is suggested by "adoptionism" and radical forms of "kenoticism," which are types of christological thinking inconsistent with the orthodoxy of the church). Thus what he was like in his historical life was in some sense a disclosure of God. For an excellent and accessible study of the church's various understandings of Jesus as both human and divine, see John Baillie, *God Was in Christ* (New York: Scribner, 1948); for a study of the New Testament period, see John Knox, *The Humanity and Divinity of Christ* (Cambridge: Cambridge University Press, 1967).

3. In Leander Keck's striking phrase, the historical Jesus is a "parable of God." See his *A Future for the Historical Jesus* (New York and Nashville: Abingdon, 1971).

4. For Jesus as "image of God" in the New Testament, see 2 Corinthians 4:4, Colossians 1:15.

5. "Icon" is the Greek word for "image." Within the Eastern Orthodox tradition of the church, icons are "sacred images," highly stylized paintings of religious subjects. As objects of contemplation, they function as "windows into the other world"; they *mediate* the Spirit.

6. See especially Walter Brueggemann, *The Prophetic Imagination* (Philadelphia: Fortress, 1978), and Abraham Heschel, *The Prophets* (New York: Harper & Row, 1962).

7. Discipleship is not equally emphasized by all Christians. Some imply (or even state) that following Jesus is not important at all because Jesus "has done it all"—his death on the cross atones for my sins, and therefore I need do nothing but rest confidently in his blood and righteousness. There is some truth in this; the mainstream of the Christian theological tradition over the centuries has persistently insisted that we are saved by grace and not by our own effort, known by God long before we know that we are known, and loved by God long before we return that love. But once one *sees* that, *believes* that, *knows* that, then what? Discipleship is the response; it does not challenge the priority of grace, but is the response to grace.

8. 1 Corinthians 11:1. Paul actually wrote, "Be imitators of me, as I am of Christ." See also Philippians 2:5–8, which is dominated by an *imitatio Christi* motif; the self-emptying, servanthood, and "obedience unto death" of Jesus are held up as a model to be emulated.

9. I am not arguing that historical knowledge about Jesus is *essential* for the life of Christian discipleship. Ever since the death of Jesus, discipleship has been a response to the living Christ and not to the historical Jesus. It is the living Christ who is still known as lord, still issues the call to "follow me," and still stands in the relation of master and disciples with his followers. Moreover, centuries of Christians have lived lives of discipleship without knowledge of the historical Jesus; prior to the modern period, no distinction had yet been made between the Christ of the gospels and Jesus as a figure of history. Clearly, historical knowledge about Jesus is no more necessary for the life of discipleship than it is for Christian faith (see chapter 1, page 13). Nevertheless, what Jesus was like is

not irrelevant to discipleship. Indeed, we may suppose that for the earliest Christians in the first decades after Easter, the still-vivid historical memory of what he was like must have shaped their understanding of what it meant to "follow him." My claim is simply that an image of the historical Jesus *illuminates* the path of discipleship.

10. Mark 8:34; see chapter 6, pages 112–114.

11. See chapter 6, note 67. Bonhoeffer (1906–1945), a German Lutheran pastor and theologian, was martyred by the Nazis in the last month of the Third Reich. Thus for him the words had a literal meaning which he probably did not anticipate when he wrote them some eight years before his death.

12. This birth is not to be identified only with a narrowly defined understanding of the "baptism of the Spirit"; clearly, the lives of the saints indicate that being "born to the Spirit" cannot be restricted to sharply defined experiences that fit a certain formula. But neither is it to be denied as central to the Christian life; at its more mature levels, that life intrinsically involves a "lived" relationship to the Spirit.

13. That is, community is an intrinsic part of it. Though there have been exceptions in the Christian tradition (hermit monks and Christians isolated by circumstance), both Jesus and his followers used rich communal images to describe the new life: family, Israel, kingdom, a banquet, a vine with many branches, a single body with many organs.

14. Matthew 5:14.

15. "Babylon" in the Bible has both a literal and symbolic meaning. On the one hand, it refers literally to the empire which destroyed the people of God in 586 B.C. In the New Testament (as well as in other Jewish writings of the time), it becomes a symbol for Rome, described as "Babylon," "the great whore drunk with the blood of the saints" (Revelation 17), the "new" imperial power which stood opposed to the people of God. Babylon thus stands for culture in so far as it is opposed to God.

16. See John 17:14–18.

17. The classic study is H. Richard Niebuhr's masterfully insightful *Christ and Culture* (New York: Harper, 1951). Niebuhr actually catalogs five ways the relationship has been seen; for the sake of simplicity, I have reduced those five to four. His more subtle distinctions are illuminating at a more refined level of analysis.

18. This case for a Christian involvement in politics should not be confused with current attempts by some Christian groups to legislate a sharply defined understanding of righteousness which is often the historically conditioned product of an earlier cultural period, and which seems more like a "politics of holiness." Rather, the "politics of compassion" is an ethos which is to shape all programs and all legislation.

19. We often think of "ideals" as politically irrelevant, but this is not so. Even though one cannot imagine a perfect incarnation of the politics of compassion in any historical future we can foresee, it (like "freedom" or "justice") can have the "relevance of an impossible ideal," a phrase central to the thinking of Reinhold Niebuhr (1892–1971), the most influential Christian social ethicist in North America (and the world?) in this century.

20. Twentieth-century scholarship has regularly treated it as *the* central element of Jesus' preaching and ministry, indeed seeing it as the "key" to understanding

the ministry of Jesus. Many studies of the historical Jesus thus focus on it. I have deliberately avoided referring to it until now, except incidentally, for two reasons. First, it does not seem to be a good beginning point for the historical study of Jesus. Rather, as a century of scholarship devoted to it has demonstrated, it is a phrase capable of very diverse interpretations. When this is the case, it is a sound procedure to begin one's historical study in another place where matters are clearer, and then move to the less clear. This is the procedure I have sought to follow. What Jesus said about the Kingdom of God becomes tolerably clear when seen within the *gestalt* of Jesus sketched in the book as a whole. Second, its centrality may be overemphasized. Burton Mack has argued perceptively and persuasively that a century of scholarship has been bewitched by Mark's advance summary of Jesus' message ("The time is fulfilled, the Kingdom of God is at hand"), treating it as if it were accurate historical recollection rather than the Marcan redaction it clearly is. See B. Mack, "The Kingdom Sayings in Mark," *Foundations and Facets Forum*, 3, no. 1 (March 1987): 3–47.

The literature on the Kingdom of God is voluminous. Three especially important recent books are Norman Perrin, *Jesus and the Language of the Kingdom* (Philadelphia: Fortress, 1976); Bruce Chilton, *God in Strength* (Linz: Plochl, 1979); and an anthology and history of research edited by Chilton, *The Kingdom of God in the Teaching of Jesus* (Philadelphia: Fortress, 1984). For my own more detailed treatment, see Marcus Borg, *Conflict, Holiness and Politics in the Teaching of Jesus* (New York and Toronto: Edwin Mellen Press, 1984), 248–263, and "A Temperate Case for a Non-Eschatological Jesus," *Foundations and Facets Forum*, no. 2, 3 (September 1986): 81–102, especially 92–95.

21. Perrin's work (see note 20, above) is especially helpful for understanding the phrase "Kingdom of God" as a symbol which evoked the "story" of God's kingship.

22. Matthew 12:28 = Luke 11:20.

23. The double expression renders two ways of speaking found in the gospels. Some texts clearly speak of the Kingdom as a present reality, others as "coming" or being "at hand."

24. Matthew 8:11–12 = Luke 13:28–29. Jesus thus does speak of "Kingdom-as-end," though it is only one nuance of "Kingdom of God," and present in only a relatively few texts. Jesus does not speak of the "final" kingdom as often as one might expect, given the emphasis of twentieth-century scholarship. Moreover, it is not said that "Kingdom-as-end" is *imminent*, as scholars are increasingly recognizing (see chapter 1, page 14). When Jesus does speak of the last judgment, it is *not* said that it will be soon (see, for example, Matthew 12:41–42 = Luke 11:31–32; Matthew 11:20–24 = Luke 10:13–15). Moreover, it is interesting that what he says consistently *reverses* the expectations of his hearers: you will be shut out, you will fare badly in the judgment. That is, the "function " of end-of-the-world discourse in the gospels is not to announce the imminence of the Kingdom, but to invite a change in perception. It is as if Jesus had said, "You believe in a last judgment. Well, in the last judgment, let me tell you how it will be." The point is not that the judgment is imminent, but a reversal of the taken-for-granted expectations of that judgment.

25. It is not to be identified with the institutional church, of course, for the "visible" church is a radically imperfect community. In its brightest historical moments,

it has sometimes incarnated the new way; and even in its darker periods, it at least preserved the symbols of the tradition. Nevertheless, the struggle between the Kingdom of God as life in the Spirit and the dominant consciousness of conventional wisdom goes on in the history of the church, just as it did in the history of Israel before.

26. "Life in the Spirit" and "life in the Kingdom of God" as two phrases which speak of the same reality complement and qualify each other in an interesting way. Thinking of the new life as "life in the Spirit" helps to prevent "life in the Kingdom of God" from having only a moral or ethical meaning; and "Kingdom of God" with its rich communal meaning prevents "life in the Spirit" from becoming simply spiritual, unconnected to history and human community.

27. See Stanley Hauerwas and William Willimon, "Embarrassed by God's Presence," *The Christian Century* (January 30, 1985): 98–100.

Select Bibliography

This bibliography has been prepared for general readers, including students in undergraduate and introductory graduate level courses. It has been limited to two elements: first, English versions of the primary ancient sources in editions especially useful for study; and second, relatively recent books within mainstream scholarship that focus on the historical Jesus. Works on particular topics (for example, parables, miracles, the trial of Jesus, worldview, conventional wisdom, and so forth) are referred to in footnotes to the relevant sections of this book.

ANCIENT SOURCES

The Bible. The single most valuable study edition is *The New Oxford Annotated Bible with the Apocrypha*, edited by H. G. May and B. M. Metzger (New York: Oxford University Press, 1973, 1977). In addition to using the text of the Revised Standard Version (most widely used in scholarly books and mainstream churches), this edition includes helpful introductory essays and explanatory footnotes.

Gospel Parallels. There are three major types of Gospel parallels that display the texts of the Gospels with their relevant parallel texts. The most widely used is *Gospel Parallels*, edited by B. H. Throckmorton (New York: Thomas Nelson, 1949, 1957, 1967), which concentrates primarily on Matthew, Mark, and Luke, and basically follows Mark's order. Robert Funk's two volume *New Gospel Parallels* (Philadelphia: Fortress, 1985) includes John and noncanonical sources as well as the synoptics, and organizes its presentation with each Gospel in turn serving as the main text. John Dominic Crossan's *Sayings Parallels: A Workbook for the Jesus Tradition* (Philadelphia: Fortress, 1986) focuses on the sayings of Jesus, including all relevant canonical and noncanonical parallels.

Other Jewish and Early Christian Literature. For Jewish writings produced between about 200 B.C. and A.D. 100, see *The Old Testament Pseudepigrapha*, two volumes, edited by James H. Charlesworth (Garden City, NY: Doubleday, 1983, 1985). For the Dead Sea Scrolls, see Geza Vermes, *The Dead Sea Scrolls in English* (Baltimore: Penguin, 1968). For the first-century Jewish historian Josephus, see the Loeb Classical Library edition, translated by H. St. J. Thackeray, R. Marcus, and A. Wikgrin, nine volumes, (Cambridge, MA: Harvard University Press, 1958–1965). There is no single primary source for the rabbinic tradition in the first century, since most of it was written down only later. The earliest authoritative compilation is *The Mishnah*, put together about A.D. 200; the standard English edition is translated by H. Danby (London: Oxford University Press, 1933).

For early Christian writings not included in the New Testament, see E. Hennecke and W. Schneemelcher, *New Testament Apocrypha*, two volumes (Philadelphia: Westminster, 1963, 1965); and James Robinson, *The Nag Hammadi Library in English* (San Francisco: Harper & Row, 1977), a collection of early Christian literature discovered in upper Egypt shortly after World War II, including the important Gospel of Thomas.

SELECTED RECENT WORKS ON JESUS

Günther Bornkamm, *Jesus of Nazareth* (New York: Harper & Row, 1960). Representing the "German school" of Jesus research and existentialist interpretation, this book was the first and most important sustained study of Jesus emerging during the period of the "new quest" for the historical Jesus.

Walter Brueggemann, *The Prophetic Imagination* (Philadelphia: Fortress, 1978). The last third of this book on the prophetic tradition in Israel treats the ministry of Jesus.

C. H. Dodd, *The Founder of Christianity* (New York: Macmillan, 1970). Written by the foremost twentieth-century British New Testament scholar near the end of his distinguished career and life, this well-balanced book remains one of the best.

Donald Goergen, *The Mission and Ministry of Jesus* (Wilmington: Michael Glazier, 1986). Readable and well documented, the study emphasizes Jesus' spirituality and compassion, his solidarity with God, and his solidarity with the people. Volume one of a projected five-volume "theology of Jesus" (volume two treats Jesus' death and resurrection).

A. E. Harvey, *Jesus and the Constraints of History* (Philadelphia: Westminster, 1982). Based on lectures given at Oxford, the book concentrates on Jesus' linkages to the circumstances of his own time.

John Hayes, *Son of God to Superstar* (Nashville: Abingdon, 1976). A survey of twentieth-century portraits of Jesus, including some of the "eccentric" ones.

Hans Küng, *On Being a Christian* (Garden City, NY: Doubleday, 1984; originally published in German in 1974). About half of this engaging and provocative "introduction" to the Christian faith is a substantial and lively treatment of the historical Jesus.

E. P. Sanders, *Jesus and Judaism* (Philadelphia: Fortress, 1985). Perhaps the most technical of the works cited here, the book argues that Jesus sought the restoration of Israel within the framework of an imminent eschatological expectation.

Edward Schillebeeckx, *Jesus: An Experiment in Christology* (New York: Crossroad, 1979; originally published in Dutch in 1974). Because of its lucid insights, comprehensive treatment of scholarship, and massive size (over 700 pages), this is the single most impressive volume presently available.

Juan Luis Segundo, *The Historical Jesus of the Synoptics* (Maryknoll, NY: Orbis, 1985; originally published in Spanish in 1982). Informed by the insights and perspectives of liberation theology, Segundo's treatment of the historical Jesus is volume two of his five-volume *Jesus of Nazareth Yesterday and Today.*

G. S. Sloyan, *Jesus in Focus: A Life in Its Setting* (Mystic, CN: Twenty-Third Publications, 1983). Informed by scholarship, generally readable, useful and accessible at the introductory level, this book speaks primarily of Jesus as a mystic and sage within the tradition of Judaism.

W. Barnes Tatum, *In Quest of Jesus: A Guidebook* (Atlanta: John Knox, 1982). Though Tatum does not develop his own portrait of Jesus, his book is perhaps the best popular level introduction to the central questions of the quest for the historical Jesus: the nature of the gospels and their sources, the history of research, and selected themes, such as birth, resurrection, parables, miracles.

Geza Vermes, *Jesus the Jew* (New York: Macmillan, 1973). Not a comprehensive portrait of Jesus but a series of studies of the Jesus tradition within a Jewish background, this important book emphasizes Galilean holy men in the milieu out of which Jesus came, and the Jewish origin of the "titles" of Jesus.

John Yoder, *The Politics of Jesus* (Grand Rapids, MI: Eerdmans, 1972). Emphasizes the social and political radicalism of Jesus, including pacifism.

For a more extensive annotated bibliography, see James H. Charlesworth, "From Barren Mazes to Gentle Rappings: The Emergence of Jesus Research," in *Princeton Seminary Bulletin* 7 (1986), pp. 225–230. Charlesworth's own book on Jesus, *Jesus within Judaism* (Garden City, NY: Doubleday), is forthcoming.

Subject Index

Modern Author Index

Scripture Index

Only texts that are either quoted or commented upon are indexed; texts that appear only as cross-references in footnotes are not. Books are listed in biblical order, beginning with the Hebrew Bible.